OFFICE MANAGEMENT

For B.Com. Students of Indian Universities

OFFICE MANAGEMENT

For B.Com. Students of Indian Universities

R.S.N. PILLAI

M.A., M.Com., LLB,

Prof. & Head of the Department of Commerce,
Arignar Anna College, Aramboly
KANYAKUMARI – 629 301

BAGAVATHI

M.A., M.Com.,

240, Chidambaranager,
Nagercoil
KANYAKUMARI – 629 002

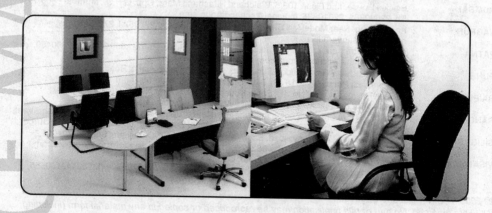

S. CHAND & COMPANY PVT. LTD.

(An ISO 9001 : 2008 Company)

RAM NAGAR, NEW DELHI - 110055

S. CHAND & COMPANY PVT. LTD.

(An ISO 9001 : 2008 Company)
Head Office: 7361, RAM NAGAR, NEW DELHI - 110 055
Phone: 23672080-81-82, 9899107446, 9911310888
Fax: 91-11-23677446
Shop at: **schandgroup.com**; e-mail: **info@schandgroup.com**

Branches:

AHMEDABAD : 1st Floor, Heritage, Near Gujarat Vidhyapeeth, Ashram Road, **Ahmedabad** - 380 014,
Ph: 27541965, 27542369, ahmedabad@schandgroup.com

BENGALURU : No. 6, Ahuja Chambers, 1st Cross, Kumara Krupa Road, **Bengaluru** - 560 001,
Ph: 22268048, 22354008, bangalore@schandgroup.com

BHOPAL : Bajaj Tower, Plot No. 2&3, Lala Lajpat Rai Colony, Raisen Road, **Bhopal** - 462 011,
Ph: 4274723, 4209587. bhopal@schandgroup.com

CHANDIGARH : S.C.O. 2419-20, First Floor, Sector - 22-C (Near Aroma Hotel), **Chandigarh** -160 022,
Ph: 2725443, 2725446, chandigarh@schandgroup.com

CHENNAI : No.1, Whites Road, Opposite Express Avenue, Royapettah, **Chennai** - 600014
Ph. 28410027, 28410058, chennai@schandgroup.com

COIMBATORE : 1790, Trichy Road, LGB Colony, Ramanathapuram, **Coimbatore** -6410045,
Ph: 2323620, 4217136 coimbatore@schandgroup.com **(Marketing Office)**

CUTTACK : 1st Floor, Bhartia Tower, Badambadi, **Cuttack** - 753 009, Ph: 2332580; 2332581,
cuttack@schandgroup.com

DEHRADUN : 1st Floor, 20, New Road, Near Dwarka Store, **Dehradun** 248 001,
Ph: 2711101, 2710861, dehradun@schandgroup.com

GUWAHATI : Dilip Commercial (Ist floor), M.N. Road, Pan Bazar, **Guwahati** - 781 001,
Ph: 2738811, 2735640 guwahati@schandgroup.com

HYDERABAD : Padma Plaza, H.No. 3-4-630, Opp. Ratna College, Narayanaguda, **Hyderabad** - 500 029,
Ph: 27550194, 27550195, hyderabad@schandgroup.com

JAIPUR : 1st Floor, Nand Plaza, Hawa Sadak, Ajmer Road, **Jaipur** - 302 006,
Ph: 2219175, 2219176, jaipur@schandgroup.com

JALANDHAR : Mai Hiran Gate, **Jalandhar** - 144 008, Ph: 2401630, 5000630, jalandhar@schandgroup.com

KOCHI : Kachapilly Square, Mullassery Canal Road, Ernakulam, **Kochi** - 682 011,
Ph: 2378740, 2378207-08, cochin@schandgroup.com

KOLKATA : 285/J, Bipin Bihari Ganguli Street, **Kolkata** - 700 012, Ph: 22367459, 22373914,
kolkata@schandgroup.com

LUCKNOW : Mahabeer Market, 25 Gwynne Road, Aminabad, **Lucknow** - 226 018, Ph: 4076971, 4026791,
4065646, 4027188, lucknow@schandgroup.com

MUMBAI : Blackie House, IInd Floor, 103/5, Walchand Hirachand Marg, Opp. G.P.O., **Mumbai** - 400 001,
Ph: 22690881, 22610885, mumbai@schandgroup.com

NAGPUR : Karnal Bagh, Near Model Mill Chowk, **Nagpur** - 440 032, Ph: 2720523, 2777666
nagpur@schandgroup.com

PATNA : 104, Citicentre Ashok, Mahima Palace , Govind Mitra Road, **Patna** - 800 004, Ph: 2300489,
2302100, patna@schandgroup.com

PUNE : Sadguru Enclave, Ground floor, Survey No. 114/3, Plot no. 8 Alandi Road ,
Vishrantwadi **Pune** – 411015 Ph: 64017298 pune@schandgroup.com

RAIPUR : Kailash Residency, Plot No. 4B, Bottle House Road, Shankar Nagar, **Raipur** - 492 007,
Ph: 2443142,Mb. : 09981200834, raipur@schandgroup.com **(Marketing Office)**

RANCHI : Flat No. 104, Sri Draupadi Smriti Apartments, (Near of Jaipal Singh Stadium) Neel Ratan Street,
Upper Bazar, **Ranchi** - 834 001, Ph: 2208761, ranchi@schandgroup.com **(Marketing Office)**

SILIGURI : 122, Raja Ram Mohan Roy Road, East Vivekanandapally, P.O., Siliguri, **Siliguri**-734001,
Dist., Jalpaiguri, (W.B.) Ph. 0353-2520750 **(Marketing Office)** siliguri@schandgroup.com

VISAKHAPATNAM: No. 49-54-15/53/8, Plot No. 7, 1st Floor, Opp. Radhakrishna Towers,
Seethammadhara North Extn., **Visakhapatnam** - 530 013, Ph-2782609 (M) 09440100555,
visakhapatnam@schandgroup.com **(Marketing Office)**

First Edition 2003
Reprints 2005, 2007, 2008, 2010, 2012, 2013
Reprint 2014
ISBN : 81-219-2252-6   Code : 07B 370

PRINTED IN INDIA
*By Goyal Offset Printers, A-60/1, G.T. Karnal Road, Indu. Area, Delhi-110 033
and published by S. Chand & Company Pvt. Ltd., 7361, Ram Nagar, New Delhi -110 055.*

PREFACE TO THE SECOND REVISED EDITION

We are pleased to present the fifth revised and enlarged edition of 'OFFICE MANAGEMENT' book to the students of Commerce and other examinations leading to Diplomas in Office Management or Office Supervision. The basic structure of the book remains the same. Several new topics have been added in different chapters. Three new Chapters–Work Measurement and Standards, Modern Technology and Precis Writing. Thereby, the book now covers the entire syllabus of OFFICE MANAGEMENT of different Universities on All India basis.

The book has been written in a simple language and lucid style. Obsolete materials have been deleted and new concepts and information have been incorporated wherever found necessary. The present edition is a compact volume containing latest information about Office Management or Office Administration.

The book has been revised in the light of the comments and suggestions from a large number of our friends and readers for which we are really grateful to them.

We express our thanks to Mrs. Nirmala Gupta, CMD; Mr. Navin Joshi, Vice President (Publishing) and Mr. R.S. Saxena, Advisor of S. Chand and Company Ltd., New Delhi for their support and encouragement.

We are fully confident that the book would prove useful to the students of Commerce. Suggestions for further improvement of the book are welcome and shall be gratefully acknowledged.

Kanyakumari   **AUTHORS**
9566367303
9994045593

PREFACE TO THE FIRST EDITION

We take pleasure, in introducing the book of **Office Management** in a new get up for the students of Commerce. This book is a key paper for the students of Graduation Courses of Commerce and Management of various universities.

Owing to the greatly fettneed efforts had been taken to enlarge the existing material. There are chapters of Prime importance—office organisation, office accommodation and layout office environment service, office supervision, collection of data, presentation of data, cost education and cost saving have been recently incorporated. The book is ideal for executives as well.

We are thankful to Shri. Ravinder Kumar Gupta, Managing Director of S. Chand & Co. Ltd., for taking interest in the publication of this book.

Suggestions for improvement and better knowledge are most welcome.

Authors

Kanyakumari

Preface to the First Edition

Authors

CONTENTS

OFFICE MANAGEMENT

CONTENTS

CHAPTER 1

Modern Office

INTRODUCTION

The complexities at business activities are increasing day-by-day. An office is a vital segment of any commercial enterprise. An office may be small or large according to the size of the concern. In olden days, all the jobs of the organisation had been done mostly by the proprietors. If the work was more, two or three persons were to be appointed. They sat in small rooms and worked in poorly lighted and congested places. There were no modern office amenities as today; clerks were found copying letters tiresomely turning leather bound registers etc. Since the typewriters had not come into general use, most of the office work had to be performed manually and clerks would be found in spending most of their time in copying letters for despatch to customers. All the internal 'and external communications were performed through human agency. The telephones and intercom systems were not generally in use. The proprietor of a business would be found sitting in the office room and supervising the office work. He personally deals with the customers and visitors. In earlier period, production was generally from a limited number

"A well organised office makes it possible for the management to plan its operations intelligently, to put its plans into effect surely, to follow their progress currently, to determine their effectiveness promptly, to appraise their result without delay and to co-ordinate all the activities of the business."

—*Leffingwell and Robinson*

1

of raw materials, that too available locally, and marketing the products was also, in most cases, confined to local market. Thus, in those days, the businessmen were interested in maximising profits through the two important profit centres, *i.e.* production and marketing. A few decades ago, the office had been defined as a place where clerical work is performed for the successful operation of an institution. Office work may be done by a clerk within the four walls of a building.

Office activities have undergone vast changes in the last few decades. The world has witnessed spectacular developments and advances in the field of science, technology, industrialisation, transport, communication etc., In modern concept is to view office as a function. When it is taken as a function, it (office) may direct, control and coordinate the office work wherever it is done and whosoever does it. Here it may be noted that in the modern time, offices are developed on scientific principles and their management and administration is in the hands of qualified and trained managerial personnel.

CHANGING OFFICE SCENE

Office activities have undergone a vast change in the last four or five decades. The old dingy, cluttered, stuffy office rooms have vanished and in their place we have well ventilated, well-lighted, airconditioned offices with upto date furnishings in alluring designs. Gone are the days when the head of the concern personally supervised the work of clerks. Today, modern offices are organised on scientific principles and their management and administration are in the hands of specialised office manager. Managers do not share the same room with clerks but sit in separate rooms. The clerks are supervised and controlled with the help of supervisors and through standard office systems, routines, office manuals etc.

The vast changes have led to an expansion in the scale of production and business activities. As the size of business enterprises grows, there is corresponding increase in the volume of office work. The office activities of today are not performed by general clerks but by specialised clerks— Receptionist, Cashier, Typist, Telephone Operators etc. There is also a greater division of labour. Departmentalisation of office has been effected. The office managers of today welcome greater use of machines and minimal use of human beings in the office work. Machines—typewriter, telephones, computers, calculators, duplicating machines, dictaphones, accounting machines, intercom, cellular phones, internet system etc. help to save time and labour. Computers are the latest additions to the long list of office machines. They are capable of performing most clerical operations at high speed without errors. Thus modern offices are becoming more and more high-tech.

Office is an important section of a business. The term business implies office work. The dictionary meaning of office is "a place for the transaction of business, the room or department, where the clerical work is done," or we can say "a place where business is carried on", or it is "a place where all sorts of activities of organisation are dealt with." Office is the centre of an organization. Commercial Office acts as a central directing and co-ordinating agency of the various activities of any business.

An office is understood to be a place where clerical work is performed and where all kinds of paper work (letters, correspondence, files, records etc.) is maintained and dealt with. It is a central place where all sorts of clerical work is done to co-ordinate and control the affairs of the whole organisation.

"Office is a unit where relevant records for the purpose of control, planning and efficient management of the organisation are prepared, handled and preserved. Office provides facilities for internal and external communication and co-ordinates activities of different departments of the organisation."

—*Littlefield, Rachel and Caruth.*

In modern age, the 'office' is used in a broader sense. *Prof. Dicksee* states, " An office is to a business what the mainspring is to a watch". An organization cannot be carried on without an office, as a watch without the mainspring is useless. In the present times, the modern office organization has so much importance as the brain in a human body. Thus a commercial office can be called "a clearing house of all essential business information." The office has to receive or collect all information of the business, process the collected information (analyse, arrange and classify) and put them into understandable form on the one hand. On the other hand, the processed information has to be presented or communicated to the management of the business, as and when required.

According to the Random House Dictionary, "An office is a place where business is transacted or professional services are available." An office is the place where the control mechanisms for an enterprise are located, where records are initiated for communication, control and efficient operation of the enterprise. According to Mills and Standing Ford, "The office is the administrative centre of a business. The purpose of an office has been defined as the providing of a service of communication and record."

"An office is the place where work in connection with the preparing and furnishing of information is done."

It is generally seen, in commercial offices, there are some persons to receive information, process them (made understandable in form) and supply the processed information to the management. Doing so, can be called clerical job. Clerical job includes correspondence (to collect information or clarify the information received) serving (filing), typing, book-keeping, handling of money etc. So it is confirmed that an efficient management of the organisation helps the managers or executives to formulate planning, organising, controlling and supervising the activities of a business concern. Prompt and accurate decision depend upon timely information.

An office is a place to record the information for the purposes of control through collection (of information) handled and serviced and where the control mechanism for a business is located—Paper work is to attain an aimed result. One must give importance to the office function rather than to the place. An office is a place of paper processing and memory centre for all its departments. In office, policies and ideas are formulated through collection and analysis of obtained information. An office maintains all these records. And these readymade, scrutinised and processed information are made available to the management to attain the best result. On the other hand, if the office supplies incomplete, wrong, misleading or delayed information, decisions taken on these defective pieces of information, are bound to be wrong. In small firms, the proprietor himself does all the jobs, but in large and complex firms, the proprietor or the Board of Directors alone cannot run the concern. Therefore, the office is there to assist the management in their day-to-day business. The office is the servant of the management.

Most of the definitions underline "paper work done" at a particular place as the main and perhaps the only function of an office. However, today the word "office" is used in a broader sense. The modern approach to the study of an office is to view it as a function instead of a certain place. When it is taken as a function, the office can plan, organise, direct,

---

"Any place where procedure concerned with the receipt, transmittal, production, reproduction, processing, storage and retrieval of information are carried out. The cab of a lorry where the driver completes his log, the corner of a factory workshop where the foreman completes the production returns, the massive headquarters of an international organisation employing thousands of people who service field operations–each of these is an office."

—*Josephine.*

control and coordinate the office work wherever it is done and whosoever does it. But if it is restricted to a certain place only, it will not cover the work which by its nature is office work, but is done outside the boundaries of that place. Therefore, the term' office' should be used broadly to represent the functions which it performs rather than the place where they are performed.

A few **definitions of office** are given below :

"The essential feature of the office is the work itself, not who does it or where it is done. If it is office or clerical work in one place, it is office or clerical work everywhere regardless of where the work is done or who does it."   *—Leffingwell and Robinson.*

"The office is not in one place; no matter how much we centralise its services, there will still be office work at the point of use. Some enterprises are almost all office. The activities of the office do not, strictly speaking, constitute a function, they are parts of all functions."

—Chalres O. Libbey.

"If it is office work in one place, it is office work everywhere, regardless of office work as such, wherever it is done and whoever performs it, is often the first step towards improving the performance of that work. That is, the principles applicable to the performance of office work in one place are usually applicable to the performance of the same work elsewhere." *—Leffingwell and Robinson.*

"Office is a unit where relevant records for the purpose of control, planning and efficient management of the organisation are prepared, handled and preserved. Office provides facilities for internal and external communication and co-ordinates activities of different departments of the organization."   *—Littlefield and Rachel.*

In a business organisation, the chief executive and his management team cannot deal personally with all the communications and cannot remember all the facts connected with it. There, the office comes to their rescue by providing with relevant facts and figures on the basis of which the management exercises its managerial functions of planning, co-ordination and control. According to Leffingwell and Robinson, "A well organised office makes it possible for the management to plan its operations intelligently, to put its plans into effect surely, to follow their progress currently, to determine their effectiveness promptly, to appraise the results without delay and to co-ordinate all the activities of the business."

OFFICE WORK

Office work is mainly concerned with clerical work or paper work. But this is a very narrow view and is an old concept of office work. Now-a-days, office work has a very wide scope. Office work is primarily concerned with making, preserving and using records. The records are concerned about purchasing, producing, selling, accounting and correspondence, inventories and written or printed memorandum of all kinds. These records are essential for an efficient and effective control of operation of the organisation.

An office serves as the memory centre and control centre of an organisation. The office performs many services like communication, reproduction, mechanical data, processing, procuring of stationery, furniture and equipment, secretarial assistance etc. to other departments in an organisation.

Office is a unit where relevant records for the purpose of control, planning and efficient management of the organisation are prepared, handled and preserved. Office provides

---

"The office of a successful business organisation must be the brain of the whole concern."   *Donald Causins.*

facilities for internal and external communication and co-ordinates activities of different departments of the organisation.

The purpose of an office is :

1. To preserve all the records of the business.
2. To handle incoming correspondence.
3. To plan the policies of the business and ensure their implementation.
4. To direct and co-ordinate the activities of the various departments, and
5. To maintain accounts, statutory and non-statutory books etc. of the business.

FUNCTIONS OF AN OFFICE

The efficiency of an office should be judged by the degree of promptness in supplying correct information. The information dealt with by an office will be on accounts, orders, prices, complaints, personal matters, etc. It will go to the credit of the manager, if his office gives out needed information at a moment's notice. George R. Terry says, "the act of collecting, processing, storing and distributing information comprise functions of the office."

Modern business is complex. A business organisation today is faced with the ever-changing conditions. The present decade is the decade of change and challenge. With the developments and advances in the field of science and technology, the manufacturing techniques have undergone a rapid change. The ever-widening markets also pose a challenge by themselves. All the problems can be satisfactorily tackled only when adequate information is available. Thus man's greatest tool today is information. To identify new markets, to design new products, to make decisions, to keep people informed and to keep abreast of knowledge, requires information. It is not only man's greatest tool, but it is also one of the greatest needs. Information is required by all members of enterprise and one of the problems in its management is to determine the nature of the information required, by whom, and in what form. Information is to help; it should assist its recipient in performing his assigned job. In short, the acts of controlling, processing, storing, striving and distributing information comprise the function of the OFFICE.

The functions of a modern office can be divided into the following categories; and they are:

1. Basic or routine functions.
2. Administrative management functions or ancillary functions.

The following are the basic functions of an office :

1. To receive or collect information.
2. To prepare a record of such information.
3. To process and arrange such information.
4. To supply readymade information to the authorities when asked for.

1. To receive or collect information :

The primary function of the office is to receive information from the various departments of the organisation or from outside through enquiries, reports, orders, circulars, complaints, messages etc. If the information received is not complete, the office tries to collect information by sending out enquiries of clarifications. There may be different types of meeting within or

"The essential features of the office is the work itself, not who does it or where it is done. If it is office or clerical work in one place, it is office or clerical work everywhere regardless of where the work is done or who does it.
—*Leffingwell.*

outside the organisation and pieces of information will be helpful to the management and therefore the office has to collect it.

2. To prepare records of information :

Information is usually received in the form of letters, enquiries, phone calls etc. and this information has to be converted into other forms, which can easily be followed by the management. These are orders, quotations, price-lists, replies to enquiries and complaints, account books, etc., within the organisation. All these records will be retained for further reference. According to the nature of the information, the record may be retained for many years or they may be safely kept for a few years, after which they can be destroyed. The records of information prepared in the office must be preserved safely, made available to the management within no time and must be easy to understand. These records maintained by the office will be reference for further dealings. Moreover, every business has to keep up-to-date books of accounts which are required to record all business transactions. The books like cash-book, purchase book, sales-book, goods returns book, productive expense and other ledgers are to be kept by every office. Besides the account-books, other books will have to be maintained by the office—in order to have a smooth function of the organisation.

3. To process and arrange information :

The information received by the office may be lengthy and the same in its original form may not be much useful to the management. Therefore, after collecting such information, it will be processed, categorised, arranged and systematically kept for readymade information. Certain letters will have to be converted into charts, statements etc. by doing calculations or analysis over such information. For instance, orders have been received every day and complied. The orders themselves will not serve any purpose to the departmental head because the orders may be in the form of letters. Therefore, it will be most useful to the Sales Manager, if these have been shown in a compact form, say sales weekwise. This can be done through charts, statements etc. Then the sales manager is at ease to understand the position of the sales by looking at the statements or charts and come to a decision within no time. Thus it is possible for all the departments or the management to understand the position easily and quickly and come to certain conclusion. If the information is not properly analysed or arranged, much time will have to be spent. An efficient office supplies readymade information to departments or managers who take proper decisions on the basis of such information supplied. Therefore, a good office is the foundation of a business organisation.

4. To supply readymade information to the authorities :

An office is a machine which receives raw materials (scattered information) and produces various items through processes (compiled and talliable). The office receives information through letters, phones, meetings, complaints, business transactions, etc. These pieces of information are further recorded in proper books processed and thus converted into charts, graphs, statements, diagrams etc. which show the complete picture of one type of dealings. The processed information is ready made information and is easy to understand at a glance. Usually, the office supplies information relating to estimates, statements of accounts, progress report, book debts, sales, costings etc. The information kept by the office must be complete and accurate and supplied to the authorities as and when required, without

---

"The office is not in one place; no matter how much we centralise its services, there will still be office work at the point of use. Some enterprises are almost all office. The activities of the office do not, strictly speaking, constitute a function; they are parts of all functions."

— Charles O. Libbey.

wasting time. If the supply of information is also kept in such place where it is easily visible and available at any time, it is a great advantage.

Administrative and Management Functions :

1. **Management function :** The most important administrative functions of the manager include planning, organising, staffing, directing, communicating, controlling, co-ordinating and motivating. The office manager must organise the office on modern lines for the efficient and effective performance.

2. **Development of office systems and procedures :** All the jobs in the office are interrelated and interdependent. As such an office must provide better services to interrelated departments. For a smooth flow of work, development of office system and procedures is essential.

3. **Form designing and control :** Forms are the basic tools for all types of office work. There are many operations which can be systematized with the use of printed forms. Besides, the use of the forms saves time and energy at every operation. Information can be collected, recorded or processed systematically and effectively with the help of office forms. Therefore, it is the task of the management to design and to control the forms.

4. **Selection and purchase of office appliances :** The office manager must purchase the appropriate machines, equipment or furniture for the office. Office work requires adequate equipment, machines and furniture and they must be maintained properly for the efficient working order. Appliances must be selected for full and proper uses. They must be suitable for the purpose. They must be simple in operation and maintenance. They must be flexible and adaptable to different uses. The cost and benefit must be compared when the appliances are purchased.

5. **Personnel functions :** The personnel function is performed by the personnel department. It is assisted by the office. It recruits and selects the personnel. It places them in different jobs in the office. For the efficient performance of the basic functions of the office, provision of adequate and trained staff is necessary. The staff must get reasonable salary. Staff must be properly motivated to achieve the best performance.

6. **Controlling office costs :** Office costs may be controlled by using machines in the office, using labour-saving devices and adopting improved methods of management.

7. **Maintenance of records :** This is a secondary function of an office. Copies of all the correspondence must be retained for further reference. From a business firm, a number of letters go out daily and a number of replies are received, and if the copies of the original letters against which the replies have been received, are not available, the decision cannot be taken wisely. Therefore all the records must be maintained through proper filing system and preserved for number of years. Certain documents need not be kept for more than a year while certain documents have to be kept for a number of years.

8. **Planning schemes and policies :** In the present stage, production is always in anticipation of demand. Therefore for a manufacturing concern, it has become essential to plan the activities of the concern for the future period. One cannot take a decision or

---

1. "The basic functions of an office can be said to be receiving, recording, arranging (and analysing) and the giving of information."
   —*Denyer*
2. "The office has come to be recognised as a production unit whose efficieny is relatively as important as that of the manufacturing division."
   —*Henry.*

plan unless one goes into the previous records and relevant statistical data, studies the present market trends, and takes decisions on basis of all information of the past period. When a proper plan has been chalked out, it will be adopted as a policy. Planning and policies will be good, when they have been drawn out carefully with the help of the office, through collecting and processing information.

9. **Safeguarding the assets :** The job of an office is not only extended from the receipt of information to the supply of processed information, but also to take care of various assets. To keep the record of customers (debtors) and keep the management to be informed of about the doubtful debts so that necessary steps may be taken to prevent the occurrence of bad debts.

    Books of accounts of all types (personal, real and nominal) are to be kept regularly. Among them the most important are fixed assets—plant, machinery, fixtures, buildings and current assets—goods, stationery, debtors, bills receivable, cash in hand, cash at bank, etc. All these are the properties of the concern and the office must arrange to protect and safeguard the assets against destruction, damage, loss by theft, fire etc. The management must be informed of all types of misappropriation matters so that its occurrence will be prevented in future through investigations.

10. **Public relations :** Public relations signify the relations of a business organisation with the general public, usually through the distribution of information. Public relations guide business enterprise. Public relations are guided by public opinions.

The functions of Public Relations are :

(a) To inform managers of the current status and the changes in the opinions of public. The public can be divided into two–internal and external. The internal public are key policy makers, supervisory personnel, employees and shareholders. The external public are customers, suppliers and the general public.

(b) To suggest purposeful relations with the public and to warn unfavourable reactions.

(c) To communicate to the public the company's policies and actions. Public interest is an essential element for any good public relations. Office is the eyes and ears of a business. It is the hand which makes friends for a company.

IS OFFICE WORK NON-PRODUCTIVE ?

From the above discussion, one can understand that office is a service as well as an administrative unit, and it assists all departments of an organisation in achieving their objectives. Thus, the ability of profit making of an organisation is contributed by an office. But no tangible goods have been created by an office, it is true. However, an office plays a positive role, in the absence of which, the production or distribution would not have taken place.

The office work is facilitating in nature. Office is a service as well as administrative unit, helping all the departments of an organisation. It is not easy to measure the office work as a work in a factory. This is because office work is mainly a brain work. And it is difficult to standardise the office work.

The office work is not confined to a particular area as production or marketing function. Every department is dependent on the office for information and other services. It is true

---

"The importance of the office to a business cannot be managed efficiently without clerical assistance in some form or other.

that an office does not produce tangible products and therefore there is no direct contribution in the earning of profits.

Modern office provides so many supportive services to the other departments in the organisation without which they cannot function efficiently. Thus, it can be said that office is an important instrument in achieving the objectives of any business concern. Henry remarked," the office has come to be recognised as a production unit whose efficiency is relatively as important as that of the manufacturing divisions."

Every order represents a margin of profit. When the order is handled by the office, a part of the profit is reduced. At the same time, if the order is not handled properly and efficiently, there may be no profit at all. At the same time, some people say that the paper work is unnecessary and therefore, it should be eliminated for keeping the profit intact. This view is wrong. But it is very difficult to conduct the business without the very help of office as it provides supporting services and administrative functions. Moreover, human memory has its own shortcomings. Many transactions cannot be memorised for a long time. Because of the complexities in business, it is not possible to run a business without an office. A well organised office can materialise the policies and plan to achieve more efficiency, in modern business conditions. The office facilitates :

1. To work according to plan anticipated.
2. To help in the performance of various functions.
3. To translate the policies into action.
4. To co-ordinate the works of all departments of a firm.
5. To have ready reference of all matters.

Thus, it has rightly been described as the hub or nerve centre of the entire organisation.

FACTORS CONTRIBUTING TO THE GROWTH OF OFFICE WORK

The office work has tremendously grown in the modern economy. Due to the expansion of economic activities, the work has been increased manifold. The following factors have contributed to the growth of office work :

1. The management needs proper and timely information on all aspects of business operations in order to arrive at intelligent decision-making.
2. When the business grows, office work also grows proportionately.
3. The work concerned with the preparation of returns to government, financial statements, dealings with employees etc., increase office work.
4. With increase of service activities such as accounting, banking, advertising, marketing, insurance damages etc., the paper work has increased tremendously.
5. The importance of office in relation to customers is of great significance. Office acts as the channel that links the business organisation with its customers.

ACTIVITIES OF A MODERN OFFICE

Office work differs from enterprise to enterprise. However, there are certain activities, which are performed by all the offices. Some of these activities are listed below :

1. Handling incoming and outgoing mail.
2. Developing office systems, procedures and methods.

The essential feature (of the office) is the work itself, not who does it or where it is done. If it is office or clerical work in one place, it is office or clerical work everywhere regardless of where the work is done or who does it."

3. Maintenance of records (filing and indexing)
4. Establishing standard at office work.
5. Designing and procuring at office forms, stationery etc.
6. Recruitment and training of office staff.
7. Maintenance of furniture, machines, appliances etc.
8. Preparation of statements, reports etc.
9. Maintaining of accounts and other financial records.
10. Handling telephone calls and enquiries.
11. Preparing upto date information for the whole firm.
12. Arranging the data in a quickly accessible form for use.
13. Safeguarding the assets.
14. Keeping a prompt and accurate handling of enquiries orders etc.
15. Maintaining efficient flow of work in the office.

RELATION OF OFFICE WITH OTHER DEPARTMENTS

Large organisations are divided into various departments such as office, production, purchase, sales, finance, personnel etc. It is the office which is concerned with receiving, recording, arranging, analysing and giving of information. All the departments depend upon the office for various information needs. The office serves as the co-ordinating link in any organisation. For co-ordinating the activities of different departments in an organisation, office has to keep relations with each and every department. For example, orders for raw materials, sales, complaints, appointments etc. are passed through office only. Office needs

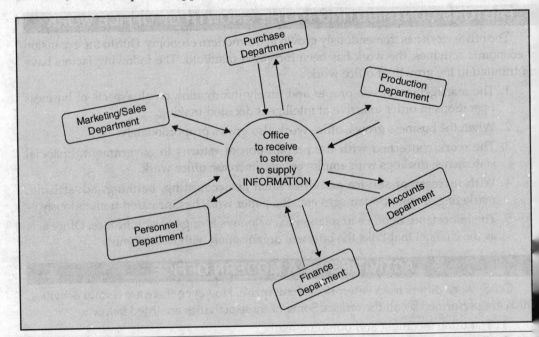

"A commercial office can be called "a clearing house of all essential business information." The office has to receive or collect all information of the business, process the collected information (analyse, arrange and classify) and put them into understandable form on the one hand. On the other hand, the processed information has to be presented or communicated to the management of the business, as and when required.

information of many kinds from different functional departments for framing general policies. Office supplies information needed in performing the functions of production, sales, personnel etc. and collects information from these departments for general policy framing and co-ordination. Relationship of office with other departments of an organisation is given below :

Office and Production Department

The production department is concerned with the production of goods and services. Raw materials, machines, equipments etc. are needed to produce goods. They depend upon office to get their requirements. The office makes purchases on behalf of the production department and also inform the production department the requirements of consumers and customers. The office is also provide common services to the production department, like, purchases correspondence, filing, market research, the trend of the market etc.

Office and Marketing/Sales Department

The office is always keep relations with customers. It is the office receives enquiries, orders etc. Enquiries are replied. Orders are executed by the sales department and the bill is sent through office. Complaints from customers are received by the office and conveys them to sales department. When sales go down, the office helps in marketing research to find out the reasons for low sales. The reasons are known to departmental heads, who take step to overcome the situations. Office receives information on behalf of sales department and office gives information to sales department, apart from general or common service, such as mailing, filing, communication etc.

Office and Purchase Department

Materials, stores, plant, machineries etc. needed for the purchase department is arranged by the office. Office assists the purchase department in inviting quotations or tenders, in sending orders, receiving invoices, making payments etc. It also gives general services to purchase department and maintains purchase journals, ledgers etc.

Office and Accounts/Finance Department

The accounts department maintains all the records of all business transactions with the help of office. The office prepares various financial statements and reports for the top management. Correspondence on behalf of accounts department is conducted by the office. It renders assistance to maintain the books of accounts, budgets, salaries and wage bills, invoices, collection of debt etc.

Office and Personnel Department

The personnel department is created only to provide necessary help to the managers in performing the staffing function. Without the productive efforts of human being, material resources would be meaningless and idle. Recruitment, training etc. are routed through office. The office maintains the records of all the employees. The workers or the employees can communicate with the management through office. There is a close link between the office and personnel department.

IMPORTANCE OF OFFICE

No business concern can exist without an office. An office can be described as the nerve centre of the whole concern. The importance of the office is as follows:

Office as a Service Centre

1. **Office renders valuable services to all other departments :** Often an office is referred to as the service department. The important services provided by the office include clerical and other services to other departments, divisions, sections etc. of the organisation and they cannot operate without an office.

2. **Office as an information centre or memory centre :** Office is the information centre of a business. In an organisation, office is as important as the brain in the human body. As such office is the brain of the organisation. It collects useful pieces of information from different sources, *i.e.* internal and external, and records them. It arranges and analyses them and makes them available to the management whenever needed. Thus office acts as an information centre or store house or memory centre. All kinds of information, past or present, are available in the office.

3. **Office as an intermediary :** An office connects outsiders with different departments and vice versa. All the sales orders are received through the office. It connects the organisation with the customers, suppliers, Government and general public. Public relations are a very important aspect of the Functions of modern office. The importance of office in relation to customers is of great significance. Office acts as a channel that link the business organisation with its customers. Their enquiries, orders, complaints etc. are taken care of by the office. The office acts as the link between different government departments and the organisation. Office is responsible for creating a good image for the organisation in the minds of the people, Danny Griswold describes public relations thus: "The management function which evaluates public attitudes, identifies the policies and procedures of an individual or an organisation with the public interest, and executes a programme of action to earn public understanding and acceptance." Thus the office conveys to the public the objectives, policies and programmes of the business. The suggestions and response of the public are gathered by the office and are conveyed to the management; thereby management reviews its plan and policies to meet the aspirations of the public in turn the public image of the business is enhanced.

4. **Office as a co-ordinator :** Office aids management to bring about co-ordination. A central office co-ordinates the activities of departmental offices. The office provides the necessary data. The management brings about co-ordination. The processing of information in an office is as follows:

   (*a*) **Communication :** Office provides essential records and communication services. Communication of correspondence is done through the office. The central office receives letters from outside, records them and sends them to the concerned department for necessary action. So the office is the brain of a business organisation.

   (*b*) **Store of records :** Office keeps adequate and up-to-date records of the business institution. It is the source of information for conducting, directing and controlling the business activities. To the management the records are the tools to direct the activities of the business. As such, the office plays an important role in the efficient management of the business.

   (*c*) **Cost reduction :** Office assists all departments in achieving their objectives. Generally customers send their orders to be executed. Of course, there is an additional cost when these orders are handled by the office. But if the orders are not handled properly and effectively, it is possible that some of the customers may stop further orders. And this leads to reduction in the profit. A well organised office with its business policies and plans will surely add to the earning capacity of the business.

These are essential for the efficient co-ordination of production, distribution and financing of the services in the business organisation. It is the co-ordinating link between all the departments of the organisation. For that it has to keep a good relation with every department.

5. **Office as an administrative nerve centre:** An office is the heart of all business activities. From here information on purchase, sales, finance and communication gets circulated.

6. **Office as control centre:** It is the medium for translating the policies into action. When the business grows, different departments come up with different jobs to be done. Each departmental head will have delegated power with which he takes actions and decisions. Each department will have its own office. Each office is responsible for the task entrusted to it. Each department gives readymade information to the management which takes final decision on the basis of the information supplied by the offices. The management makes out plans and policies and directs business activities in profitable ways and each departmental office is responsible for the function entrusted to it.

A good office facilitates the management to chalk out plans and policies. Dicksee has correctly said, "The office is to a business what the mainspring is to the watch." Prof. Donald Cousins says, The office of a successful business organisation must be the brain of the whole concern."

No organisation worth its name can exist without an office. The office can rightly termed as the nerve-centre or brain of a business organisation, for it exercises complete control over the organisation. It is its business to take policy decisions, drawing up plans and execute them competently. It keeps a vigilant eye on the functioning of the organisation and detects even the slightest deviation and applies corrections wherever and whenever necessary. It sets and resets procedures so that the organisation targets are fully met. Any failure of the organisation will be attributed to the incompetence or mismanagement of the office. An efficient office ensures unhampered growth and sustained prosperity.

The importance of the office to a business concern can be explained as, "The efficient management of a business enterprise depends on the effective performance of certain basic managerial functions, *viz.,* planning, formulation of policies and executive decisions for the employees and workers, directing and guiding the workers, co-ordinating the activities of different departments, controlling business activities and evaluating the results. To carry out these functions properly, the management needs accurate information and factual data, effective ways and means of executing the plans and policies, as well as of communicating the decisions and evaluating the results. The office provides the necessary information on the basis of which plans and policies may be formulated and results assessed. It also provides different means of communication which help management in directing, guiding and co-ordinating the activities of the different departments, executives and employees. Again it is with the help of the factual information supplied by the office that the management maintains effective control over the business operations. "According to *Leffingwell*," a well-organised office makes it possible for management to plan its operations intelligently, to put its plans into effect surely, to follow their progress currently, to determine their effectiveness promptly, to appraise the results without delay, and to co-ordinate all the activities of the business.

Leffingwell and *Robinson* have summed up the importance of an office thus' "A well organised office makes it possible for the management to plan its operations intelligently, to put its plans into effect surely, to follow their progress currently, to determine their effectiveness promptly, to appraise their result without delay and to co-ordinate all the activities of the business."

CHALLENGES BEFORE THE OFFICE

The importance of the office has enhanced in our country due to industrialisation, increased economic activities etc. The office in our country faces challenges of different kinds—social, political, economical etc. Some of the challenges are stated below:

1. **Mechanisation :** In the modern day, the office activity is becoming more and more mechanised, say for example, sophisticated machines, like computers. The challenge before the management lies is installing these machines with the co-operation of the employees and their maintenance and proper use.

2. **Growth :** Owners (share-holders) are no longer in direct control of the business of a company form of business organisation. The top management aims the business to grow even when expansion is not accompanied by adequate profits. However, growth is accompanied by adequate return to the share-holders of the company.

3. **Statutes :** Various laws concerning the management are being changed frequently to achieve the social and economic objectives. It is essential for the office of an organisation to gear itself to face such changes. The problem lies on the office in running the enterprise without evading the various laws.

4. **Recruitment of staff :** By the introduction of sophisticated machines, it is an important problem to attract better entrants and train them properly. There must be a provision of proper incentive system and promotional opportunities.

5. **Reduction of paper work :** The office should distinguish between essential and non-essential records. Some records may be essential. Such records may be retained and other non-essential records should be destroyed.

QUESTIONS

1. What is an office ? What are the functions of an office?   (B. Com.,M.S.)
2. "The office is to a business, what the mainspring is to a watch." Explain.
                                                                    (B. Com., Delhi, Punjab)
3. "Office work is unproductive clerical work." Explain.
                                                            (B. Com. MK, Bangalore, Chennai)
4. "The office is a co-ordinating factor." Explain.   (B. Com., Delhi)
5. "The office is the nerve centre of an organisation." Explain.
                                                            (B. Com., Punjab, ICWA, Delhi)
6. What is an office ? Bring out its importance.   (B.Com., Madurai)
7. What are the functions of a modern office? Explain its organisation and management.   (B.Com., Madurai)
8. "An office may be regarded as a place where the central mechanism for an organisation is located." Comment on this statement and explain the importance of modern office.   (B. Com., Delhi, ICWA)
9. "No organisation worth the name can exist without an efficient office." Comment on this statement and bring out clearly the functions of modern office.
                                                                    (B. Com., Mumbai, ICWA)

10. "Office does not produce any article for sale: therefore, office work is relatively unimportant." Do you agree? Give reasons for your answer.

(B. Com., Punjab, ICWA, MS)

11. "Office work is concerned with records and statistics, with computing with planning and scheduling." In the light of this statement, discuss the administrative management functions of an office. *(B. Com., M.S., MK, Mumbai, ICWA)*

12. "The essential feature of the office is the work itself, not who does it or where it is done." Discuss. *(B. Com., Chennai, ICWA, Punjab)*

13. Describe the functions of a modern office. *(B.Com. Delhi)*

14. "An office is to a business what the mainspring is to a watch". Comment on this statement and explain the importance and functions of a modern office.

(B.Com.Gujarat, Delhi)

15. What is the relationship of office with other departments in a business firm ?

(B. Com., Delhi)

CHAPTER

2

Office Management

INTRODUCTION

Management simply means to control or to administer. Office management means the method of controlling an office so as to enable to achieve a given aim. In our modern society, all kinds of business are carried on by a group of people, who have enough knowledge in their respective fields. But group of people, who are working for a common object must be guided and controlled by a leader or an authority. This is the function of the management. Management is a technique of leadership or control of an office in order to attain the aimed result through the efforts of other people in grouped activities. This is possible when the office is properly organised and managed. Office function is carried on by a group of people for a common result, by giving services to the organisation. The management has to organise the office in such a way as to attain the objectives. It is the function of the management to organise, guide and control the whole activities of the office personnel for a common aim. That is why in the present era, the personnel management has become a specialised subject.

Before entering into the next topic, it would be essential to understand the meaning of administration, management and organisation. *Sheldon* summarise them in the following words :

16

"Administration is the function in industry concerned in the determination of the corporate policy, the co-ordination of finance, production and distribution, the settlement of the compass of the organisation and the ultimate control of the executive."

"Management proper is the function in industry concerned in the execution of policy, within the limits set up by the administration and the employment of the organisation for the particular objects set before it."

"Organisation is the process of so combining the work which individuals or groups have to perform with the faculties necessary for its execution that the duties, so framed, provide the best channels for the efficient, systematic, positive and co-ordinated application of the available effort.

"Organisation is the formation of an effective 'machine; management of an effective executive; administration of an effective direction. Administration determines the organisation; management uses it. Administration defines the goal; management strives towards it. Organisation is the machine of management in its achievement of the ends determined by administration."

Thus "Determination of policy and co-ordination (Administration), the execution of policy and employment of organisation (Management) and the combination of the work of individuals or groups with the faculties necessary for its execution (Organisation)".

According to *Schulze*, "*Administration* is the force which lays down the object for which an organisation and its management are to strive and the broad policies under which they are to operate. *Management* is the force which leads, guides and direct an organisation in the accomplishment of a predetermined object. *Organisation* is the combination of the necessary human beings, materials, tools, equipment, working space and appurtenances, brought together in systematic and effective correlation, to accomplish some desired object."

According to *Milward*, "*Administration* is primarily the process and the agency used to establish the object or purpose which an undertaking and its staff are to achieve; secondarily, administration has to plan and to stabilise the broad lines or principles which will govern action. These broad lines are in their turn usually called policies. *Management* is the process and the agency through which the execution of policy is planned and supervised. *Organisation* is the process of dividing work into convenient tasks or duties, of grouping such duties in the form of posts, of delegating authority to each post and of appointing qualified staff to be responsible that the work is carried out as planned."

It is known through economics that the factors of production are divided into four— Land, Labour. Capital and Entrepreneur. The last is important under the present study. The entrepreneur is the man, who brings together the other factors in a business. The other factors can be called as organisation. For example consider a human body. Human body can be compared as an organisation. It has various organs—ears to hear, eyes to see, hands to work, legs to walk, etc. Each organ has a specific work. Each of the organs of course works in co-ordination with the other organs. All the activities of the different organs combined, can be considered as an organisation. Finally, there is a top administrator—the brain. Similarly in business, production department, sales department, personnel department etc., have to do the proper functions as directed by the management. The organisation may refer to the function of organisation or to the plans carried out through persons. Organisation is concerned with and exists when an employee is selected, assigned jobs within his ability to work through a clear understanding. He must understand what he should do, how he should do and when he should do.

Office administration denotes the function of giving birth to major policies upon which the enterprise is to be functioned. In a joint-stock company, the Board of Directors makes the major policies and in a partnership firm, the partners lay down the policies. In all kinds of business the function of administration is the same. Making the policies is the function of the administration.

The word management has been defined variously by different authors and some of these definitions are given below :

1. "Management is an executive function which is primarily concerned with carrying out of the broad policies laid down by the administration. It is that function of an enterprise which concerns itself with the direction and control of the various activities to attain the business objectives."   —*Spriegel*

2. "Management is the force which leads, guides and directs an organisation in the accomplishment of a pre-determined goals."   —*Schulze*

3. "Management proper is the function in industry concerned in the execution of policy, within the limits set up by the administration and the employment of the organisation for the particular objects set before it."   —*Liver Sheldon*

4. "The job of management is to make co-operative endeavour to function properly. A manager is one who gets things done by working with people and other resources in order to reach an objective."   —*Newman and Warren*

5. "Management consists of getting things done through others. Manager is one who accomplishes the objectives by directing the efforts of others."   —*George*

6. "Management may be defined as the art of securing maximum, prosperity with a minimum of effort so as to secure maximum prosperity and happiness for both employer and employee and give the public the best possible service."

7. "Management is simply the process of decision-making and control over the action of human beings for the express purpose of attaining predetermined goals."

8. "Management is the art and science of decision-making and leadership."

Definition of Office Management : The term office management has been defined in the following ways by different authors :

1. "Office management is that branch of management which is concerned with the services of obtaining, recording and analysing information of planning and communicating, by means of which the management of a business safeguards its assets, promotes its affairs and achieves its objectives." Institute of Administrative Management, England.

2. "Office management may be defined as the manipulation and control of men, methods, machines and materials to achieve the best possible result—result of the highest possible quality with the best possible effort and expense, in the shortest practicable time and in a manner acceptable to the top management."   —*Wylie Brecht*

3. "Office management is mainly concerned with the organisation of an office in order to achieve a specific performance, and to make the best use of the personnel by using the most appropriate machines and equipment, the best possible methods and by providing the most suitable environment."

4. "Office management as a function is that branch of the art and science of management which is concerned with the efficient performances of office work, whenever and wherever that work is done."   —*Leffingwell & Robinson.*

5. "Office management may be defined as the art of guiding the personnel of the office in the use of materials, methods, machines and equipment appropriate to their environment in order to achieve its specified purposes." *—Mill & Standingford*
6. "Office management as a task of planning, co-ordinating, motivating the efforts of others towards the specific objectives in the office". *—George R. Terry.*

We can understand from these definitions that office management means planning, organising, co-ordinating and controlling the activities of an office. The other names used for office management are : Administrative office management, Scientific office management, Information management etc.

> **Functions of Office Management :**
> 1. Planning   2. Organising
> 3. Staffing   4. Directing
> 5. Motivating   6. Co-ordinating
> 7. Controlling   8. Communication

FUNCTIONS OF OFFICE MANAGEMENT

There is no universally accepted classification of management functions. This is because different authors who were considering different organisations, gave separate classification of management functions. Office management is similar to the general or administrative management, it performs the same functions as are performed by the management. The functions of office management in brief, are given below :

I. Planning

Planning is a fundamental function of office management. All types of organisations prepare plans. Planning our studies, our careers, new products etc. are examples of planning. It is the determination of a course of action to achieve a desired result. Planning concentrates on setting and achieving objectives of an organisation. It is an intellectual process. It is characterised as the process of thinking before doing. Planning function of management precedes all other managerial functions. "Planning is deciding in advance what is to be done. When a manager plans, he projects a course of action for the future, attempting to achieve a consistent, co-ordinated structure of operations aimed at the desired results." Planning involves projecting the future course of action for the business as a whole and also for different sections within it. Planning is thus the preparatory step for actions and helps in bridging the gap between the present and the future. Since planning is essentially choosing, it is dependent upon the availability of alternatives. It is through this process of choosing that office manager can obviously be seen as an important aspect of planning. Planning process comprises determination and laying down of objectives, policies, procedures, rules, programmes, budget and strategies etc. The operations of the office will not run smoothly if they are not planned adequately. Planning makes it possible to occur which would not otherwise happen.

Benefits of Planning
1. The business objectives can easily be secured through plans.
2. Planning gives direction to activities in the office.
3. It focuses attention on objectives.
4. It provides co-ordinated efforts and reduces risk and uncertainties.
5. It facilitates the process of decision-making.
6. It encourages innovation and creativity.

7. It serves as a basis of control.
8. It encourages the sense of involvement and team spirit.
9. It eliminates unproductive office work and thus helps to minimise cost.
10. It helps in economical operations.

II. Organising

It is an important managerial activity by which management brings together the human and material resources for the achievement of certain objectives. Organisation is the foundation upon which the whole structure of management is built. It may be conceived of as the structuring of functions and duties to be performed by a group of people for the purpose of attaining enterprise objectives. Organising is the determining, grouping and arranging of the various activities deemed necessary for the attainment of the objectives, the assigning of people to these activities, the providing of suitable physical factors of environment and the indicating of the relative authority delegated to each individual charged with the execution of each respective activity.

According to *Louis A Allen*, "Organisation is the process of identifying and grouping the work to be performed, defining and delegating responsibility and authority, and establishing relationships for the purpose of enabling people to work most effectively together in accomplishing objectives."

According to *Oliver Sheldon*, "Organisation is the process of combining the work which individuals and groups have to perform with the faculties necessary for its execution that the duties so formed provide the best channels for efficient, systematic, positive and co-ordinated application of the available effort."

Steps of Organisation

The important steps involved in the process of an organisation are :

1. Identification of Activities

Organisation structure is developed to achieve objectives. Organisation as a process of management is concerned with identifying and grouping of activities to be performed.

2. Grouping of Activities

Closely related and similar activities are grouped together to form departments, divisions or sections. Grouping may be done on several bases depending on the requirements of the situation. Such grouping of activities is called departmentation.

3. Assignment of Duties

Each group of related activities is assigned a position most suited for it. Every position is occupied by an individual. While assigning duties, the requirements of the job and the competence of the individual should be properly matched together. The process of assigning duties goes on till the last level of the organisation.

4. Delegation of Authority

Authority without responsibility is a dangerous thing and similarly responsibility without authority is an empty vessel. Hence corresponding to the responsibility authority is delegated to the sub-ordinates for enabling them to show work performance.

5. Fitting Individuals

Having determined the various parts and portions of the job to be done, the next step will be to fix suitable and well-qualified persons into these activities. Each person in the group will be given a specific part of the job to do and will be made responsible for it.

III. Staffing

'Staffing' is concerned with the recruitment, selection, placement, training, growth and development of all those members of the organisation whose function is to get things done through the efforts of other individuals. After determining the number and type of personnel to be appointed to fill different jobs management starts recruiting, selecting the training the people to fulfil the requirements of the enterprise. According to *Franklin Moore,* "Staffing is a forward looking activity because tomorrow keeps becoming today. Attrition constantly reduces executive ranks through retirement, death, resignations and occasional dismissal; so young men keep moving up. Besides this, most enterprise grow, providing new openings for managers." The function of staffing was considered to be a part of organising but recently it has developed into a distinct function of management, and is, therefore treated separately in the chapter relating to Personnel Management.

IV. Directing

Once plans are drawn up to pre-determined objectives competent persons are appointed, the organisation is ready to go into action. Directing is the managerial function of guiding, inspiring, instructing and harnessing people towards the accomplishment of desired results. It is that part of the management process which actuates the members of an organisation to work effectively and efficiently for the achievement of the goals. Direction in the words of *Koentz* and *Q 'donnel,* "the interpersonal aspect of managing by which subordinates are led to understand and contribute effectively and efficiently to the attainment of enterprise objectives." According to *Haimann,* "Directing consists of the process and techniques utilised in issuing instructions and making certain that operations are carried on as originally planned. Directing is the process around which all performance revolves. It is the essence of operations, and co-ordination is a necessary by-product of good managerial directing." Directing consists of the following steps :

1. Issuing orders and instructions to sub-ordinates;
2. Guiding and teaching the sub-ordinates the proper method of doing work;
3. Supervising the work of sub-ordinates to ensure that it conforms to plan;
4. Motivation of sub-ordinates by providing incentives.

V. Motivating

The term motivation has been derived from the word motive. Motive is anything that initiates or sustains activity. It is an inner state that energises, activates or moves and that directs or channels behaviour towards goals. Motive is a psychological force within an individual that sets him in motion. Behind every human action there is a motive. According to *Brech,* "Motivation is a general inspirational process which gets the members of the team to pull their weight effectively, to give their loyalty to the group, to carry out properly the tasks that they have accepted and generally to play an effective part in the job that the group has undertaken." The important task of office management is to motivate employees so that they may direct their efforts towards the accomplishment of organisational goals.

Motivating may be achieved by :

1. Providing inducements and incentives to employees;
2. Keeping morals high;
3. Satisfying the needs of the employees.

VI. Co-ordinating

Along with specialisation there must be conscious efforts on the part of the management to see that all activities, carried on by experts and different departments, should contribute to the achievement of the objective of the business. Smooth working of an enterprise and the definite achievement of its objectives depend on sound co-ordination. According to *Lundy,* "Co-ordination involves the development of unity of purpose and the harmonious implementation of plans for the achievement of desired ends." According to *Mooney* and *Reiley,* "Orderly arrangement of group efforts to provide unit of action in pursuit of a common purpose." Thus co-ordination may be achieved by:-

1. Simplified Organisation.
2. Harmonised programmes and policies.
3. Well designed method of communication.
4. Voluntary co-operation.
5. Co-ordination through supervision.
6. Clear cut objectives.
7. Clear definition of authority and responsibility.
8. Effective leadership.

VII. Controlling

"To control is to determine what is being accomplished; that is to evaluate performance and, if necessary, to apply corrective measures so that performance takes place according to plan. After the plans are put into action, there can be several hurdles in the achievement of goals. Results may fall short of targets. Direction may be faulty. Therefore, management must find out what is going wrong, what changes in plans and directions are required and what must be done to set things right. This is the function of control. In words of *Anthony,* "Management control is the process by which managers assure that resources are obtained and used effectively and efficiently in the accomplishment of an organisation's objectives."

Basic elements of the control process :

1. Establishment of standards or objectives.
2. Measurement of actual performance.
3. Comparing actual performance against the standard set.
4. Determining the reason for deviation.
5. Taking corrective action.
6. Feedback.

Control is thus closely related to the planning job of the manager. But it should not be viewed merely as a postmortem of past achievements and performance. In practice, a good control system should suggest corrective measures so that negative deviations may not recur in future.

VIII. Communication

Communication is a means by which different persons are linked together in a group or organisation to attain a common goal. No group activity is possible without communication. It enables the members to co-ordinate, to exchange and to make progress. A good communication should aim at making everyone concerned aware of the goal which the organisation wants to achieve.

The two main objectives of communication are to inform and to persuade. Communication is the means by which behaviour is modified, change is effected, and goals are achieved. Communication is essential for effective control and motivation.

SCIENTIFIC OFFICE MANAGEMENT

Scientific management, as the name implies, means the application of the scientific method for the solution of the problems of management. In its application, the scientific approach is used in meeting problems of all types instead of depending on tradition. In view of the present day complexities and growing magnitude of management responsibilities, scientific office management is perhaps the best solution. It does not mean that office management is a pure science. It is the application of scientific principles to management decision-making. In the words of *Frederick W. Taylor, the Father of Scientific Movement*, "the scientific management means knowing exactly what you want men to do and seeing that they do it in the best and cheapest way." Scientific management is characterised by a scientific method of attack in the solution of business problems and the development of managerial techniques. It looks, considers and evaluates customs and traditions, personal intuition and experience, and inductive deductive thinking.

Techniques of scientific management involve the following steps :

1. Setting up of standard tasks through scientific investigation and research (time, motion and method of studies)
2. Analysis of operations to evolve the best method of doing the standard task.
3. Scientific selection of personnel and their training in the methods involved.
4. Standardisation of materials, equipment and working environment for workers.
5. Introduction of specialisation in the administrative and organisational set up.
6. Improvement of worker-management relations through good faith, perfect understanding and better incentive wage plans.

The principles and techniques of scientific management are equally applicable to office management and lead to increased productivity of labour. Elimination of waste of all types, whether men or materials, is aimed at.

Elements of the Management

The four elements of office management are :

1. **Purpose :** The office manager must be fully aware of the aims and objectives of the organisation in order to make correct decisions. If he knows the purpose of office, he will provide direction to the office activities and thus make it easy to evaluate the performance of different individuals.
2. **Environment :** The office environment is not only the physical environment but also the external factors such as the laws and customs of the community within which the firm operates. Efficiency of office personnel depends upon the perfect understanding of office environment. The environment is always changing and the officer must take decisions accordingly.
3. **Personnel :** It is the most important element. The office manager must select suitable personnel and place them in appropriate jobs. They must be given proper training and then only they can increase their efficiency. To realize the desired objective of the office, the personnel must be provided with sufficient incentives to motivate them to contribute their efforts whole-heartedly.
4. **Means :** It is a tool and includes materials, methods, machines and equipments with the help of which office activities are performed by the office employees. The office manager must know how to use these means in the best manner. The best use of means leads to greater efficiency and effectiveness in the work.

DEPARTMENTATION

Departmentation is the process which is used to group business activities into units for the purpose of efficient administration at all levels. The process of organising an enterprise consists of (a) dividing and grouping the work to be done and (b) assigning different duties and responsibility to different people. In other words, the total activities of the business are divided into a number of functional departments, each entrusted with a particular type of business activity. A large business house has, therefore, as many sectional offices as there are functional or operating departments. It is difficult to function for a business enterprise unless its activities are divided into group of functions, for example, production, purchasing, financing, accounting etc. These classified functions are performed by a group of specialised employees. A section is a group of workers under one supervisor. There is a general office, under the control of the Secretary, which co-ordinates the activities of the functional departments as well as those of sectional offices.

Basis of Departmentation

Different concerns follow different bases of departmentation depending upon their size and nature of operations. The bases of departmentation usually followed by most business enterprises are :

1. Product Basis : When a firm produces large number of products and the volume of business done in each product is sufficiently large, then internal organisation may be formed on the basis of products handled or service rendered. One department is in charge of one line of products. For instance, a firm dealing with paints, chemicals, plastics and fertilizers, it may have four departments each dealing with one product.

2. Geographical Basis : When an organisation is large and geographically dispersed, departmentation on territorial basis may be made. For instance, a large Fan Manufacturing Company doing business in all the states of India may have separate departments for each state.

3. Functional Basis : Most business enterprises, however, prefer to segregate their departments on the basis of the major activities or functions of the enterprise, *viz.* production, purchase, marketing, accounts etc. The various activities of the business enterprise are divided into a number of functional departments. Thus matters relating to production are dealt with by the production department, matters relating to accounts by accounts department and so on.

4. Customer Basis : Under this basis of departmentation, activities are grouped according to the type of customers. For example, a large cloth store may be divided into wholesale, retail and export divisions. Each department specialises in serving a particular class of customers. For example, a large ready made store may have a separate department each for women, men and children.

5. Process or Equipment Basis : Manufacturing activities may be sub-divided on the basis of their process of production. For example, production department of a textile mill may be divided on the basis of processes of production, like, designing, spinning, weaving, dyeing, bleaching etc.

Advantages of Departmentalisation

1. An organisation can avail benefits of specialisation.
2. The efficiency of the management increases.

3. It is easy to fix accountability for the results.

4. Better control is facilitated.

5. It is easy to fix responsibility on workers.

6. It facilitates co-ordination.

The main purpose of the office is to provide efficient clerical work to the functional departments and the top management. For reasons of efficiency and economy and to secure specialisation, various activities to be performed by an office are divided into different departments. Each department of the office performs a specific function and the clerical staff attached to it becomes specialised in that particular function through constant dealing with the same work. Thus departmentation leads to greater efficiency which reduces the cost of office. Generally, a modern office has cash department, accounts department, filing department, typing department, mail department etc.

OFFICE MANAGER

It is already seen that the office work is a function of service. The job of the office manager is to control the activities in the office so as to get the maximum benefit out of them.

The manager plans, organises, directs and controls the activities of his sub-ordinates in the organisation. He brings the human resource or human talent of a firm into combination with non-human resources viz. money, materials and machine.

Qualities of a Manager

1. In addition to general education, he must have undergone management training. There is no hard and fast rule as to the minimum qualifications to be possessed. The qualifications are based on the job he does.

2. He must have a good command of language.

3. He must be a good organiser.

4. He must have an ability to teach others.

5. He must be tactful and skilful in his dealings.

6. He must be sincere to do his duties.

7. He must be a good leader. He must be able to create team spirit.

8. He must have ability to delegate the job and work to his staff according to the abilities of the workers.

9. He must be calm and confident in all situations. He should have self-control. He should not be irritable.

10. He must be constantly in touch with the new facts and methods to increase the efficiency.

> **Functions of Office Manager**
> 1. Leadership
> 2. Co-ordination
> 3. Recruitment of staff
> 4. Training of staff
> 5. Motivation
> 6. Discipline
> 7. Accounting
> 8. Controls stationery
> 9. Secretarial services
> 10. Organising office activities

Functions of an Office Manager

1. **Leadership :** He has to control his office. The office manager is important for the smooth running of the organisation. He is in-charge of the public relations. He helps other

departments to achieve their goals. He has complete control over the work done in the office.

2. **Co-ordination :** He has to select the persons–right persons for the right jobs.

    (a) He will have to work and carefully see that the policies laid down by the management are implemented.

    (b) He is the connecting link between the top management and the workers. Workers approach him for their grievances and difficulties and manager has to redress them. If he is not able to do the needful, he must place it before the management.

    (c) He has to work and safeguard the firm, where he is an office manager.

    (d) His primary duty is to the management and secondary duty to the workers. He must please both the parties. If either one of the parties is annoyed or neglected, he will be regarded as a bad manager.

3. **Recruitment of Staff :** He has to select the right person for the right job. For that he invites applications, conducts interviews and selects personnel.

4. **Training of Staff :** He provides training to the new employees as well as old employees to improve their skill in the latest techniques of management.

5. **Motivation :** He measures the employees' work and output and offers rewards which increase their efficiency and ensure their better co-operation and lead to the promotion of the staff.

6. **Discipline :** Discipline in the office depends upon him. The rules and principles of the management should be followed by the sub-ordinates. He must have ability to speak. New methods cannot be accepted, unless full explanation is followed. He has to convince others about the fact findings.

7. **Accounting :** He has to keep a close touch with the accounting and costing section.

8. **Controls Stationery :** He has to safeguard the furniture, fittings, machines, equipments and various types of records.

9. **Secretarial Services :** He maintains statutory and accounts books, holds meetings, drafts reports and minutes etc. Thus he does the secretary's functions.

10. **Organiser and Supervisor :** He organises and supervises the office correspondence, messenger services, communication system, filing and indexing, protection of records etc.

There is no hard and fast rule as to the functions of an office manager. His functions depend upon the type and size of the organisation.

He has to face difficult situations very tactfully, and must have pleasing manners always in dealing with critical positions and in suggesting suitable ideas. He must be tactful.

Some drawbacks of Office Managers :

1. Some managers do not delegate proper authority to others for fear of losing power. If they do not delegate authority they may be unnecessarily approached even for unimportant matters. Only if authority is delegated, the sub-ordinates will feel the responsibility and work sincerely. Sometimes sub-ordinates assume authority which creates unpleasantness.

2. If the office manager delegates all the power to his sub-ordinates they may think that they are overburdened with the work, while the manager is resting in his chair. This should not happen. He must also work along with others, as he is the leader.

3. When the office work is delegated, the office manager looks for the result. The result will not be good unless the work is simplified and made easy to execute. Therefore, it is the prime duty of the office manager to make his sub-ordinates to understand the work and suggest good and easy methods through which the work can be performed.

4. If he is not punctual towards his duties, then naturally his sub-ordinates will also follow his bad example. If he is punctual, he can maintain punctuality in his office.

5. If any employee–sub-ordinate–comes to him with grievances, he has to hear them politely and suggest suitable remedies. A patient is often much more relieved not by the medicine, the doctor prescribes, but by his pleasing attention.

Leffingwell lists down twelve control measures for the Office Manager :

1. Plan and schedule the day's work in writing.
2. See that the work is started on time.
3. Determine the amount of unfinished work.
4. Determine the amount of current work to be done.
5. Measure the working force by the work.
6. Check up on the daily output.
7. Insist on a full day's work.
8. Check up on your standard practice instructions.
9. Plan your daily supervision for the week.
10. Establish overall daily inspection of maintenance.
11. Establish overall inspection of filing and record keeping.
12. Get acquainted with your personnel.

Status of Office Manager

The executive, who is put in charge of the management of the office is known as Office Manager. He performs the managerial functions of planning organising, directing and control in relation to the office operations. The scope of functions of an office manager vary from organisation to organisation. This is because of nature and size of organisation, volume of work etc. Business conditions, both internal and external, do not remain constant for long. Therefore he should constantly occupy himself in the task of innovating, *i.e.* introducing new changes. According to *Neuner and Keeling,* "Today's office executives direct the nerve centre of their companies. With knowledge of technological developments, office systems and procedures, and human relations, they greatly influence the growth or progress of their firms, to reflect their new status of office responsibility, new titles have come upon the scene: no longer is it possible to categorise all office executives by the title of office manager. Today among other titles, the office executives may be known as the controller, director of finance and services, manager of office services, treasurer, systems and procedures manager - director, operations manager and administrative manager".

TRAINING OF OFFICE MANAGER

Every office manager must possess leadership quality. Leadership is the process by which a manager guides and influences the work of others in choosing and attaining specified goals by mediating between the individual and the organisation in such a manner that both will obtain maximum satisfaction. So the office manager must have the quality to mould the people working under him into a unified team dedicated to the realisation of objectives of the office. Another essential quality of an office manager is his ability to delegate authority to do work. If he is able to delegate his ability efficiently, he will become the most successful office manager.

Training is an organised process for increasing the knowledge and skills of people for definite purpose. The purpose of training is to improve the employee's current job performance. Training is a continuous process because a person never stops learning. Training should be differentiated from education and development.

The training methods usually adopted for training office managers are of two types :

(*i*) **On-the-job-training :** Under this method, the office manager is trained and developed while he is working on the present job. The usual methods are coaching and counselling, understudy, job rotation, temporary promotion to higher posts etc. While working on the job, the office manager gathers valuable experience in coping with various managerial problems. Alongwith this, he may receive advice and counsel from senior managers on methods of tackling special problems. Sometimes, he may be asked to act as the understudy of a senior manager or may be temporarily promoted to a higher position in exposure to new responsibilities. These methods will enable him to exercise his own managerial skill and judgement in new situations.

(*ii*) **Off-the-job-training :** Under this system, the office manager receives instruction and training away from his job, that is from outside agencies. The usual methods of such training are: lectures and conferences, training programmes conducted by management institutes and associations, universities other agencies. Office managers may receive such training in their off-duty hours on their own initiative or they may be encouraged to take such training by the top management of his organisation. It makes them more responsive to the objectives of the enterprise and more responsible in their performance. They begin to accept the goals of the enterprise as their own, which motivates them to higher and higher levels of performance. This results in higher efficiency and productivity. It also gives them a sense of dignity and self satisfaction, which encourages them to think creatively and develop themselves for higher responsibility.

Devices to promote Office Productivity :
  1. Use window envelope.
  2. Type on both sides of the paper.
  3. Use maximum cyclostyled materials.
  4. Review the existing form.
  5. Do not rush through work.
  6. Avoid using old files and folders.
  7. Selected clerks must be trained to do all jobs.
  8. Visitors should not be allowed to enter the place of work. If permitted, with the permission of the section head.
  9. Post-cards and inland letters are to be used wherever possible.
  10. Clerks should not disturb executives too often.

ORGANISATION

Organisation means a form of human association for the attainment of common objectives. Organisation is expected to facilitate better relationship among people, work and resources. Industrial organisation also denotes a type of association of persons for a common purpose.

According to *Sheldon*, "Organisation is the process of so combining the work which individuals or groups have to perform with facilities necessary for its execution, that the duties so performed provide the best channels for efficient, systematic, positive and co-ordinated application of available effort." As is the organisation is the result. Better organisation brings about better results, and poor organisation fails to get desired results.

OFFICE ORGANISATION

An office organisation involves the division of office activities into certain departments as well as persons. The office manager defines, and assigns activities, so that they can be most effectively executed. It means the determination and assignment of duties to the workers, and also the establishment and the maintenance of authoritative relationship among these grouped activities. Each department works in co-ordination with the other departments. Organisation is the backbone of the management. With proper care at all levels, it is possible for the management to attain the aimed goal.

Further each department splits the job into many simple processes; and each process is operated by a person. The sub-division of a sub-divided job makes the work simple, easy to understand and quick to perform. The office may be divided on the basis of size and nature of a concern. However, for big concerns there may be the following departments : (1) Accounts Department, (2) Cash Department, (3) Correspondence Department, (4) Purchase Department, (5) Sales Department, (6) Advertising Department, (7) Filing (Record) Department, etc. Further if the concern is very large, there may be Credit Department, Personnel Department, etc. In practice, the principle of division of labour to an office organisation means the division of office (work) into as many departments as necessary and each department is made responsible to increase the sales. The purchase department is responsible for good purchases and is answerable if bad quality of goods are purchased. The credit department is answerable if bad debt increases, so on and so forth. Thus, the responsibility is being fixed on all departments. In addition, a person, who deals in one item continuously becomes an expert and specialist. Through him better and quicker result is possible for the management.

Therefore, by division of labour, responsibility can be fixed on individuals. People gain more efficiency in the work, (*e.g.*, cashier of a bank).

QUESTIONS

1. What do you mean by Office Management? Discuss the functions of Office Manager.
   (B. Com., M.S.)
2. Give a suitable definition of Office Management. What are the elements of Office Management? *(B. Com., Madurai)*
3. "Office Management is the task of planning, co-ordinating and motivating the efforts of others towards the specific objectives in the office." Discuss. *(B. Com., Kerala)*
4. What are the functions of Office Manager ? *(B. Com., Madurai)*
5. Bring out the qualities of a good office manager and comment upon the role of Office Manager. *(I.C.W.A.)*
6. What do you understand by Departmentation ? *(B. Com., M.S)*
7. What are the functions of Office Management ? *(B. Com., Chennai)*
8. Bring out the advantages of scientific Office Management. *(B. Com., Kerala)*
9. Discuss the main departments of a Modern Office. *(I.C.W.A.)*
10. Define the concept of organisation and state the Principles of an organisation.
    (B. Com., Punjab, Delhi)

CHAPTER 3

Office Organisation

INTRODUCTION

Organisation structure has two complementary aspects :

(*i*) The form of structure where we can apply the principles of organisation. (*ii*) The functions to be performed, *i.e.* activities to be pursued and the degree of specialisation needed for such a pursuit. A planned or an effective organisation defines functions, relates these functions in a systematic manner, and assigns authority and degree of responsibility for each function. Sound organisation is essential to the existence of an enterprise or institution–economic or social. Organisation structure has human beings as links who are responsible for planning, direction, co-ordination and controlling etc. Thus it is true to state that organisation is the foundation of management as well as its chief tool.

PRINCIPLES OF ORGANISATION

The following principles are helpful in developing a sound and efficient organisation structure:

1. Objectives and Purpose
2. Specialisation and Definiteness
3. Delegation and Authority
4. Span of Control
5. Co-ordination and Balance

    6. Decision Making and Continuity
    7. Responsibility
    8. Efficiency
    9. Grouping
  10. Personal Ability
  11. Flexibility
  12. Scalar Principles.

1. Objectives and Purpose

Organisation is the mechanism through which management directs, co-ordinates and controls the business. Therefore, organisation is the foundation of management. Orderly planning is necessary for a good organisation. The entire organisation, at all levels of the organisation structure, must be geared in order to obtain the maximum results. It provides the framework within which all activities of the various connected works are carried out. The purpose of organisation is to avoid waste of time and duplication of work, and at the same time it aims at maximum co-ordination among departments. There must be unity of objectives so that all efforts can be concentrated on the set goals.

2. Specialisation and Definiteness

The principle of specialisation is the division of work aiming at maximum results. The effective attainment of the objectives needs specialisation in organisational functions through the division of labour. The activities of a concern are divided into many units and sub-units and suitable groupings into departmental activities, sectional activities, etc. In a small business, the manager does all the functions. But in modern business, the activities have become more involving complex specialised function. Through a good organisation, each job is well defined and is distributed on the basis of skill, experience and ability of the persons concerned. Fixed responsibilities aid in speeding up the work. Every employee must definitely know of his position in the firm and purpose thereof, so that he realises his responsibility and works accordingly.

3. Delegation and Authority

A clerk gets his authority from his section-head, to whom the worker is responsible for the proper performance of the job assigned. Therefore authority always flows downward, while responsibility always moves upward. A clear definition of authority and responsibility is essential. In the lack of clear definition, the management cannot have a smooth function of office work. A busy management allocates task among the sub-ordinates. A successful office manager never performs the task himself, but gets the work done by others.

4. Span of Control

No executive must have too many sub-ordinates reporting to him. If an office manager has many sub-ordinates under him, then the control becomes defective. The span of supervision or the span of authority or span of control limits the number of sub-ordinates reporting to a chief. An office manager should be expected to supervise a reasonable number of sub-ordinates. A sound organisation requires a proper balance between a section-head and workers. The ratio between the section-heads and the workers may depend upon factors: say, size of the units, nature of organisation, individual differences, etc.

5. Co-ordination and Balance

Co-ordination is essential to bring unity of action in the organisation. Centralisation of control of an organisation can be achieved through interlocking all units of the organisation. To secure co-ordination, working relationship should be established. Each worker should be known by the organisational structure, his designation in it and the relationship of his work with other departments as well as his executive. Work of all departments should be balanced in order to avoid conflict or overlapping of functions; with the object of ensuring smooth and efficient working of functions. Co-ordination aims at higher efficiency and effectiveness. It is a facilitative function. It helps the integration of the basic managerial functions *i.e.* planning, organising, motivation and control.

6. Decision-Making and Continuity

The organisational structure should be capable of ensuring the continuity of existence of an enterprise, and must permit the growth and expansion without dislocation of existing methods. The decision making process should be moved from bottom to upwards.

7. Responsibility

Without authority there cannot be any responsibility. Assignment of responsibility should be coupled with authority sufficient to carry them out. There must be parity between authority and responsibility. Each worker must have sufficient authority to discharge the responsibility assigned to him.

No superior should be allowed to avoid his responsibility by delegating authority to his sub-ordinates. He must be held accountable for the acts of his sub-ordinates.

8. Efficiency

Available human resources should be utilised to the best and fullest capacity in order to achieve the highest efficiency through operations.

The structure formulated should enable the enterprise to function efficiently and to achieve its objectives with minimum cost and effort.

9. Grouping

The work of the enterprise is divided into certain groups of activities and placed in charge of different departments or sections. The work load must be equally distributed to ensure smooth working of the enterprise. A periodical evaluation of the work load of departments and the workers should be made by the management.

10. Personal Ability

As people constitute an organisation, proper selection, placement and training are necessary. Organisational structure must ensure optimum use of human resources.

11. Flexibility

Organisation must be flexible so that it can be adjusted to changing conditions. It must permit expansion, replacement, merger etc. It should not be rigid.

12. Scalar Principle

The line of authority, called the chain of command, from the top executive to the lowest level executive should be clear and unbroken. Every individual should know whom he reports and who reports to him.

FORMS OF ORGANISATION

When there is one man, there is hardly any need for any organisation. When the enterprise expands, some pattern of organisation should be adopted. Generally, the following are the types of organisation.

1. Line Organisation

This is the simplest and oldest form of organisation. It is also referred as the 'Military' or 'Traditional' or 'Scalar' or 'Hierarchical" form of organisation. An important feature of such types of organisation is the superior– sub-ordinate relationship. In this type of organisation authority descends from the top to its bottom level through downward delegation of authority. Sub-ordinates become responsible to their immediate superiors. All decisions and orders are made by the top executives and handed down to sub-ordinates. This type of organisation is as that of military administration. The topmost management has full control over the entire enterprise.

This form is suitable:

(a) If the business is comparatively small.
(b) If the labour management problems are easy to solve.
(c) If the processes are easily directed.
(d) If the work is of a routine nature.

Merits of Line Organisation

1. It is simple to work.
2. It is economical and effective.
3. It is easy to fix responsibility.
4. It facilitates quick decisions and prompt actions.
5. Quick communication is easy.
6. Discipline can easily be maintained.

Demerits of Line Organisation

1. The organisation is rigid and inflexible.
2. It works on a dictatorial basis.
3. Departmental heads act in their own whims and desires; as such it is difficult to secure co-ordination of the activities of workers and department.
4. In big business it does not operate satisfactorily.

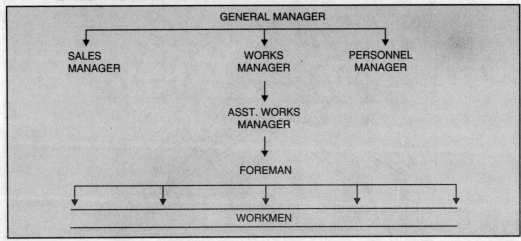

2. Functional Organisation

The limitations of line organisation have been removed under this system. All types of work of the organisation are grouped and managed by the top executive. There are separate functional departments for major functions of the enterprise, for example personnel department, sales department, purchase department, finance department, etc. Each department does its function for the entire organisation. Sales department does its function for the whole organisation. Purchase department does its function for the whole enterprise. The functional organisation works through the line organisation. Functional organisation is based on expert knowledge and makes the greatest use of division of labour resulting in high efficiency and specialisation.

Features (Functional Organisation)

1. The whole task of the enterprise is divided into specialised functions.
2. Each function is performed by a specialist.
3. The specialist incharge of a functional department has the authority over all other employees for his function.
4. Specialists operate with considerable independence.

Merits of Functional Organisation

1. Greatest use of division of labour is possible.
2. The system is based on expert knowledge.
3. Functional efficiency of the worker can be maintained.
4. Mass production is made by standardisation and specialisation.
5. Separation of mental and manual functions is possible.
6. Methods and operations can be standardised.

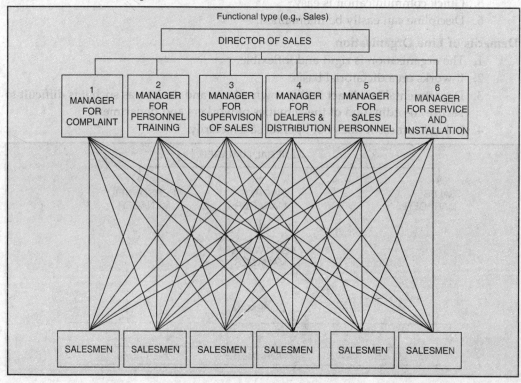

Functional type (e.g., Sales)

DIRECTOR OF SALES

| 1 MANAGER FOR COMPLAINT | 2 MANAGER FOR PERSONNEL TRAINING | 3 MANAGER FOR SUPERVISION OF SALES | 4 MANAGER FOR DEALERS & DISTRIBUTION | 5 MANAGER FOR SALES PERSONNEL | 6 MANAGER FOR SERVICE AND INSTALLATION |

SALESMEN | SALESMEN | SALESMEN | SALESMEN | SALESMEN | SALESMEN

Demerits of Functional Organisation

1. Too many experts and bosses (high officials) create confusions in the minds of the worker.
2. It is difficult to fix responsibility on workers .
3. Discipline and morale of the workers are seriously affected, because of contradictory orders from different experts.
4. There are heavy overhead expenses.

3. Line and Staff Organisation

In this type, the organisation is based on the line organisation and the functional experts advice the line officers as to the functions of the enterprise. The line officers are the executives and the staff officers are their advisors. Though the staff officers do not have the power to command the line officers, their advice is generally adhered to. The combination of line organisation with this expert staff forms the type of organisation–line and staff. The 'line' keeps the discipline and the staff provides expert information. The line gets out the production and the staff carries on research, planning, fixing standard etc. This type of organisation is suitable for large concerns. The line officers give orders, decisions etc., to sub-ordinates in consultations or guidance with the staff officers. The underlying idea of this method is that specialised work is to be left to experts, who will give advice on specialised grounds– investigation, research, etc. The staff officers have no executive positions in the concern and are the thinkers, while the line officers are the doers.

Merits of Line and Staff Organisation

1. This type is based on specialisation.
2. It brings expert knowledge upon the whole concern.
3. Increased efficiency of operations may be possible.
4. Mass production is possible.

Demerits of Line and Staff Organisation

1. There arises confusion unless the duties and responsibilities are clearly/Indicated by charts and office manuals.
2. Advice and expert information are given to the workers through the line officers. It is possible that the workers may misunderstand or misinterpret.

Line and Staff :

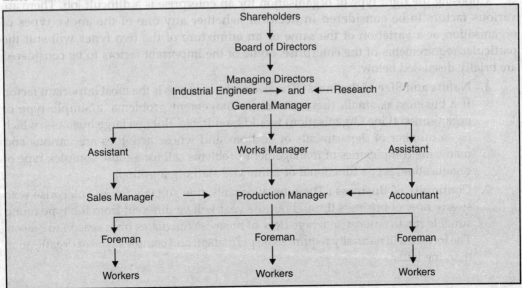

4. Committee Organisation

Committee organisation is widely used for the purpose of discharging advisory functions of the management. Committees are found in different levels of organisation. A committee is a group of people who meet by plan to discuss or make a decision on a particular subject. Because of its advantages, committee organisation is preferred. Committee means a body of persons, for example, Management committee consisting of General Manager and Departmental heads.

Committees have become an important instrument of management in modern organisations; they may be used for the following objectives :

1. To secure view-point and consultation of various persons in the organisations.
2. To give participation and representation to different groups or interests;
3. To co-ordinate the activities of different departments;
4. To review the performance of certain units;
5. To facilitate communication and co-operation among diverse groups.

Merits of committee organisation

1. It facilitates co-ordination of activity of various departments.
2. Pooled knowledge and judgement become available to the business thus its efficiency increases.
3. It is a good media of training and educating employees.
4. It helps to improve the motivation and morale of employees.
5. It promotes mutual understanding, teamwork and co-operation among employees.

Demerits of Committee Organisation

1. It is not only costly in terms of time it consumes, but also in terms of money involved.
2. Difficulty in reaching agreement results in indecision.
3. Compromise at the cost of efficiency is often affected.
4. Indecision may lead to a breakdown of group action.
5. Committee management is slower in reaching decisions than a one-man rule.

WHAT TYPE OF ORGANISATION TO CHOOSE ?

Choosing the right type of organisation for an enterprise is a difficult job. There are various factors to be considered in deciding whether any one of the above types of organisation or a variation of the same or an admixture of the two types will suit the particular requirements of the enterprise. Some of the important factors to be considered are briefly discussed below.

1. **Nature and Size of Business :** The size of the business is the most important factor. If a business is small, there are few management problems, a simple type of organisation (Line Organisation) would be suitable. But in a large business, which has a number of departments or sections and whose activities are various and many, the complexities of management problems call for a more complex type of organisation, *viz.,* a functional or a line and staff organisation.

2. **Continuity of Business :** The type of organisation suitable for an enterprise with steady flow of business throughout the year will be different from the type found suitable for an enterprise where flow of business fluctuates from season to season. The former will naturally require more permanent and complex type of organisation than the latter.

3. **Geographical Locations :** The geographical location of the various divisions or units of the enterprise is also an important factor in choosing the type of organisation. If the units, for example, factory, sales division,* marketing division etc., are located in the same premises or in close proximity to one another, a comprehensive but more complex type of organisation will be suitable. But if the units are located in separate buildings situated kilometers apart, separate organisations based on line and staff type may be more suitable.

4. **Staff Strength and Degree of Mechanisation :** The degree of supervision needed and the placement of different functions at different levels will depend on the ratio of unskilled to supervisory staff. Again the degree of mechanisation (ratio of machines to operatives) is also an important factor. Both these factors will have to be taken into consideration in choosing the type of organisation.

5. **Period of Establishment :** An old established business is in a better position to evolve and develop its own kind of organisation over the course of years than a newly established business. A greater effort is required to set up even a simple type of organisation in a newly established business.

OFFICE SYSTEM AND ROUTINE

To do office work, persons are required. These persons can work through forms and equipment. Therefore, three factors–persons, forms and equipment are involved in office work. An office has its own systems through which the work is carried out. System means a pre-planned approach to the day-to-day work to attain the aimed goal. A firm operates through systems. Again system indicates that right persons should be chosen for particular jobs.

There may be specific systems for office work, *viz.,* filing system, mailing system, purchasing system, etc. Filing system indicates the systematic maintenance (preservation) of documents, reports, etc. After looking up a paper it is filed in the proper file and kept in the proper place. All these jobs can be called as operations by persons. That is, before a paper is filed, operation takes place; that is finding out the proper file, checking the code of the file, tallying with the code mentioned in the paper to be filed, filing it datewise, keeping it in the place where it was, etc., are to be performed. These are the operations, whereas system refers to the filing of papers alone. Therefore system is broad division of work, and operations are within the system or comprising it. For example, when a mail is received, operation involves opening the letters, stamping them, dating them, registering them, giving them to the concerned departments, etc. The book-keeper also operates and finds the balance.

According to *Zene K. Quible,* "A system represents inter-related procedures necessary to achieve a well-designed goal." Each system is composed of a number of procedures. Procedures or routines or operations may be called the steps in a system.

According to *Terry.* "A system is a network of procedures which are integrated and designed to carry out a major activity."

According to *Carl Heyel,* "A system is an orderly arrangement of inter-dependent

---

The term *'system'* is a planned approach to the activities needed to attain desired objectives.

The term *'procedure'* or *'routine'* signifies a planned sequence of operations for handling recurring business transactions uniformily and consistently.

The term *'method'* is the manual or mechanical means and devices by which each operation is performed.

activities and related procedures which implements and facilitates the performance of a major activity of an organisation."

The definitions given above made clear that an office system is a standard sequence of operations in a particular business activity and is concerned how these operations are performed as well as when and where they are performed. In the specific context of an office, the term 'system' means the planned use of office personnel, forms and equipments for the performance of a particular phase of office work. In every office, there is a specific system for each major office activity. For example, the filing system refers to the planned manner of arranging and maintaining office records.

"A system is an organised combination of parts which form a complex entity, with interrelationships or interaction between the parts and between the system and environment."

— *Mills and Standingford*

A 'system' is a broad division or plan of work for the orderly performance of major phase of office activity. 'Procedures' or 'routines' are the smaller divisions comprising a system. The procedures comprising a system are so planned that every time a particular phase of office activity has to be performed according to the system, the same procedures have to be performed in the same sequence and in the same manner.

PROCEDURES

According to *Charles O.Libbey*, "Office procedures are a series of clerical acts organised under supervision to accomplish the purpose of the office." Office procedures may also be termed as office routines. Thus, "office routines or procedures are a series of steps to be taken for doing a particular work in the office as per the office system." The term office procedure is used to describe an office system : procedures are therefore, said to be made up of operations, an operation being the smallest step in a procedure, although the amount of work involved in an operation depends upon particular circumstances.

Carl Heyel describes, "a procedure is a series of logical steps by which all repetitive business action is initiated, performed, controlled and finalised. A procedure establishes what action is required, who is required to act, and when the action is to take place. Its essence is chronological sequence and its implementation is translated into results or actions."

The term 'procedure' or 'routine' signifies "a planned sequence of operations for handling recurring business transactions uniformly and consistently". It refers to the series of routine steps or operations needed for completing a particular phase of work according to the planned system. A procedure or routine thus stands in between a system and an operation. The procedure or routine operations required to complete the work are planned in such a way that every time that particular work has to be performed according to the system, the same operations have to be performed in the same sequence and in the same manner. Thus, a system is a broad division or plan of work, whereas procedures or routines are the smaller divisions comprising it.

METHOD

"A Method is the manual or mechanical means and devices by which each operation is performed. For each operation within a procedure, there is a method for accomplishing that phase of work. For example, in the procedure for classifying records, there is method for receiving the records; for examining them, filing them and arranging them in proper order.

The following figure illustrates the relationship–systems, procedures and methods.

PURCHASE SYSTEM

Procedure	1.	**Initiate Requisition**
Methods		A - Fill the purchase requisition
		B - Get necessary authorisation
Procedure	2.	**Selection of Supply Source**
Methods		A - Fill out quotation form
		B - Send the form to vendors
		C - Get quotation from vendors
		D - Prepare comparative statement
Procedure	3.	**Order for Purchase**
Methods		A - Fill purchase order
		B - Get signature of Purchasing Officer
		C - Send it to vendors
Procedure	4.	**Receive Supplies**
Methods		A - Verify quantity and quality of goods
		B - Send the goods to departments
		C - Verify the bill
Procedure	5.	**Payment**
Methods		A - Verify bill with the order
		B - Prepare voucher
		C - Get approval of Accounts Section
		D - Prepare cheque
		E - Send the cheque

CHARACTERISTICS OF A WELL-DESIGNED SYSTEM:

1. Flexibility
2. Adaptable
3. Systematic
4. Functional
5. Simple
6. Resourceful
7. Dependability
8. Acceptability

IMPORTANCE OF SYSTEMS AND PROCEDURES:

1. A goods system reduces delay and avoid delays.
2. Systems, based on methods employed, assist in speedy despatch of work.
3. A system involves internal check.
4. Saving in labour and overheads is brought about.
5. Delay, errors and unsatisfactory results are eliminated.

6. Improvements are constantly made.
7. A good system makes easier to train staff.
8. A uniform procedure is followed for each similar transaction.
9. Responsibility is more easily fixed for unsatisfactory performance.
10. A good system assists in the prevention of fraud and better control over work.

J.C. DENYER HAS LAID DOWN ELEVEN PRINCIPLES OF OFFICE SYSTEMS:

1. To have a good flow of work without bottle-necks.
2. To avoid duplication of work and records.
3. To keep the movements of the staff to the minimum.
4. To avoid unnecessary writing.
5. To make the best use of specialisation.
6. To keep the amount of paper work to the minimum.
7. To use the principle of management by exception.
8. To make as few exceptions to the rule as possible.
9. To avoid unnecessary checking.
10. To make the best use of machines, but not to use them unnecessarily, and
11. To seek simplicity, for complicated systems usually lead to mistakes.

ADVANTAGES OF SYSTEMS AND PROCEDURES :

1. Delay and bottlenecks can be avoided.
2. Errors can easily be eliminated.
3. Office efficiency is stepped up.
4. Office personnel can easily be trained.
5. Responsibility can be fixed for each employee.
6. Better form design and form control is possible.
7. Better control over work is facilitated.
8. Better co-ordination is possible.
9. Staff can perform their job independently.
10. A good system liberate the management.
11. Possible to achieve economy and efficiency.
12. Serves as a basis of control.

A 'routine' is a series of steps constituting a planned method of doing any particular work according to system. The same steps are taken in the same order and in the same way whenever the work is performed. A number of routines make a system. So a system is a broader division of work rather than a routine.

Suggestions for a Sound Office System :

1. The office system should be simple.
2. Co-related sections should be housed in close proximity.
3. The system should avoid chances of mistakes.

4. It should facilitate uninterrupted flow of work.
5. Available space should be utilised fully.
6. The system should serve the purpose for which it is meant.
7. It should be flexible.
8. It should maintain safety and secrecy.
9. It should facilitate effective internal control.
10. The system should be free from breakdowns.
11. It should avoid duplication and delay of work.
12. Unnecessary operations should be eliminated.
13. The system should achieve maximum economy in office operations.
14. Responsibility should be fixed on each employee.
15. Personnel must perform their duties independently, as far as possible.
16. Writing work of the staff should be minimised.
17. Procedure and system must be simple, economic, efficient and practicable.
18. Forms, proformas etc. must be simple to fill in.
19. Labour-saving machines should be adopted to get quick results.
20. Movement of persons should be brought down to the minimum.

JOB

Job is a collection of tasks, and responsibilities as a whole assigned to an individual.

Job Analysis is a procedure designed to discover the facts about jobs including each job's requirement in terms of the personal qualities of a satisfactory job-holder.

Job Description is an abstract of work performed, the responsibilities involved, the skill or training required and the type of personnel required for the job.

Job Specification specifies the type of employee required and assists in the selection of appropriate personnel by outlining the particular working condition. It is a product of **Job Description.**

Job Standardisation involves the establishment of uniform mechanical facilities and methods and combines the specifications of human standards with the specification of physical standard, so that efficiency can be maintained in keeping with the human element.

Job Classification deals with comparative study of jobs. Similar jobs are grouped into classes so that identical and consistent titles may be assigned.

Job Grading is the process by which the relative levels of various jobs are determined to establish the relative place of each job in the organisation.

Job Evaluation is the study of a job's worth in relation to other jobs. This involves the direct assignment of rupee value to jobs depending upon the method used.

Worker Analysis focuses attention on appraisal of the characteristics of employees using physical examination, tests, interviews and other procedures for the purpose.

Merit Rating is the relative value of the men as related to particular jobs. It is also known as "Efficiency Rating", "Employee Rating", "Service Rating", "Performance Rating", "Experience Rating".

OFFICE MANUAL

The office system, when it takes the shape of a book, is called office manual. The office manual contains the details of the work to be done in the office and other particulars of the concern. Generally, it will be helpful to the employees (especially new-comers) to understand the work without any delay. The office manual contains all the details of the whole office work. If a new man is appointed to do a particular job, he has to know the details relating to the job to be performed. Therefore, it would be enough to give instructions which are necessary for his job. This can be copied from the office manual and handed over to the person. This is enough. These written instructions as to the job to be performed can also be called as a Duty List. This is common in government offices.

An office manual is an authoritative guide to office organisation. It is a source of information, a knowledge of which is essential for the performance of office work. It may be in the form of a book or booklet and contains for the benefit of the office staff, information on operating office systems and procedures, methods and routines, executive decisions, standard practices, organisational policies and so on. If office employees are supplied with copies of the office manual, they do not have to approach their superiors again and again for necessary guidance, instructions and decisions; they do not, therefore, cause any interruption of work, nor waste their own time and the time of the executives. Office manuals are used not only to fix responsibility for the performance of office jobs, but also to set up procedures for the performance of office jobs.

Because instructions, rules and regulations are written down, each employee receiving a manual can be held responsible for them and for manner in which they are carried out.

TYPES OF OFFICE MANUALS

The main types of office manuals are given below :

1. **Policy Manual :** It contains a basic policies of the company. It describes the overall limitations within which managerial actions can take place. A policy manual lays down the decision, resolutions and pronouncements of the Board of Directors regarding the policies of the company. The main objective of policy manual is to inform all decision makers regarding their limits in the matter. This does not allow anyone to cross his limits and also provides guidelines.

2. **Organisational Manual :** The organisational manual contains the organisational structure, duties, rights and powers of the officials, the liabilities of each one and mutual relationships between the two of the officials, departments etc. and their interrelationship.

3. **Administrative Practice Manual :** This manual consists of administrative structure, systems, procedures, methods of work of each department in the organisation. This also spells out the duties, rights and responsibilities of the departments concerned. This also gives the proforma records returns etc. to be prepared from time to time.

4. **Departmental Practice Manual :** It contains detailed information about the organisation, policies and procedures of one department. Inter-departmental relationships are also shown with the help of charts and diagrams. Each department has its own manual.

5. **Multipurpose Manual :** This type of manuals helps the management to explain the personnel policies, rules and regulations to all employees. And this type of manual helps in eliminating misunderstanding and frictions between the management and employees.

Purpose of Office Manuals : Three purposes of office manuals are: to make instructions definite, to find answers in connection with procedures and to improve administrative control. For the successful controlling of office, there must be complete and up-to-date office manuals which inform the employees what they have to do, when and how.

An office manual contains general information, general office rules and regulations, safety instructions, organisational policies, job description, office facilities, executive relationship, standard practices and general instructions etc.

Advantages of Office Manuals :

1. It is easy for the office manager to supervise the work.
2. Doubts can be referred to office manuals.
3. Changes can be made whenever necessary.
4. It includes delegations of authority along with assignment of job.
5. Expensive training is reduced.
6. The worker understands the job to be performed, because the method is also written in it.
7. Responsibility can be fixed on individuals.
8. Good manuals lead to reduction of office costs.
9. The employees can get necessary information at any time they want.

Disadvantages of Office Manuals :

1. Office manuals are costly and time-consuming.
2. It is difficult to keep a manual up-to-date.
3. It may discourage team work because somebody may not like the recorded relationship.
4. A manual may be misinterpreted if it is not written clearly.
5. Sometimes the details given in the manuals are inadequate or incomplete or vague.

PREPARATION OF OFFICE MANUAL

The task of preparing the office manual is generally entrusted to a committee consisting of departmental heads. If the organisation plans to have a manual of a particular department, say. Sales Department, then the Sales manager will be a member of the committee. And he who takes initiative of supervising the preparation as well as revision of the manual. Revision of office manuals is as important as the preparation of the manuals. The committee will prepare the manual by following the steps :

1. An outline of subjects to be covered should be prepared. It will include history of the organisation, its products, objectives, office rules affecting office hours, holidays etc. Suggestions, ideas etc. as to the subjects to be collected in the manual should be invited from departmental heads, supervisors and employees etc. of the enterprise.

2. The number and types of manual to be prepared and their contents will be determined. This will help in determining procedures being used in different departments to be standardised.

3. The committee will consult the important executives and employees from each department regarding the flow of work and the job analysis of each position. It will assemble the information and compile it for proper use in preparing the manual.

4. The committee will study the data to determine the overlapping of jobs and duplication of functions. The information and data included should be accurate and complete. The language should be simple. As far as possible short sentences and words should be used.

5. Lastly, the draft manual will be prepared and edited. It may be either in bound or loose leaf form depending upon the use to be made of the manual.

A limited number of copies of the draft manual should be prepared for key executives, supervisors, employees, union representatives. Criticisms and suggestions should be received from them and in the light of which the manual should be given final shape by the committee and send it to the top management for approval.

The work of revising the manuals becomes easier and less expensive if the manuals are prepared in the form of loose-leaf books, rather than bound books. If it is in loose-leaf form the pages requiring revision can be extracted from the book and substituted easily.

ORGANISATION CHART

Organisation is made up of a group of persons working together towards the accomplishment of certain specified objectives. It has a structure of planned relationships among the group members. These relationships can be shown in an organisation chart.

"An organisation chart portrays managerial positions and relationships in a company or a department unit."   –Henry HAlbers

"The organisation chart is a graphic means of showing organisation data. Organisation charts are snap shots: they show only the formal organisation and they take it for only a given moment of time."   –Allen

"An organisation chart is a plan of working relationships. It shows who is to do the work that is to be done and who is to direct and supervise the efforts of those who are to do the work."   –Leffingwell

"An organisation chart is a diagram of the formal authority structure." –Ernest Dale

It is made clear that an organisation chart shows the different departments, divisions and units into which the activities of the organisation have been grouped.

It also shows the positions held by the different executives and their sub-ordinates in the departments and units, the relationship between their functions and the lines of authority and responsibility among them. It enables each executive and employee to understand what is his position in the organisation structure, what are his functions, to whom he is responsible for his work and who is responsible to him.

"An organisational chart is a diagrammatical form, which shows important aspects of an organisation including the major functions and their respective relationships, the channels of supervision, and the relative authority of each employee who is in charge of each respective function.   George Terry

Contents of Organisation Chart

An organisation chart may contain a variety of information. But, generally speaking, it includes the following:

1. Structure of the organisation.
2. Flow of authority.
3. Spheres of responsibility.
4. Line and Staff relationship.
5. Names and status of personnel in different positions.
6. Number of personnel, proposed promotions or transfers, salary etc. of staff.

An organisation chart should be as simple as possible and as soon as it becomes complicated, it may defeat the purposes for which it is created.

Advantages of Organisation Chart

1. It shows the whole organisation structure at a glance.
2. It defines the line of authority and responsibility.
3. It enables the management to locate defects.
4. It gives guidance to new employees.

Disadvantages of Organisation Chart

1. It reveals only a partial picture of the organisation.
2. It shows only the formal relationship and not the informal relationship.
3. Charts often lacks flexibility.

TYPES OF ORGANISATION CHART

Organisation charts can be prepared in different forms. However, all organisation charts may be classified into three broad categories :

1. Vertical Chart : This is the most widely used form. It shows the organisation structure in the form of a pyramid, the lines of command proceeding from top to bottom in lines. The highest position or person is placed at the top and after that the next highest. This process goes on upto the lowest level.

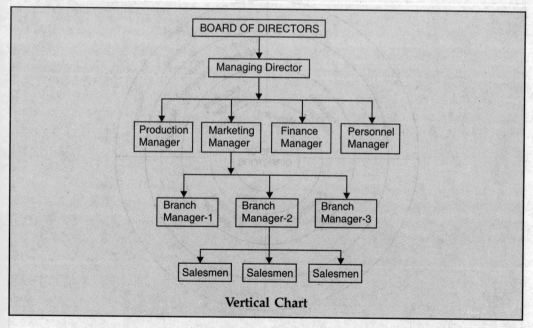

Vertical Chart

2. Horizontal Chart : In a horizontal chart the pyramid lies horizontally instead of standing vertically. The highest position is shown at the extreme left and the lowest position at the extreme right. In between each successive sub-ordinate position extends from left to right. Therefore, this chart is also called Left to Right chart.

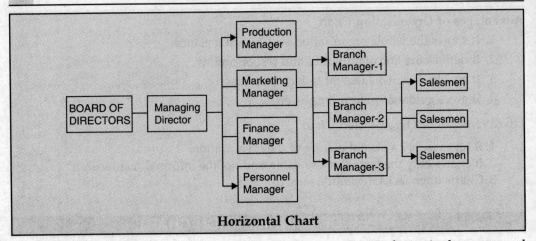

Horizontal Chart

3. Circular Chart : In a circular chart, the highest position is shown in the centre and the lowest position at the outermost circle. Positions at successive echelons extend in all directions outward from the centre. Distance of a position from the centre indicates the degree of closeness to the top position. Positions of equal status lie at the same distance from the centre. This form is, however, rarely used.

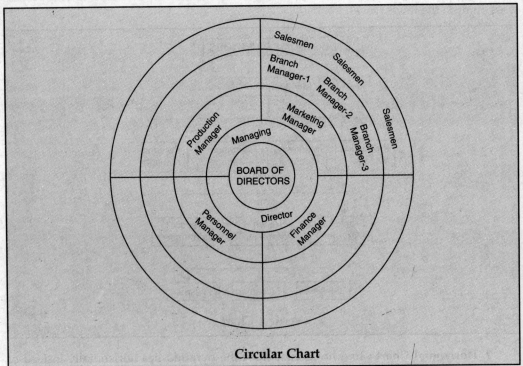

Circular Chart

FLOW OF WORK

"Flow of work is concerned with the way, work moves along from one operation to another–the quantity or volume of work gone through, the rate at which it moves along and the smoothness of its passage." –*Leffingwell*. The flow of work should be so planned that there is no interruption in the flow of work and there is no wastage of time of the staff waiting for the work. A steady, constant flow of work following a routine results in high efficiency. The study of the flow of work is basically a study aimed at greater efficiency in every sphere of office activity so that not only costs are cut down but delays are also eliminated.

Flow of work refers to the movement of office work from one place to another place without any interruption. If the flow of work is interrupted in its movement, there will be waste of time. In offices, some works reach the final stage quickly, while others move here and there in the whole organisation, perhaps for days. Such obstruction affects the flow of work. Office manual must be drawn up in such a way as to enable the flow of work through many hands. If the first man is quick, the second man slow and the third quick, then naturally the third man has to wait for the work; *i.e.* he has to waste his time because the flow of the work is interrupted by the second man. The following obstructions may cause interruptions:

1. Information required is not readily available and therefore the work is held up.
2. Unequal volume of work to be done causes delay in the flow of work.
3. Non-availability of work in hand means his job time is wasted.
4. Unnecessary movements of papers (or file) here and there in department affect the speedy result.
5. Laziness and carelessness of the staff will result in slowing down the flow of work.
6. Visitors to the office, calls from supervisors, telephone calls, etc., interrupt the work.
7. Lack of careful planning and backward movement of work affect the flow of work.
8. Unequal times required for different operations.
9. If the amount of work to be done by different workers of the same rank is unequal, the person who is burdened with a greater load of work will slow down the flow of work.
10. If work has to pass through wrong or unnecessary points, there may be a slowdown in the flow.

Straight Line Flow of Work

"Straight-Line flow of work is a method in which the work while progressing from one operation to another, should follow a course which is approximately, or nearly as may be possible, a straight line." This means that the work must always move forward from the beginning to the end of each operation. As far as possible, the straight-line flow of work, which involve very few backward movements should be adopted.

Merits :
1. Speed of work increases.
2. The method reduces messenger work.
3. Papers are rarely lost.
4. Keeps clerks and executives at their desks.

Office operations are continuous and repetitive in nature. Waste of time, in any stage results in a serious waste of time. Delay breeds delay. Therefore, the flow of work must be quick and continuation without interruption.

PROCESS OF DELEGATION

Performance of a function or service by an individual is called duty or the activities that an individual is required to perform are a duty on him. He is answerable for the work he has done. Authority is a right of power required to perform a job on the basis of duty assigned to one. An authorised person is empowered to do the assigned job and take a decision. Power means an ability to do things or get things done by others. Delegation means assigning work to others and giving them authority to do it.

The Board of Directors or the partners or the sole trader possesses all the power or authority to run the firm concerned. If the top management goes for doing the works of the concern, it becomes difficult for it to conduct the business, because of lack of time. Therefore, the work is divided and entrusted to persons who are appointed to look after it. When persons have been appointed to do a particular job, it can be said that a duty has been assigned to them. The assignment of duty is not complete unless authority has also been given to them. Therefore, assignment of duty is followed by authority. When the authority is passed on to the employees, there is a transfer of power to the sub-ordinates; *i.e.,* delegation of powers. Delegation of required authority to the sub-ordinates is necessary to discharge their assigned duty. Delegation of authority is made on the basis of duty one does. When one is delegated the authority, it means permission is given to do the duties. To be short it can be defined that authority is power to command others to do an act in a manner desired. When authority is conferred on a person, he knows the responsibility. If authority is not delegated, the assigned duty will not be done by the entrusted person, because he has no authority. It may also happen that sometimes he assumes authority and does the job. In both the cases the position becomes bad. Therefore, responsibility must always be followed by corresponding authority or power.

The difference between authority and responsibility is that they move in opposite directions. Authority always moves from the top downward, whereas responsibility moves upward. Authority is derived from supervisors, to whom the employee is responsible for the proper performance of his work. An executive working in a particular position cannot transfer to his sub-ordinates greater power than he himself possesses. One can transfer what one possesses. Sometimes, the sub-ordinates may not be willing to accept the orders from the supervisors, and then the delegation of authority has no meaning.

Delegation of Authority

According to *Allen*, "Delegation is the dynamics of management, it is the process a manager follows in dividing the work assigned to him so that he performs that part which only he, because of his unique organisational placement, can perform effectively and so that he can get others to help him with what remains."

According to *G.R.Terry*, "to delegate means to grant or confer, and delegation means conferring authority from one executive or organisational unit to another in order to accomplish particular assignment".

"Delegation means the passing on to others of a share in the essential elements of the management process a share, that is to say, in the judgement/decision for determining specific objectives, plans and targets for directing given operations, and in the command/control of the activities of the persons performing those operations."   *–Brech.*

"To delegate means to grant or confer; and delegation means conferring authority from one executive or organisation unit to another in order to accomplish particular assignment."   *–Terry.*

"Delegation is the process where an individual or group transfer to some other individual organs the duty of carrying out some particular action and, at the same time, taking some particular decision."   *–Mills and Standingfbord.*

If concern is a medium or large one, it becomes difficult for the office manager to do the works of the organisation. When he feels the lack of time to do a particular job within a specified time, he entrusts the work to his sub-ordinates. Now the sub-ordinates have the delegation of authority in doing the entrusted work. If the office manager divides the works among his sub-ordinates, he gets time to look after his managerial functions, which are more important to him.

In business concerns, the source of authority originates from the top of the firm; and the authority part by part, is delegated to the following persons–directors, secretary, managers, etc., and further from these persons delegation of authority is transmitted to various sub-ordinates. Delegation of authority shares the managerial work and operating work between a manager and his sub-ordinates. At the top of concern the scope of authority is wider and as it passes to the sub-ordinates, the scope of authority becomes narrower.

IMPORTANCE OF DELEGATION

1. For every organisation, small or big, delegation is essential.
2. Managers and supervisors at all levels can lessen their burden by delegating authority.
3. Ability of sub-ordinates increases as they are given some responsibility.
4. Delegation of authority reduces the work load. Hence work is done very quickly and efficiently.
5. Delegation of authority helps trained sub-ordinates also.

The delegation of authority may be done in the following manner.

1. The duty of a sub-ordinate should be defined clearly by the supervisor (duty list) and must be understood by the former.
2. Secondly, necessary authority may also be conferred upon him corresponding to the duty list, so that he knows his accountability and responsibility to the superiors.
3. Thirdly, though a manager may delegate certain authority on his sub-ordinates to perform certain acts, still he is responsible to his superiors *i.e.,* the manager cannot delegate his responsibility, but work can be assigned to his sub-ordinates. Therefore, in the initial stages, counter check by the assigning officer prevents unpleasant results.

The delegation of authority means fixing up of responsibility on the sub-ordinates by the superiors. Sub-ordinates cannot disown the responsibility. If a sub-ordinate neglects the responsibility after the delegation of authority, he is doing so at the cost of his job. The assigning officer has the authority to remove him from service.

The three components of delegation are Responsibility, Authority and Accountability. Each component depends on the others. They are equally important, interrelated and interdependent, and the three are inseparable features of process of delegation.

Responsibility : The work or duty of the sub-ordinates in the organisation is called responsibility. Responsibility is expressed in terms of functions, when a person is asked to control the working of a machine. Responsibility is expressed in terms of objectives, when a person is to produce a particular piece of product.

A manager assigns a certain function, work or duty to his sub-ordinate for performance. This is termed as assignment or responsibility.

Allen states, "Responsibility is the work assigned to a position. Responsibility refers to the mental and physical activities which must be performed to carry out a task or duty."

Donnell states, "Responsibility may be defined as the obligation of a sub-ordinate, to whom duty has been assigned to perform the duty."

Davis states, "Responsibility is the obligation of an individual to perform assigned duties to the best of his ability under the direction of his executive leader."

Authority : It means the powers and rights entrusted to a person to supervise the performance of work delegated. A manager grants authority *i.e.,* rights and powers to be exercised by the sub-ordinate. It is the right to perform certain assigned work or duties. The supervisor should delegate sufficient authority to do the assigned work.

Mooney stated, "Co-ordination is the all inclusive principle of organisation and finds its foundation in authority, the supreme co-ordinating power."

According to *Simon*, "Authority may be defined as the power to make decisions which guide the actions of another. It is a relationship between two individuals, one superior and the other sub-ordinate. The superior frames and the transmits decisions with the expectation that these will be accepted by the sub-ordinate. The sub-ordinate executes such decisions and his conduct is determined by them."

According to *George R Terry*, "Authority is the official and legal right to command action by others and to enforce compliance. Compliance is obtained in a number of ways– through persuasion, sanctions, requests, coercion, constraint or force."

Accountability : It is an obligation to account for and report upon the discharge of responsibility, or use of authority. Accountability is the liability created for the use of authority. It is the answerability for performance of the assigned duties. Authority flows downwards whereas accountability flows upwards.

CENTRALISATION OF AUTHORITY

According to *Allen*, "Centralistion is the systematic and consistent reservation of authority at central points within an organisation".

Centralisation of authority means all office works are carried on in a central place and managed by a single top official. It implies that decisions pertaining to office matters are taken at the top level. The other departments will have to do duties assigned to them. Centralisation may be physical and functional.

Centralisation increases the importance of the central authority in the organisation and reduces the importance of sub-ordinates.

Centralisation is desirable in the planning and control of the management. It is desirable in the determination of objectives of the organisation. It is desirable in legal and governmental relationship. It is desirable in diversification, modernisation, expansion or contraction of the business activities of the organisation.

Advantages of Centralisation

1. The manager of office can distribute the work equally amongst the members of the staff. In decentralised method, some members of the staff have less work while some are overloaded. This unpleasant situation is avoided by equal distribution.

2. Under centralisation, duplication of work and expenditure are eliminated, *e.g.*, typewriter, duplicators, typists, stenos, etc. In centralisation, there will be one Section consisting of typewriters and typists–typist pool. Otherwise in decentralisation, every department has a typist and a typewriter. Therefore, there is less expenditure.

3. Better supervision is possible by a single man, because similar job is centralised; otherwise many supervisors have to be appointed.

4. Each worker will have to perform a particular type of work. He has to do it again and again. When he does a job over and again, naturally he gets speed in the job and becomes a specialist in the particular work.

5. Centralisation brings uniformity of action. Uniformity of action can be attained when a centralised authority manages the operating units.

6. There is no need to give overtime work to any department, as there are many clerks to handle the work without difficulty.

7. Quick decisions can be taken. Expert advice can be made available for managing the system.

Thus centralisation results in greater productivity, low cost, personal utilisation and greater administrative convenience.

Disadvantages of Centralisation

1. If one requires any information, he will have to approach the central office. If the central office is far, then there is a delay in getting the information.

2. The section-heads suffer from an inferiority complex for every information, the central office (supreme) is to be approached.

3. The staff working in the central office may feel proud, at the same time such feelings may wound the staff working in different sections.

4. Since the central office is overloaded, it is possible that mistakes or errors will creep in.

5. Too much concentration of authority or control over others may spoil the interest and initiative of the sub-ordinates.

6. Delays in accomplishing the work owing to the transmitting of the records from and to centralised units.

DECENTRALISATION OF AUTHORITY

According to *Allen*, "Decentralisation means the systematic effort to delegate to the lowest levels all authority except that which can only be exercised at the central points". Everything that goes to increase the importance of the sub-ordinates' role is decentralisation. In a large and complex organisation, management cannot centrally control for everything.

Decentralisation of office means each department of the concern possesses its own office. There is no central office. Each department has supervisors, clerks, typists, etc. There is a delegation of authority to the lower levels. Thus the authority to take decision is delegated to the managers, Purchase Managers, Sales Managers, Works Managers, etc. The Managers are responsible to their superiors.

The reasons for the decentralisation of authority in an organisation are:

1. Larger size of an enterprise needs decentralisation. It is difficult for the top management to make all the decisions at a time.
2. Growth and diversification of activities leads to overburdened work. It is difficult to have an effective direction when the work is unwieldy.
3. The increase in competitive market calls for decentralisation.
4. Training of executives leads to decentralisation.
5. External and internal factors lead to decentralisation.

Advantages of Decentralisation

1. The chief executive of the firm will be free from the burden of overloaded problems arising in different departments. To make the top officials free, the adoption of decentralisation is needed. They, then, can attend to major problems.
2. Secrecy can be maintained, because all the papers of a department are kept by the department itself. In a centralised one, secrecy cannot be maintained.
3. Research can be facilitated to have more efficiency in production.
4. Co-ordination takes place from the low level which is preferred. In a centralised one, co-ordination takes place at the top level.
5. Since each department is assigned duties and is answerable, each department takes initiative so that better results are produced.
6. It avoids confusion and promotes speed in decision-making.
7. Lower level executives can introduce new ideas and techniques.
8. It is easy to achieve flexibility at all levels of management.
9. Achievement of better management-employee relation is possible.
10. Efficient practice of management principles is possible.

Limitations of Decentralisation

1. Many competent executives are required to work because many departments may be there.
2. The operating cost is very high, because many persons are employed.
3. Co-ordination amongst the departments becomes a problem.
4. Chance of uniformity of action becomes less.

In process of delegation, three actions are involved :

(a) **Assignment of duties:** The manager or supervisor conveys what the sub-ordinate is expected to do.
(b) **Grant of authority:** The superior gives permission to the sub-ordinates to do his part of the assigned task and grants him certain rights like asking for implements or other requirements necessary for performing the task.
(c) **Creation of accountability:** The sub-ordinate takes upon himself the obligation to complete the task as desired by the superior and makes himself accountable to the superior.

Authority is delegated, responsibility is assumed and accountability is imposed. Responsibility is derived from authority and accountability is derived from responsibility. Authority is the medium for creating responsibility and for imposing accountability.

QUESTIONS

1. What is office organisation? State briefly the principles of organisation.

   (B. Com., Mumbai, M.S.)

2. What is the importance of sound organisation structure?   (B. Com., Madurai)

3. What is the line type of organisation ? Discuss its characteristic features.

   (B. Com., Andhra)

4. What is the Line and Staff system of organisation ? Do you feel that this system is an improvement over the pure line system?   (B. Com., Delhi)

5. What is organisation ? What are the different types of organisation? (B. A. Kerala)

6. What is delegation of authority? State the limit of authority.   (B. Com., Kolkata)

7. Distinguish between authority, responsibility and accountability. (B. Com., Jabalpur)

8. Define decentralisation of authority. To what extent is decentralisation of authority helpful in office administration.   (B. Com., Chennai)

9. Explain the term 'office systems'. Explain their importance and limitations.

   (B. Com., M.S.)

10. What is the meaning of the term 'flow of work'? Discuss the problems in the smooth flow of work.   (B. Com., M.S. & Madurai)

11. What are the merits of office manual?   (B. Com., M.S.)

12. What is an organisation chart ?   (B. Com., M.S. and Chennai)

Office Accommodation and Layout

INTRODUCTION

Office manager aims at getting the work done in the office at the lowest possible cost through proper selection and training of staff. Office staff work efficiently if they are properly accommodated. Employees have to spend long hours in the office. Bad and insufficient accommodation can cause boredom, monotony and frustration among them which will affect their efficiency adversely. Suitable accommodation, modern equipment and proper working conditions are important factors in improving efficiency and reducing costs.

A scientific arrangement of office will naturally fetch maximum efficiency at a minimum cost on all occasions. The management of the concern or the in-charge of the office of the firm aims at getting maximum benefit by a proper arrangement of office at minimum expenses. The efficiency of the modern and up-to-date office will depend upon many factors—location, layout, light, ventilation, office equipments, undisturbed atmosphere, etc. apart from the persons working in. The best result can be had by recruiting an efficient personnel and proper selection of machines and equipments. The office people can work well when there is a good and pleasing atmosphere in the office, because the clerks who are engaged in the office, use their mind and brain in the work. Concentration of their mind is an essential point. Therefore, the important factor of office management is to provide proper and adequate office facilities to the staff so as to get maximum result.

The office manager has to play the major role in determining the arrangement of office. The following points are to be considered :

1. The site or location of office building,
2. Size and shape of office,
3. Layout of office,
4. Open office or private office,
5. Convenience to staff and visitors,
6. Physical conditions of office,
7. Ventilation and aircondition,
8. Light,
9. Sanitation,
10. Noise,
11. Health,
12. Safety.

Note : *These points are discussed in detail in this chapter and the next chapter.* **(4 and 5)**

THE SITE OR LOCATION OF THE OFFICE BUILDING

The following factors are to be considered in providing the right type of office accommodation:

1. Location of office building.
2. Size, shape and cost of office accommodation.
3. Lighting and ventilation of the space.
4. Layout and facilities for office organisation.
5. Customer and staff conveniences.
6. Safety of the staff, etc.

While selecting a building for office, present as well as future requirements will be considered. In future the office may have to be expanded. If office is situated unsuitably, it may cause inconveniences both to the staff and to the customers. Each enterprise or business must select the proper location of the office building according to its requirements. Before finding out a location, it would be better to finalise the place as regards to choice of urban or rural area. The location of the office can be chosen in an urban (city) or rural (suburb) area. Both have their relative merits and demerits. The decision of selecting a place depends upon circumstances.

Merits of an office in Urban Areas :

1. The staff and the customers can easily reach the office because of the transport facilities prevailing in the city.
2. It facilitates to make purchases and sales in city rather than in suburban area, because city abounds in dwellers, shops, etc. When buyers want to make purchases they go to cities.
3. One is able to enjoy the available facilities such as post offices, banks, insurance companies, etc. In rural areas such facilities are not easily available.

4. There is a general tendency among the staff to prefer to work in a city; therefore a good recruitment of staff can be easily made for the office, if it is in the city. Always the first preference of the staff is to work in a city rather than in rural areas.

5. A goodwill can be created in the minds of the buyers by providing service after sales at the proper time. Immediate action can be taken and customers too are satisfied.

6. Almost all important government offices are situated in cities. The important offices are Income Tax, Sales Tax, Registrar of Companies, etc. It will be convenient to make easy contact with such offices. Regular contact may be needed.

7. Electricity, water supply, skilled labourers, easy communication, specialised agency, etc. are easily available.

Demerits of an office in Urban area :
1. It is experienced that the rent of a building or the cost of construction of an office becomes heavy. In the initial stage the firm may not be able to construct its own building, and will have to go for rented accommodation. Often heavy rent will have to be paid.

2. Since cities are overcrowded, it may not be possible always to have adequate space for the office. Small accommodation with many workers looks overcrowded.

3. Expansion facilities are also limited, because of the non-availability of building, high rent etc.

4. Generally in cities, dust and noise prevail in the atmosphere; hence the concentration of mind and physical condition which are necessary for smooth working in the office are affected.

5. With higher cost of living, the staff may demand higher wages, resulting in high expenditure.

Merits of an office in Rural Area :
1. The wages of the labourer will be low.
2. The rent of building will be low. The cost of construction of a building will also be low.
3. There will be possibilities of expansion, because of the space available.
4. The atmosphere will be clear and good for health.
5. Insanitary conditions will not prevail.
6. Cost of living is lower for the employees.

Demerits of an office in Rural Area
1. There will be no proper transport and communication.
2. Electricity will not be available.
3. There will not be any facilities for repairs and maintenance.
4. Skilled labourers will not be available.
5. There will be delay in getting the essential materials, because shops may not be there.
6. Specialised agencies–banking, engineering, insurance, etc. will not be available.
7. Important government offices may be situated in cities, as such regular contact is impossible.
8. Odd sales or purchases are not possible.
9. Staff may not be willing to serve in the rural area.
10. There will be no scope for the expansion of business, because of the low sales.

After having decided the area–rural or urban for office purpose–the next step should be, to decide whether to rent or own premises. Both have merits and demerits, which are discussed next in detail.

OWNED VS. RENTED PREMISES

Own Premises	Rented Premises
(1) According to one's own will and pleasure a building of any size and space can be constructed.	One must adjust and satisfy oneself with the size of the building and the space available.
(2) Initial expenses will be high and so it may not be wise always to go in for construction. large amount of capital has to be invested.	There will be nominal expenses in the shape of rent—monthly or quarterly. In the initial stage of a firm, it is better to have rented premises rather than owned premises, which will consume a large amount.
(3) Municipal Taxes, maintenance expenses have to be met.	There are no such expenses.
(4) If the business is large, there will be a stable demand for the products; naturally there will be good sales. Forecasting these conditions premises can be owned.	The available money can be used on the firm.
(5) A good attractive building owned by the firm will naturally add to the prestige of the firm, staff and customers.	A rented building does not add to the prestige of the firm.
(6) Subletting is possible.	Subletting is not possible always.
(7) The office premises cannot be shifted anywhere as they are permanently fixed.	When a more suitable location is found, the office can be shifted very easily.
(8) It is not convenient for medium and small offices and newly started firms because they have less finance.	It is convenient for medium and small offices and newly started firms.

FACTORS IN CHOICE OF LOCATION

While choosing the location for office, consider the following:
1. It is desirable to choose the location where same line of trade engaged.
2. The locality must have been adequately served by transport services of all kind.
3. The locality must have service facilities–banks, post office, insurance etc.
4. Office should be located near the source of availability of labour.
5. "Cost should be minimum and efficiency must be maximum" must be looked for.
6. The location must provide healthy environment.
7. If necessary, the location of office should be preferred nearer to other units– godown, branches, factory etc., for better function.
8. It should be ensured that the municipality laws allow the construction of the building according to the requirements of the company.
9. The office building must be located in a quiet and healthy neighbourhood from noise, dust-fumes, bad smell etc.

THE SIZE AND SHAPE OF THE OFFICE

After having fixed the site, the size and shape of the building are to be considered. The size and shape of the office should be conducive to the present requirement as well as for the future expansion. Ample room is a prerequisite for the most efficient performance of the staff and the optimum utilisation of equipment. Each worker in the office must be given facilities to do his job freely. In deciding the size of the building both the area and shape are also to be considered. Lengthy narrow space is undesirable, because time will be wasted in walking. It will be good to select a square or rectangular space for office.

LAYOUT OF THE OFFICE

"The determination of the space requirements and of the detailed utilisation of this space in order to provide a practical arrangement of the physical factors considered necessary for the execution of the office work within reasonable cost."   —Terry

"The problem of layout relates to the arrangement in the space involved so that all the equipment, supplies, procedures and personnel can function at maximum efficiency.

—Hicks and Place

Systematic and scientific arrangement of different departments and equipments on a well defined plan, so as to get the maximum benefit from the space available can be called as office layout. In an average firm, it is not possible for the management to do all the jobs. In many cases division of labour has to be applied. When the division of labour is applied, the job of an entire office is divided into as many sections or departments as necessary. It may also be not possible to accommodate all the sections in one room or on the same floor. While making the office arrangement, the following objectives are to be noted :

1. Office layout should ensure an effective, steady and smooth flow of work. A straight line flow of work is preferred for the work will move forward from the beginning to the end. It will increase the speed of work. There is less danger of losing papers due to regularity. It will keep clerks and executives at their desks and check unnecessary movement of papers and enable maximum control.

2. Arrangement of the department must facilitate speed and smoothness of the flow of work. A proper and constant flow of work means that the work moves from one operation to the other through a system which will fetch high result. This must borne in mind and facilities should be made for regular flow of work which adds to efficiency,

3. The receptionist section should be near the main gate or entrance, so that the customers may feel convenient and easy.

4. Preferably the different sections or departments of the office must be nearer to each other, because the sections may be interconnected and one section cannot work without seeking or referring to the other department. If the interlinked departments are located far apart, much time is wasted to go over and come back.

5. The office of the Secretary or the General Manager or section-heads whom outsiders have to visit, may be placed near the receptionist's room, so as to provide easy approach.

6. While dividing the whole space, each department may be given adequate space so as to enable the clerks to work freely and move freely during the course of work. As far as possible, any space of the floor should not be left out.

7. The office records, equipments, machines, etc., may as far as possible be kept in their respective sections. This will facilitate to speed up the work. If the files or machines are kept at a place, which is far off from his seat, the employee will have to waste his time.

8. Certain sections such as interview section, enquiry section etc. dealing with the progress report of the staff, etc., require privacy. These departments or sections will be provided with privacy by allotting separate rooms.

9. The position of the supervisors must be so adjusted that they can easily observe the activities of their staff and watch whether they are engaged in work or chitchat.

10. The equipments or machines which make noise in their operations should be placed away from the clerks, who do paper work. If space is not available, sound proof walls or partitions must be erected to reduce the noise.

11. There will also be noise from external sources. If there is much disturbance, double-glazed windows and doors may be fixed.

12. Adequate facilities must be provided to the executives and the staff to work in comfort. The facility may also refer to systematic arrangement of furniture and good atmosphere.

13. There must be sufficient, natural or artificial light.

14. As mentioned in 8 and 9, let it be remembered that most of the office work is done mentally. If there is much disturbance it will be an obstruction to the clerks to do their jobs. There will be delay in doing the work. Clerks may feel irritated. This must be avoided to maximise efficiency.

MERITS OF GOOD LAYOUT

A good layout is a good investment. A good office layout offers and the following advantages:

1. A good layout makes supervision more effective.

2. A good layout promotes efficiency as it follows the flow of work.

3. A good layout aims at making the most economic and effective use of available floor space.

4. There is better communication among all departments.

5. The layout provides for joint use of machines and equipment, optimum use.

6. The process of production, planning and control is greatly facilitated.

7. It is easy to bring about co-ordination in the organisation.

8. It reduces the cost of cooling, heating, air-conditioning etc. and their maintenance costs.

9. A good layout aims at providing best working conditions. This improves morale of staff.

10. A good layout projects a good impression about the enterprise on customers and visitors. This results in better goodwill.

Betts suggests the following checklist for an office layout.
1. Avoid overcrowding.
2. Ease of daily cleaning.
3. Staff not facing directly into light.
4. Proximity of cloakrooms and toilets.
5. Comfortable furniture.
6. Non-slip floors and stairs.
7. Fencing any exposed moving part of office machines.
8. Minimise staff movements.
9. Place filing cabinets near staff using them.
10. Group together staff with related activities.
11. Adequate space between desks.
12. Positioning supervisors at appropriate points.
13. Separate noisy machines from staff who are engaged in work requiring high concentration
14. Put close work near to natural lights.
15. Minimise paper movement by designing according to work flow.
16. Adequate space for main aisles and sideways.

Re-layout means changing the existing layout, that is, planning the layout afresh. A re-layout may become necessary for the purpose of improving the existing layout or adjusting it to the changed environment. *Dartell* has mentioned the circumstances in which the present layout should be reviewed:
1. When there is an increase or decrease in personnel;
2. When the flow of work is changed by new procedures;
3. When more working space is required;
4. When work piles up at one table while others wait;
5. When work is lost in transit;
6. When employees complain of bad lighting or ventilation;
7. When employees appear to have difficulty in moving about the office;
8. When overcrowding of personnel and record room is apparent;
9. When buying new equipment or replacing the old ones;
10. When there is a change in the organisation–when there is new personnel, new authority and new responsibilities etc.;
11. When alterations to the space are to be made;
12. Where there are lease difficulties;
13. When functions have been added or taken away from a section;
14. When the balance of the sexes changes radically;
15. When some persons have been promoted.

OPEN OFFICE AND PRIVATE OFFICE

Now the question is whether each department will be provided with separate rooms or all the departments of the office will be accommodated in one large hall. There is a tendency among the office personnel to prefer open office rather than private or separate rooms for each section. Both the systems have advantages and disadvantages.

Advantages of open office
1. Better space utilisation is possible, because space has not been lost by partitions.

2. The section-heads or supervisors feel easy to watch the office. It is also possible to reduce the number of supervisors.
3. The layout of the office can be altered or changed without any expense.
4. There is more economy in arrangement of light.
5. Easy communication from department to department is possible.
6. Decoration, cleaning and maintenance can be done inexpensively.
7. Better working condition is possible.
8. It reduces the movement of staff.

Disadvantages of open office

1. Work will be affected by visitors and movement of the staff themselves.
2. There will be internal noise, because of the conversation and talks in the office by staff themselves or visitors.
3. Infections and disease may spread quickly.
4. A big hall may not be efficiently supervised.
5. The office may appear to be a crowded place.
6. Secrecy cannot be maintained.
7. Top executives may not feel comfortable in the open office.

Private Office

Private offices are small rooms occupied by departments. Each department will be placed in each room. Such rooms are allotted by considering the nature of confidential matter to be dealt in, or for top officials etc. Nature of the work determines the private office. Then secrecy and security can be maintained.

Advantages of private office

1. It gives prestige and importance to the top executive in the organisation.
2. Confidential work and discussion is possible. General privacy is ensured.
3. Concentration of mind on accounting and statistical work is possible. It leads to increased efficiency in their work.
4. Better ventilation is possible and it ensures better health of the workers.

Disadvantages of private office

1. Much space is wasted for partitons.
2. It affects the flow of work.
3. More supervisors are needed to watch the work done in office. Thus supervision becomes more costly.
4. It is more expensive to build separate offices.
5. There will be more expenses to provide adequate light.
6. Cleaning of the office becomes a tedious work.
7. The office layout will be a complicated one.
8. More expensive furniture arrangement is needed than the open office or general office.
9. Extra means of communication are needed for each room.
10. Clerks, messengers have to waste time to see whether the concerned man is there or not in the private room.

Both advantages and disadvantages of open and private office have been discussed. At present, there is a tendency of preferring open office to have smoothness, forward flow of work and greater efficiency. In all cases, open office system may not be suitable. The persons, who are holding major positions, are advised to occupy the private office because of the nature of their work. The positions of high executives need privacy, security, concentration of mind and avoidance of disturbances from others. The question of their own status also comes in. Therefore, it is advisable to have private office. Apart from the preferences, take the example, of a bank, where open office system is adopted. Therefore, as far as possible private office may be replaced by open office accommodation; but private offices may be provided wherever they are essential.

STAFF-VISITORS CONVENIENCE

While assigning accommodation to different sections, there must be an easy access to different sections. Clerks will have to make frequent visits to certain sections of the office; cash department, sales department, etc. Sufficient space must be provided for clerks to move from department to department. The Office Manager should take care of the arrangement of office.

In business firms it is usual that visitors may pay visits often. Sometimes, the visitors have to wait till the executive is free. Waiting will often prove to be much tedious. If there is a reception room for the customers or the public, it will be convenient for them to wait. The location of the reception room must be, as far as possible, near the main entrance or near the private office where the visitor has to go. The first impression is the best impression therefore, the reception room should have enough light, good ventilation etc. The visitor must have a homely feeling, while he is in the reception room.

Merchandise can be displayed. There can be attractive show windows in it. It is a common practice to supply reading matters–current magazines, booklets of certain good products, booklets of the services of the company, etc. to the visitors, The reception room must be self-contained, *i.e.,* there must be facility for drinking water, toilet etc.

There must also be a canteen and toilets for the staff. The visitors or the staff must feel at home while they are in the office.

NEW TRENDS IN OFFICE LAYOUT

Now-a-days attempts are being made to minimise the disadvantages of private offices while at the same time providing some degree of privacy in work, through the use of modular desk units and movable partitions.

Modular Units

Modular units are becoming increasingly popular now. These units normally consist of a combined desk and file cabinet with a working surface on the top of each, and dwarfed partitions upto a height of 4 to 6 feet. It is especially designed to meet specific needs of employees resulting in greater productivity and efficiency. These units offer the benefits of privacy, easy access to working materials, and economy in space. These units generally uses less office space than the conventional furniture. It is compact. It eliminates unnecessary motions and speeds up work.

Movable Partitions

Movable partitions are now being used in setting up private offices. These partitions are made of metal, wood, plastic or glass. They help in maintaining privacy in office work. Partitions are available in a variety of sizes, shapes and colours. The choice of the partition depends upon the type of work to be done. They are less costly as against permanent partitions. They provide flexibility. If private offices are not needed, partitions can easily be removed. Thus quick changes in layout plan can be made to suit the changing needs of business.

QUESTIONS

1. Discuss the importance of Office Layout. What factors would you take in to account while laying out an office ?   *(B. Com., Delhi. Bangalore, M.S.)*

2. What do you understand by an "Open Office"? What are its merits and demerits?
                                                              (B. Com., Delhi, Madurai)

3. You have been asked by your employer to choose an office location. What factors will you consider in doing so ?   *(I.C.W.A., B.Com., Punjab, Delhi)*

4. Discuss the merits and demerits of an open office as compared to separate office rooms.   *(I.C.W.A., C.S., B. Com., Delhi)*

5. Define office layout and list its objectives. On what principles office layout should be based ?   *(B. Com., Punjab, Madras, Madurai)*

6. "Layout is very important for office operations." Explain.   *(B. Com., Delhi)*

7. What are the merits of own office building ?   *(B. Com,. M.S.)*

8. `What points should be taken, into consideration when arranging an office accommodation and layout ? Describe them briefly,*(I.C.W.A., B. Com., Madurai)*

9. What is meant by office accommodation? What factors influence office location?
                                                              (B. Com., M.S. Madurai)

10. What are factors that determine the size of office ?   *(B. Com., Delhi, Bangalore)*

CHAPTER

Office Environment

INTRODUCTION

Office environment has an important bearing on the efficiency of employees. Environment refers to surrounding conditions particularly those influencing development and growth. An office may be properly laid out and the best type of furniture and equipment may be installed in it but its efficiency may be low if the physical working conditions are not good. Physical working conditions are the life of an office. Environment can be described as a combination of circumstances or conditions that effect and influence the efficiency of the employees. Office work consists of mental work which is distinct from physical work. Mental work is more boring and fatiguing than physical work. Normally, a clerk spends about 8 hours in the office during any working day. The emotional response of workers is better if the environment is good.

In the words of *G.R. Terry*, "An individual's performance is significantly conditioned by the environment in which he works. The cumulative effect of his total work environment is a strong determinative of how well he marshals his abilities and skills, his attitude towards his work and his colleagues, and his enthusiasm for his work."

In the words of *Z.K. Quible*, "Failure to give proper consideration to the environment of the office is reflected in several ways. A poor office environment often results in decreased levels of

64

production and employee morale. Absenteeism and tardiness are also apt to increase, as are the number of errors, made by the employees. In the extreme cases, the employees "physical well being may actually be hampered."

The working conditions and efficiency have direct correlation between them. Therefore, one of the easiest way to improve office performance is to improve working conditions. It is the duty of the office manager to provide an environment which is pleasant, comfortable and conducive to good working habits. This is because employees spend more time at work in the office.

It is accepted fact that the work of the clerks requires more mental effort than physical. By written tests, personal interviews etc. good workers can be selected. To have better results, such selected persons should be given training in the office. Thus workers can be fully trained to do the assigned jobs to achieve better result than expected. The office people have to concentrate their minds while doing the jobs. Disturbances, if any, will lower their efficiency.

Here it is made clear that the working environment of an office include all these factors of the surrounding area which are detectable and which effect the behaviour of the employees. The following points should be taken into consideration while making effective or sound scheme of office environment:

1. Office Lighting
2. Ventilation
3. Interior Decoration and Furnishing
4. Office Furniture
5. Freedom from Noise and Dust
6. Safety
7. Sanitary Arrangements
8. Security
9. Secrecy

They are discussed in the following paragraphs.

OFFICE LIGHTING

Lighting is perhaps the most important consideration in an office. A proper designed system of lighting results in greater accuracy, improved quality of work and reduced costs. Almost all the work in the office involves paper work. Thus, it leads to great eye strain. There must be proper and adequate lighting in the office to avoid eye strain. Poor light or powerful light will cause troubles. If the light is not proper, mistakes may be committed or accidents may occur. The work of a clerk requires concentration. Improper arrangements of office light will lower the efficiency of the staff through delay, errors and mistakes. If the position of the building is so situated that natural light is not easily available, artificial lights must be arranged. Of course, it will cost more.

The natural light has its own merits. It is good for health. It is economical. Therefore, while, selecting or constructing the office building, see that as far as possible the shadow of the other buildings does not fall on the office. This may not be possible in all cases, particularly when the selection of locality is made in an over crowded area. The office manager should take more care and responsibility to see that maximum natural light is made available in the office. The clerks should be provided with seats near the windows.

Points to be borne in mind

1. Right power of light should be provided according to the nature of work. There should not be any sharp glare or dazzle either directly or indirectly.
2. There should not be any sharp shadows over the table where the clerks have to work.
3. There should not also be any glare directly or indirectly on the table.

If the building does not admit sufficient, natural light, an alternate arrangement of artificial lighting should be made, so as to have sufficient light, or supplement the available light. In a gloomy day it is difficult to get enough light in the rooms, and in such cases artificial light is the only source. When making arrangements for artificial light the office manager should see that the light provided must be proper for the particular nature of work.

Points to be remembered

1. Good lighting will facilitate an increased output, efficiently and economically.
2. Lighting arrangement should be well-designed.
3. If natural light is not available, make proper supplementary arrangement through artificial lighting.
4. Walls may be painted with suitable colours to increase the light. Care must also be taken to reduce the glare and at the same time to improve the vision.

Types of Artificial Lights

1. **Fluorescent light :** It is widely used and is popular. We get diffused or scattered light. Electricity consumption is also low. In offices, it is good system of lighting. It does not matter that the initial expenses are high.
2. **Direct light :** The lamp is fitted against the ceiling with shades. It gives a direct downward fall of light. The ceiling portion will be in the dark. This type of lighting system is giving place to fluorescent light.
3. **Indirect light :** This system is the reverse of the above. The fittings are made facing the ceiling. The fittings throw light upward and the ceiling reflects it on the tables. This system gives unshaded light without glare. But for clerical work, it is not advisable.
4. **Individual desk light :** When a particular work requires more light, then an individual desk light can be provided in addition to the common light. It is expensive. Since the light is placed on working table, it may cause fatigue and eye strain. It is not common at the present age. Benefits of good light in an office are :
   1. Output can be increased.
   2. Quality of work can be increased.
   3. Eye strain can be reduced.
   4. Improve the morale of the staff.
   5. It creates good impression on visitors.

VENTILATION

The office should be quite airy. Fresh and natural air can be had only when there is proper ventilation. Fresh air will reduce fatigue and remove the irritable feelings of the clerks. Low height of the office, small or few windows, opening to a narrow courtyard etc., obstruct the flow of air through the office. If the office has no free flow of air, particularly in summer, workers get tired or fatigued and in rainy season they feel drowsy. These will lead to low efficiency of the clerks. Artificial circulation of too cool or hot air will also cause irritation to the workers. Adequate, clean and fresh air at the required temperature can help the clerks to do their work smoothly. There are many devices to provide a comfortable atmosphere.

If the doors and windows have double shutters, to a certain extent, they will not allow the hot air to come in during summer and cool air to come in during winter.

Air conditioners can also be used to overcome these problems; but it is expensive to install and maintain them. If natural and fresh air is not freely moving, fans, exhaust fans, filters, etc. may be used to draw natural air duly filtered. This is less expensive.

INTERIOR DECORATION AND FURNISHING

Interior decoration means pleasant colouring of doors, windows and walls. The main purpose of interior decoration is to make the office look pleasant. Interior decoration stimulates better performance on the part of the staff and creates a better impression on the minds of visitors.In the words of G. Mills. "The decoration of an office can have a noticeable effect upon the morale of the staff. Drab surroundings are depressing, pleasant surroundings are conducive to good work."

The colour used on the walls must be of pleasing nature. Walls of the office should be in light colour. Dark colours will not be pleasing to the eyes. This also includes design of furnishings, floor coverings etc. It is seen that pleasant colouring and good furnishings will create cheerfulness in the minds of the workers. Furnishings (curtains etc.) should also be of pleasing colour. The floors, stairways, corridors etc. should be of attractive colour. For example, green and blue, induce the feeling of coolness, orange and yellow induce the feeling of warmth. A pleasing decoration will increase the prestige of the firm as well as of the employees.

Floor coverings are used to reduce noise and to add to the beauty of the place. Floor coverings are carpets, thin rubber, linoleum or foam mattresses.

Furnishing includes curtain, chair, table and sofa covers and floor mattresses etc. These must be pleasant looking. Chair and sofa covers may be pleasant to see. They have a protective as well as decorative value. For example, curtains not only decorate a door or window, but also prevent glare and sunshine coming into the room directly on the table of the office worker.

Some paintings and other art pieces can be attractively displayed in the office. It will add to the decor and prestige of the organisation. The office premises will look attractive and will break the monotony of the office staff. It will also have a positive effect on the visitors.

OFFICE FURNITURE : Refer Chapter 6

FREEDOM FROM NOISE AND DUST

Noise may be defined as an unwanted sound in or outside the office. Noise may be an occasional or an unusual loud sound or a constant loud sound. When employees are at work, there should not be any disturbance. Noise will create irritation to the office people.

Clerical work involves great concentration of mind. Therefore, the mental concentration of workers should not be disturbed by noise. It brings about errors, mistakes, delays, mental fatigue etc., and in turn, leads to inefficiency and lowering of the output. Unexpected sounds or loud noise will take their mood off from the work. Naturally, when people are working in an office there is some sound; but it is tolearble, because people are accustomed to it. There is internal noise as well as external noise.

Internal noise is created by the following:

1. Movements of machines.
2. Movements and conversation of clerks, peons, visitors etc.
3. Cracking doors.
4. Calling bells, telephone bells.
5. Shifting of furniture from one place to another.

Measures to prevent internal noise:

1. Carpets or rubber mats or coir mats spread on the floor will reduce the sounds caused by the movements of the clerks and other people.
2. Below the office machines which create noise in operation, feltpads can be placed which reduce the noise.
3. Calling bells can be replaced with buzzers.
4. Banging or Cracking doors should be fitted with rubber or felt stops to reduce sound. Proper oiling of the hinges of the door will also reduce noise. Automatic door springs, rubber pads, etc., can be fitted.
5. Telephones may be kept in sound-proof booths to reduce the sounds.
6. Clerks must be instructed to maintain calmness.
7. When the office is free from noise, calmness prevails, clerks will automatically be discouraged to make sounds by talk or gossip.
8. Workers must be engaged fully during the office hours, so that they don't waste their time over idle gossip.

External noise is caused by the street sounds, workshops, noisy industrial process, etc. These sounds seldom enter the office through the open windows and doors.

Measures to prevent external noise:

1. As far as possible the location of the office should be away from the noise-creating places.
2. Doors and windows may be kept closed.
3. Walls of the office should be made of sound-proof materials.

Dust : In certain area, the amount of dust in the surroundings is much greater than in other areas. For example in areas where cotton mills or jute mills or cement mills are working, the atmosphere is constantly dust laden. When dust enters the office, it spoils the decoration of the office, affect the health of staff, reduce the life of machines, equipments etc. It is difficult to check entry of dust into the office. Dust should be cleaned quite regularly.

SAFETY

Safety precautions are a must. Accidents are undesirable. Whenever any accident occurs, it leads to a wastage of time the person involved in the accident and the fellow workers.

Accident may take place because of many reasons-slip on floor, fall on staircase, leakage of electric wire etc.

Precautions

1. A first-aid box must be provided and must be under the custody of a trained person. Two or three members may be trained in case of need. It must be placed at a visible and convenient place.

2. Fire precautionary methods—fire extinguishers must be provided and the staff be trained to use them.

3. Fluorescent lamps and fans must be checked periodically. All the electrical fittings must be checked and tested to confirm the absence of leakage.

4. Floor carpets, coir-mats etc. if torn, must be removed or mended, so that people who walk over will not trip.

5. Files should not be placed on the top of the almirah, because, when taking one file, others may fall down.

6. There should be regular inspection of machines, equipments etc.

7. Smoking should not be allowed within the office premises.

SANITARY ARRANGEMENT

As far as practicable, the office and its surroundings must be kept clean and free from all bad odour and infection. Insanitary conditions affects the health of staff adversely. A large number of persons daily visit the office, there is, therefore, bound to be some dirt and dust.

Cleanness of the office contributes to a good atmosphere, and it creates a pleasant and healthy attitude to the clerks work in. The office may be well furnished and decorated, and to get its full effect, it must also be kept neat and clean. If a well-furnished office is not cleaned properly, it looks shabby; visitors will have a bad impression about the office. People who work in shabby places, will produce careless work. The unclean office affects the prestige of the clerks too. They will feel proud to work in a clean office.

Hints to be noted

1. Office must be cleaned everyday.

2. There must be special cleaning, at least once a week, so as to keep clean the filing cabinet, cupboard, shelves, furniture, equipment, etc.

3. The room should not only be clean but free from bad odour and infection.

4. Office should be sprayed often with disinfectant.

5. Waste paper and other waste materials must be placed in waste-box and disposed of daily in the evening hours; preferably after the office hours.

6. Daily after cleaning the floor of the office, the furniture should also be dusted.

7. Air purifiers must be used which must be replaced in time.

8. A sufficient number of spittons should be provided in every building at convenient places.

9. Effective arrangement should be made to provide a sufficient supply of wholesome drinking water at suitable places.

10. Adequate cloak rooms, toilets and washing facilities should be provided at convenient places.

11. Neat and clean canteen under the combined management of employers and employees, must be arranged to supply quality food to staff. Interior decoration may be done in pleasing colours, inside the canteen.

12. Office should have provision for rest rooms or retiring rooms where workers may go and rest during rest intervals.

SECURITY

One of the vital functions of a modern office is to keep and preserve documents and records for future guidance. Important and valuable documents are kept in office safes or bank lockers. Office files, correspondence etc. are kept in safe places so that outsiders may not have access to them.

The employer may, before recruiting an employee, ask for two reputable personal references from him. These references may be contacted and information sought from them regarding the past general conduct behaviour etc. of the employee. Generally speaking, the employees who handle cash are required to deposit a certain amount of money with the organisation as a security measure.

People entering the building should be properly identified and entry passes should be issued to them. For any INTRUDER the cash department or cash section is the most tempting target. It is thus necessary to locate it in a very safe part of the building and restrict entry to this part. It is essential to install alarms and warning systems so that emergencies are met with effectively and in time.

SECRECY

There are some records about the business which must be kept secret from the junior staff and outsiders. They may be known as business secrets. Disclosures of such secrets may entail heavy loss to the firm. It may lower down the reputation of the business. The management must determine what type of information must be kept secret and must make arrangements for keeping them secret.

The following information should be kept secret :

1. **Tenders :** Tenders which the organisation submits or invites should not be disclosed to anyone till the date of tenders . If disclosed, the organisation may lose valuable contracts.

2. **Cost Information :** If the clerical staff possess knowledge of cost data, there are possibilities of its leakage to competitors. Therefore, disclosure of cost information to staff should be avoided.

3. **Labour Policy :** The personal policy of the management should be kept secret and should be disclosed at appropriate time. If leaked out, it may lead to strikes, lockouts, and other unpleasant activities.

4. **Dividend Declaration :** If the rate of dividend to be declared by the company is disclosed, before its annual general meeting, such disclosures may have impact on the market value of its shares.

5. **Financial Position :** The financial position of a company is to be depicted in its balance sheet at the end of every year. If unfavourable conditions, if any, is between the year, it will reduce the credit-worthiness of the business, share prices may go down, sales may be affected adversely, etc.

QUESTIONS

1. Explain the importance of good working environment for the office staff. Discuss the consideration you will take into account while planning for office lighting, ventilation and efficiency of work. *(B. Com., Delhi, M.S.)*

2. "The efficiency of office employees is directly or indirectly affected by the conditions under which they are required to work." Elucidate this statement. *(I.C.W.A.)*

3. What is meant by 'working condition' in an office and how does it influence the employee morale? *(I.C.W.A.)*

4. "The efficiency of the office staff very greatly depends on physical facilities." Advance your arguments for and against this statement. *(B.Com.,Punjab)*

5. Discuss, the various factors which influence the physical environment of an office. *(B.Com.,Bangalore)*

6. Describe the importance of proper lighting and ventilation from the point of view of efficiency of office work. *(B.Com.,Delhi)*

7. Disuss the impact of noise in relation to clerical work and the ways in which it can be reduced. *(B.Com.,Madurai)*

8. Explain your views on the effect of good office conditions on the office worker and his work. *(B. Com., Madurai)*

9. What is environment? How does it affect human behaviour ? *(B.Com.,Jammu)*

10. "Interior decoration is now an important part of office environment" Discuss.

11. What are the different types of artificial lighting used in a modern office? *(M.S.M.K.)*

12. Explain the importance of physical surrounding in relation to concentrated mental work. *(M.S.)*

13. A scooter manufacturing company employing 3,000 factory workers and 500 office employees is contemplating the moving of its operation from Madurai city to Suburban Melur. The question has been raised whether the company should maintain its office in Madurai city or whether to house the office in the same building as the manufacturing operations in Melur. There is the prestige factor to be considered in having a Madurai city address. Discuss in the order of their importance the factors to be considered in locating the office in the suburb or in Madurai city. *(M.K. University)*

CHAPTER 6

Furniture

INTRODUCTION

After having acquired the office building, the next job is the selection of furniture–tables, chairs, cabinets, shelves, etc. The importance of furniture in a modern office cannot be overlooked. A greater part of the office work is done on desk, so suitable furniture and other equipments must be provided to the office staff to enable them to be seated comfortably and perform their work speedily and competently. One should not only pay attention to the utility of furniture, but also to its appearance. In well-furnished office, workers will feel happy to work. So selection of office furniture must be given careful consideration.

Office furniture is necessarily a part of the total environment in which an employee works. It can be described as a basic facility with which an employee identifies himself. It has been increasingly realised now that furniture is bought not only for its utility but also for its appearance and that its artistic design is worth paying for, it makes the office look more attractive, and appeals to the office workers who must use it. A good quality furniture not only improves the general efficiency of the office employees, but also increase the prestige of the organisation among its visitors.

BASIC PRINCIPLES IN SELECTING THE FURNITURE

1. Suitability

The selected furniture must be suitable for the job. The working area of the table should be sufficient. It must also have space to keep files (incoming and outgoing), stationery, etc.

2. Comfort

The seat of the workers, shape of the chairs and tables must be so designed that the workers would not feel any fatigue while doing their jobs. This will result in efficiency, in turn, more output. The equipment, forms, stationery, etc., must be within easy reach. Those items frequently used, should be placed at hand.

3. Design

Prior to purchase, one must have an idea of the size, height and design of the furniture. For example, the size, height, design, number of drawers of the table should be decided on the basis of work done on it. There are many designs of tables available in the market. One must decide whether the top of the table should be of polished wood or glass plate or laminate surface. The decision regarding the choice of the furniture, say table, desk, chairs, etc. as to its size and design depends on the officer who uses it.

4. Durability

Metal furniture is more costly than wooden furniture. But the maintenance charges of wooden furniture are more than those of the metal furniture. Nowadays, metal *i.e.*, steel furniture is more popular, because it is more durable than wooden furniture. Moreover, steel furniture is safe against fire, burglary etc.

5. Weight

As the business expands, the size of the office also increases. The existing layout of the furniture has to be rearranged according to the required comfort. It may become often necessary to move the furniture from one place to another. Therefore, it is better to have light weight furniture. If the furniture is light, there will be less breakage and wear and tear when the furniture is shifted.

6. Space saving

Furniture which would occupy minimum space should be selected. The decision regarding the design of the furniture should depend upon the space available in the office and the number of persons who work there.

7. Cost

The cost of the furniture should not be neglected when selecting it. It should be kept within the financial limit.

8. Hygiene

The outlay of the furniture should be so made that it will be easy to clean the furniture as well as the floor underneath it.

9. Usefulness

The furniture should be selected according to the nature of the particular job. When it is not needed for the department, it can be easily transferred to another department, where it may be useful.

10. Appearance

Furniture should have a good appearance and be pleasing to the eyes. This will impress the workers and visitors. Wooden furniture looks attractive. Furniture of high quality wood is durable. It has a warm look and gives comfort to the users. Many varieties and designs of furniture can easily be made.

11. Multi-purpose uses

Furniture should be adaptable to multi-purpose uses, wherever possible. This permits standardisation in the purchase of multi-purpose desks and enables office workers to perform more than one type of work with the help of the same kind of furniture.

> **Factors :** In selecting the furniture and other equipment to be used for a specific job, the following six questions should be considered.
> 1. Is the working area adequate ?
> 2. Can the clerk work comfortably ?
> 3. Can the clerk use both hands ?
> 4. Can the job be supervised ?
> 5. Is the work adequately protected against dust, loss or damage ?
> 6. Is there suitable provision for the clerk's personal effects ?

Generally, in a modern office, desks, tables, chairs, filing rack, cupboards, cabinets, safe, etc., are used. Every table should have sufficient top space to keep the incoming files and outgoing files and to keep necessary forms and stationery. Apart from the top of the table it must have enough space to work comfortably.

If the clerk is to be provided with a telephone, it must be placed on the left-hand side of the table. The writing pad will be placed on the right-hand side, so that while he is working with his right-hand, he can easily take the receiver with his left-hand. In the same way the stationery articles, should be kept on the top of the table, within easy reach.

Completed files should be placed on the right-hand side and incomplete files should be placed on the left-hand side. This will enable the supervisor to check the work done by the clerk, by a look from his seat.

The work table, machines, stationery, etc., on it should be kept free from dust. Certain files of a confidential nature should be safely placed in steel cabinets, after the work.

The clerks who come to the office may bring personal belongings, such as money purse, rain coat, lunch packets, hand-bags, etc. The clerk's table should have provision to keep the personal belongings under lock. This will be an additional advantage.

TYPES OF FURNITURE

Office furniture may be of different types, the usual types are as follows :

1. Executive furniture

High officials have different tastes for furniture. Therefore, executive furniture is purchased according to their tastes. This is mainly to impress the visitors, and it should add to the prestige of the person using it and the prestige of the firm. The term 'executive' is applied to those persons who are responsible for making decisions and policies. Generally, executives included section managers and officers above them. Therefore, different executives will prefer different types of furniture to suit their job and status.

Diagram of Executive Table

Work not completed (in)	Referece records	Stationery	Work Completed (out)
Phone	Forms to read and write	Writing place items	Equipments and other

Chair

The following factors which should be considered before acquiring new furniture. (*J.C. Denyer*)

1. **Design :** It is related to size of top, height, number of drawers etc.
2. **Capital outley :** An obvious factor when buying any equipment.
3. **Durability :** Metal furniture probably last longer than ordinary wooden furniture.
4. **Saving in space :** Some furniture is specially designed to save office space.
5. **Fire risk :** Again metal furniture is a better fire risk than wooden.
6. **Weight :** If furniture has to be moved around, as it often does in a large office, then light weight is preferable.
7. **Hygiene :** How easy it is to clean, and to clean the floor underneath it.
8. **Appearance:** Furniture which is not only pleasing to the eye, but appears workman like, is quite an important factor.
9. **Comfort of office work:** This means that more work is likely to be performed and with less distraction.
10. **Safety :** Plate glass topped furniture may not be safe in use.
11. **Finish :** If there is too high a glass, it can cause glare and distraction from work.
12. **Saving in Labour :** Some furniture has built-in file units, which can save movement and walking about the clerks.
13. **Supervision :** To work being done in office should not be overlooked due to structure of furniture.

Desks : The desk is the work-bench of the office worker. Most of office work is handled on a desk, over a desk, through a desk or across a desk. The primary function of any desk is to provide a suitable surface for writing, checking, sorting, examining and conferring; for these purposes a table top is just as good as a desk top; tables also have other advantages over desks. As far as possible, the desks selected for office should multi-purpose in use. There are different types of desks for different persons depending upon the nature of work and status.

Executive Desk : These are designed to suit individual tastes and quite often they are designed as a show piece of an organisation. Their purpose is also to impress visitors with the prestige and importance of persons using them. Executive desks are generally double pedestal. Sharp edges and corners are eliminated. Table top is covered with a sheet of glass.

Some executives use full top glass while others prefer to cover writing area only. **General purpose desk** are of less elaborate design being single pedestal with less desk space. **Typist desk** may be fitted with either a fixed sunken well for the typewritten or a collapsible well into which the typewriter is fixed.

Table : In many government and other offices, tables still serve as clerical desks and this they may be fitted with one or two drawers. Tables are ordinarily needed for sorting of mail, housing of files, file-tray, holding meetings etc. Most of the tables follow the conventional dimensions for their sizes.

Chairs : Chairs are perhaps the most important item of furniture from the point of view of the worker since he sits in them all through the day in office. Comfortable sitting in the office not only reduces fatigue but also maintains the health of the employee, thus benefitting the firm by less absenteeism, few errors and large volume of work. The back of the chair should be such which gives support to the back and sufficient relaxation. It will be better if the back is adjustable. Seat should be sufficiently large, properly designed and thinly padded. A revolving chair may be ideal in most cases since it allows for movement without getting into ground.

Fittings and Accessories

Generally office fittings include desk lamp, telephone stand, coat stand, waste basket etc. When choosing or selecting such items, their colour may be considered, because the colour of these must not ruin the pleasing atmosphere of the office. Clerks should be provided with certain accessories in order to perform their work efficiently. Such items may be penholders, sorting trays, boxes, cabinets, special lamp etc.

General furniture is designed to facilitate the **work of** the clerks. The size of a table depends upon the nature of the work to be performed. Different clerks may be doing different types of work. The clerk, who works on the ledgers, needs a big table. Each clerk will be provided with a table and chair, according to his requirement.

The following points may also be considered

    (i) Only required furniture should be purchased and its cost should be within reasonable limits.

   (ii) Multipurpose use should be considered while planning the purchase of furniture.

  (iii) The furniture should use the space economically.

  (iv) The design of the furniture should be aimed at maximum comfort and convenience to the user.

   (v) The top of the table will be adequate to work with.

  (vi) The drawers should slide in and out smoothly.

 (vii) As far as possible the table should be designed to avoid unnecessary movements– bending, stooping, standing, twisting, etc. by the clerk.

(viii) The edges of the furniture must be rounded off.

  (ix) The back of the chair should be adjustable and of the saddle seat type.

   (x) Clerks desks should not be placed face to face, because it encourages conversation.

  (xi) The furniture should be adaptable, simple, durable and of good taste.

Built-in Furniture

In the present period, buildings are constructed in space-saving method. Almirahs are commonly built in the walls of the rooms. Thus, expenditure is reduced and space is also saved. The cleaning job becomes very easy, because only the front portion needs to be cleaned.

Steel and fibre glass furniture is gaining popularity in modern offices. Wood has definite advantages over other structural materials because of its long tradition as a quality material. Modular design provides many variations in the furniture components and variation in the arrangement of components. Most modular furniture is self-contained, since the unit consists of desk space, file space and storage space. The ratio of space required for various components can be adjusted according to the nature of the job to be performed.

In addition, the following points should also be borne in mind when buying furniture: (Mills and Standingford).

1. Staff should be involved with choice, wherever possible.
2. Choice between wood and steel is not important now as often the two materials are used in construction.
3. Some systems have a choice of colours.
4. Plastic is not repairable, but is strong on drawer inners.
5. There should be no sharp or rugged edges or corners.
6. Locks should be either counter-sunk or flush.
7. Screen should be easily created or dismantled.
8. Adjustment of height of desks or tables should be possible.
9. Visual display units should be adjustable.
10. Desk tops can be made with some parts able to be tilted from 1° to 20° to make tasks easier.

QUESTIONS

1. What are the different types of furniture in an office ? *(B.Com., M.S.)*
2. What are the factors to be considered when selecting furniture for a business concern ? *(B.Com., Chennai)*
3. Discuss the principles of selection in the furniture layout. *(B.Com., Punjab)*
4. Write short note on built-in furniture, wooden furniture and steel furniture. *(B.Com., Mumbai)*

CHAPTER

Correspondence and Mail

Learning Objectives

INTRODUCTION

Correspondence and handling of mail are two basic office routines of any organisation. They are closely related to other office services-typing, duplicating, indexing, filing etc. Separate chapters have been devoted to these related activities.

CORRESPONDENCE

One of the most important departments of an organisation is correspondence department. An office receives communications and sends out communications in the form of letters, circulars, notices, telegrams, communique, etc. Again correspondence means, conveying information in writing from one person to another or between institutions on matters of common interest. Communication, again is one of the fundamental functions of the office. The prime responsibility of the office manager is the maintenance of communication service. Communication service is the part and parcel of the office organisation. Again, there cannot be a business office without correspondence. An office is a nerve-centre of an organisation and correspondence is the lifeblood of a business office. It is also possible to receive or to convey information through telephone or telegram, which is quicker than correspondence, but is more expensive. Sometimes the meaning will not be clear. Therefore, almost all the communication is made by correspondence–letters. Of course, it takes much time but it will reach the right person. Letters received or sent out are generally lucid in meaning. The success of a business office depends upon the efficiency of the correspondence department.

Advantages of written communication

(1) Accuracy can be maintained.

(2) It provides a written record of all transactions.

(3) It is less expensive than other methods.

(4) Ample time is available and therefore pre-thinking is possible; thus it is possible to minimise the errors in letters.

(5) It is more easy to send unpleasant communication.

(6) Properly drafted letters are free from doubts and confusions.

(7) It has become easy by the introduction of automatic office machines.

TYPES OF CORRESPONDENCE

Correspondence may be external and internal. *External correspondence* is that between the organisation and the outsiders (other firms, organisations, companies etc.) that is to say, all the letters received from and sent out to other firms come under external correspondence.

Internal correspondence means the correspondence between the departments of the company, between branches and head office of the same organisation. Branches are also considered as a department of the organisation and therefore, the correspondence is considered as an internal one.

The main object of correspondence is gained through an efficient and economic communication service. Every letter is a salesman. Every letter carries a certain message. It is a silent ambassador. It attracts the people. It enhances the reputation of the firm.

Nature of Correspondence

Office correspondence may be further classified into :

(*a*) **Routine Correspondence :** It includes correspondence on routine matters like enquiries, replies, orders, appointment letters, etc.

(*b*) **Sales Correspondence :** It includes correspondence on matters relating to sales, for examples, sales letters, invoices, statement of accounts, collection letters, delivery letters, debit notes, credit notes etc.

(*c*) **Personalised Correspondence :** It includes correspondence on matters involving personal or emotional matters, for examples, thanks letters, introductory letters, letters requesting favours or granting favours, letters conveying congratulations and appreciation etc.

(*d*) **Circular Letters :** Circulars are identical letters which are sent to a large number of persons and business firms, for example, such letters may be sent on matters like change of address, introduction of a new product, opening of a new branch, declaration of dividend etc.

Additional merits of Correspondence

1. It is a proper and permanent record for further reference.

2. The records are the witness if any dispute arises.

3. Verbal or oral orders may create confusions or doubts or misunderstanding. Correspondence removes all such drawbacks.

4. A good letter will promote business.

5. A good letter can create goodwill.

Nature of Correspondence

The nature of the correspondence may be of routine matters, or ordinary matters, personal matters, special matters, etc. Routine or ordinary matters are of ordinary nature e.g., enquiries and their replies, orders,circulars, acknowledgements, interviews, appointments, etc. Personal matters are in the nature of requests, introduction, appreciation, co-operation etc. Special matters are those which are concerned with the sales, complaints, collection, adjustments etc.

Cost of Correspondence

The cost of correspondence includes not only the cost of paper and postage but also the cost of:

1. The time spent on the correspondence (by the dictator and the typist).

2. Capital cost of the machines (typewriter, franking machine etc.)

3. Wasted stationery.

4. Overhead expenditure (light, rent etc.).

5. Time spent by clerks and messengers.

Organising Correspondence

A firm may send out letters and receive letters. This can be dealt with in two ways, either by centrally organised system or by decentrally organised correspondence system-centralised correspondence and decentralised correspondence.

Centralised Correspondence

Correspondence department is organised to set up an effective system of correspondence in a specialised and econonical way. Under the centralised correspondence system all the letters received are handled by a specialised department only. In big concerns it is so, because letters have been processed by trained staff and the staff work under a qualified supervisior. Correspondence is not passed to other departments. But when any correspondence needs special skill by any other department, such letters will be given to them.

Merits of Centralised Correspondence

1. Since qualified staff are appointed and are working centrally, it is possible to produce effective correspondence.

2. By sending out effective letters, goodwill can be created in the mind of the recipient.

3. Since the letters are handled by the same member it is easy to study the customers taste and needs.

4. High standards of correspondence are generally possible.

5. Specialisation generally increase productivity.

6. Staff can be trained adequately and quite easily.

Demerits of Centralised Correspondence

1. Though qualified persons are there, yet sometimes, to reply certain letters, other departments have to be approached.
2. Consultation, getting the information, drafting etc., will result in loss of time.
3. The persons of centralised correspondence department, writing out wrong replies, based on information received may create complication in future.
4. Letters relating to the policy of the business have to be approved by the management. A draft may have to be written several times before being passed and thus there is an unnecessary labour on the part of correspondent.

HOW TO WRITE GOOD LETTERS ?

1. Think about what you want to say before you start to write.
2. Jot down all the points you wish to write : never mind the order.
3. Now rearrange the points in the logical order.
4. Have a clear idea of character of the person you are going to write.
5. Begin with a short paragraph stating why you are writing; you can refer to a letter received by you and mention the subject of the correspondence.
6. The actual message can be written in the second paragraph.
7. The closing paragraph usually leads to some action on the part of the reader; it asks him to write back, or to place an order or to write to someone or to look into some complaint.
8. "You" attitude is the secret of effective letter.
9. The language must be friendly.
10. Remember, a short well-thought out letter has life.

DECENTRALISED CORRESPONDENCE (Departmental Correspondence)

The organisation has many departments and the correspondence relating to each department is entrusted to itself. Incoming letters are passed on to them and they send out replies. Such a system is called decentralised or departmental correspondence.

Merits of Decentralised Correspondence

1. Replies can be sent out without delay, because needed information is in the files, which are with them.
2. The staff have good knowledge about the matter they are dealing with.
3. Each department will try to send out letters of high quality.
4. Replies based upon first hand information will be more accurate.
5. Speedy replies can be made.
6. Promptness in sending letters can be maintained.

Demerits of Decentralised Correspondence

1. Specially trained persons cannot be appointed in each department. The departmental heads have to perform the work. As such, correspondence will not be of a good standard as in centralised correspondence.
2. It is possible that errors and mistakes creep in easily.
3. A goodwill cannot be created by writing standard correspondence.
4. It is not possible to maintain uniformity in the correspondence.

MAIL SERVICES

In good olden days there was no correspondence department as one-man-owned business alone existed. The correspondence department, nowadays, is the key to a successful firm. In the department, the whole correspondence is carried on. Therefore, the correspondence department deserves careful attention of the management. The arrangement of handling the correspondence depends upon the volume of business. In small firms, a clerk or the proprietor himself receives and sends out the letters. In big concerns, a constant contact with the customers has to be maintained. A written communication received through post office or messenger is termed as mail.

If the firm receives only a few letters a day, no machine is required to open them. If the volume of mail is large, then letter-openers or letter opening machines are used. Much time is saved if the letter openers are used, say 75% or 80% of the time is saved, through the labour-saving devices. The mail handling work can also be centralised or decentralised, according to the volume of incoming mails.

Advantages of Centralised Mail-Handling

1. Labour-saving devices can be used ; thus speedy result can be achieved. (But, it is not always possible to provide each department with the labour-saving machines).
2. By doing a particular job daily, the department will become more and more efficient.
3. Departmental clerks, stenos, etc., can be relieved from the mail-handling work.
4. Since the job is entrusted to a single department, they handle the work systematically; say. affixing date stamp, time of receipt, distribution of letters etc., without loss of time.
5. In the same way, outward letters are properly despatched. If every clerk is to send out letters, it is possible that the letters bear more than sufficient or insufficient or no postage stamps at all. This will affect the prestige of the firm.
6. Labour-saving machines can be used only if the firm has a centralised mail department; otherwise it is not economical.

The simplest way to open the incoming letter is by hand using a steel envelope opener if the letters are few. If the volume of letters is large, hand-operated machine is used. If the volume is very large, then an electric letter-opener can be used. All these methods are adopted to save time.

Business mail can be classified as :

1. Inward Mail (Incoming Correspondence)
2. Outward Mail, (Outgoing Correspondence)
3. Inter-departmental (within the organisation) Correspondence. The various methods of handling the inward mail are as follows :

1. Receiving the Mail

The inward mail is received through persons (peons), post, etc. A particular clerk is entrusted with the job of receiving letters reaching him through local people by issuing receipts against the letters received.

2. Sorting the Mail

If there is a post box, then a peon will be sent to the post office to collect the letters. He collects and hands them over to the officer concerned. In small concerns, the office-head or the superintendent will open them. In big concerns, there may be a separate section to deal with them. When a separate department is set up, labour-saving device, say, letter opener, operated by hand or electric power is adopted. The man to whom the duties are assigned, will sort out the letters. The personal letters will be handed over to the addressees concerned.

From the remaining letters, letters marked "Private, Confidential", etc., are sent to the officers concerned. The remaining letters addressed to the firm are passed on to the correspondence department.

3. Opening the Mail

All the incoming letters are placed on the table at the left-hand side and the letter-opener at the centre. The clerk takes out a letter from the left-hand side (letters are in a tray) and places it in the letter-opener and does the operation. The machine letter opener (described later) has a revolving knife edge, which will slice a very thin part from one edge of the envelope. While the cutting operation is on, the contents of the cover have to be safe; so the cover or envelope should not be shaken. After cutting all the envelopes, they are kept on the right-hand side of the clerk in a tray meant for that.

4. Scrutiny of Contents

After the letters are opened, either the same man or another clerk will empty all the covers by taking out the contents. While taking out the contents, a proper scrutiny will be done to verify whether all the contents from the cover have been taken out. With some letters there may be enclosures, concerned with them. They must be verified to find if they are in order or not. It will be more safe to attach a slip to the letter, with cheques, drafts, postal orders etc. The slip can be pinned to the letter. The slip along with cheques, drafts, etc., is to be sent to the accounts department and after taking out the cheques or drafts, the clerk in the accounts department should sign on the slip and return it to the mail opening section. The same slip, duly acknowledged by the accounts department, should be pinned to respective letter. While doing so, the amount of the cheque or draft must be verified very carefully to avoid complications in future.

In some cases the cheques or drafts are allowed to remain along with the letters. In such cases, the letters will be handled very carefully, so that the enclosed cheques or drafts should not be lost. After opening the letters they are placed one by one in a tray and the empty envelopes are thrown into a waste-basket.

5. Stamping the Mail

All the incoming letters are to be rubber-stamped, showing the date of receipt. Along with the date stamp, the name of the company is also affixed. The date, month and year in the seal can be adjusted.

If more departments have to deal the same letter, a slip should be attached to it, when it is sent for circulation. The slip should indicate the order in which it is to be circulated among the departments. After circulation the letter goes for filing.

6. Recording the Mail

All the incoming letters have to be entered in a register called 'Letter Received Book', 'Letter Received Register' or 'Receipt Register'. Specimen proof is given below.

S.No.	Date of Receipt	Name and address of the firm	Name of Correspondence	Subject-matter	Encl. if any	Section to which sent	Date of reply	Initials of Officers	Remarks

Entry in the letter-received register is a proof that a particular letter mentioned in it has actually been received. It is also a safeguard against the loss of any letter. When the letter is handed over to the section concerned, initials are obtained as an acknowledgement receipt. When telegrams are received, they are entered in red ink in the register.

7. Distribution

After registration, the letters are sorted out and kept in different trays and sent to the departments concerned. The receiving clerk should sign the register or a slip, to indicate that the letters have been received.

All the letters received are placed before the departmental head, who in turn, distributes them to the various clerks, who have to deal with such letters. In the evening hours, the departmental head has to make enquiries or verify whether replies have been sent to all the letters received. If not, he should see that replies are sent in order to save the name of his department.

(Outward correspondence has been dealt with in the same chapter, after drafting the correspondence).

The letter-writing process :
Eight ways of answering a letter

1. The correspondent may dictate the entire letter to the dictating machine or to a stenographer.

2. He may dictate certain personal paragraphs and the numbers of form paragraphs to round out the letter.

3. He may answer it by form paragraphs or by a form letter. To add a personal touch, when desired, certain fill-in paragraphs or a personal opening sentence or post-script may be written.

4. He may answer it with a printed letter/form.

5. He may jot down an outline of the proper answer and let his secretary shape it up.

6. He may turn the letter over to an intelligent secretary without comment.

7. He may dictate a special letter which is to be sent to several widely separated correspondents. Each letter may be separately typed or its copy may be put on a duplicator.

8. When he wishes to show intimate personal interest, he may add a brief note in his own hand-writing.   (*Leffingwell*)

DRAFTING OF LETTERS

All the letters received must be replied. The writing of the replies is based on the custom and size of the concern. The system of drafting must be economical and prompt. Take out one of the letter, study it properly, collect the required information and draft a reply systematically. The draft or the reply is written by the officer concerned or dictated by Manager or departmental head. The reply is typed either on post card or letter pad. The ways of giving replies or answers to a letter are as follows:

1. The Manager or the sectional head or the correspondent will dictate the replies to a stenographer, who will transcribe, type and give them for the signature of the officer concerned. This system is commonly followed. The dictation work is being done in the

early hours of the office work. After that, the officer is free to do other jobs. To take dictation, the executive, and stenographer must be present. If anyone is absent the work cannot be done. When the steno is absent a dictaphone is used.

2. The executive dictates to a stenographic machine known as dictaphone. The message recorded on tape or disc is removed from the machine and is placed in another machine; dictated replies are reproduced and thus the typist is enabled to type out the letters. The dictated message can be erased and the tape or disc can be re-used.

3. Dictating is done directly to a typist. The executive dictates the message and at the same time the typist goes on typing it. There is every possibility that the typist makes mistakes in typing or the executive makes mistakes in dictation. In some cases the executive may wish to change the message. As such, the system is not preferred.

4. Busy executives or the departmental heads note down the hints or outline or points to be covered by correspondence and the actual drafting is done by the secretary.

5. Letter forms are used.

6. Form paragraphs will be followed by the drafting or dictation of the remainder of the letters.

Merits of a Dictaphone

(a) The executive can dictate or give the reply even if the stenographer is absent.

(b) When the executive is in the mood for dictation, replies can be dictated even if the stenographer is absent.

(c) The number of clerks can be reduced.

(d) Salary of stenographers is high, whereas it is low for the typist. Instead of appointing stenographers, typists can be appointed. It is more economical.

(e) All stenographers may not be able to take dictation at a high speed. If a dictaphone is available, the executive can dictate the reply at any speed. When the typist types the speed of the tape or disc can be regulated.

(f) It is usual that visitors may come often. During a dictation to the stenographer, arrival of such visitors wastes the time of the steno. Such waste of time can be avoided.

Demerits of a Dictaphone

(a) Personal contact is neglected.

(b) It is very difficult to make corrections in a dictaphone.

(c) Since tape or disc is used again and again, original records cannot be maintained.

(d) For efficient operation of the machine, the executive must be a good dictator.

TYPING

After the matter has been dictated, it is to be typed before it is sent out. Outgoing letters from a concern must be attractive, legible and lucid. Good correspondence creates good impression on the customers and goodwill for the firm.

The draft, prepared or dictated matter is handed over to the typist who types it. When four or five copies are required, carbon paper is used. When more copies are needed, a duplicating machine can be used economically. There are two ways to arrange the type work in big concerns–Centralised and Decentralised typing.

CENTRALISED OR TYPING POOL

The typing work of each department is done at a central place, called typing pool. Each department has to send drafts to the typing pool and they, in turn, return them afterwards along with the typed matter. This method has its own merits and demerits.

FACTORS OF SELECTION OF COMMUNICATION SYSTEM
1. Speed
2. Distance
3. Accuracy
4. Secrecy
5. Safety
6. Records
7. Impression
8. Cost
9. Certainty
10. Importance

Merits of Typing Pool

1. Equal distribution of work amongst the typists will be done by the supervisor-in-charge.

2. When there is a typing pool, there is an economy of time and expense, say 25%, because the number of typists in the pool can be reduced. Otherwise each department has a typist; for example, if there are seven departments each department needs a typist. When there is pool system, the number of typists can easily be reduced to four or five.

3. Since the pool is in one place, other departments are not disturbed by the noise of typing.

4. New comers to the post of typist can easily be trained in the pool.

5. It is possible to measure the efficiency of each typist.

6. When a job is decentralised, and when the executive is away or on tour, the stenographer has to sit idly without job. In the pool there will not be any time to waste, because general works of the organisation can be attended to.

Demerits of Typing Pool

1. Personal touch with the executive is lost.

2. All the typists of the pool do not possess knowledge of technical words; hence errors may creep in.

3. Secrecy cannot be maintained.

4. Since there is no personal touch between the typist and the executive, sincerity is also lost.

DEPARTMENTAL TYPING

Under this method, each department of the organisation appoints a typist, who does the typewriting work of the department exclusively. It has its own merits and demerits as follows.

Merits of Departmental Typing

1. A Departmental typist, when doing the typewriting work of a particular department, will become familiar with the technical words.
2. The typist is always at the disposal of the executive.
3. The typist or stenographer will be more sincere and responsible when he is attached to a particular department.
4. Efficient, accurate and neat work is the result.
5. The possibility of committing errors in letters is few.
6. Stenographers attached to a particular department are familiar to the tone and pronunciation of the executive.
7. Likes and dislikes of the executives are known to the typist or stenographer, he can work with confidence.

Demerits of Departmental Typing

1. The typewriting of the whole organisation is not distributed evenly, because some may have more work and some may have less work or no work at all.
2. This method is uneconomic.
3. This system disturbs the department by the sound caused by typewriter.
4. When the executive is away or on tour, the typist has no work. He talks with his colleagues and interrupts their work.

Ways to eliminate the time waste at the typist's work

1. The typewriter and the seat of the typist must be in the correct position.
2. The paper should be inserted properly in the typewriter.
3. The carbon paper should be placed properly between the papers.
4. The tabulator of the typewriter must be in order.
5. The typewritten paper must be correctly removed from the typewriter.
6. All the fingers of the typist must possess equal force.
7. Changing paras must be done with the help of tabulator.
8. The typist must be able to concentrate his mind while at his work.
9. The typist must be thorough with the spelling of words.
10. He must have interest in his work.

OUTWARD CORRESPONDENCE

All the typewritten matters are sent to the superintendent or head-clerk who compares the typewritten script with the draft. After the verification or comparison is done, the head-clerk or the superintendent puts initials in the letter to indicate that the letter is ready for despatch or the contents are correct. The officer concerned makes his signature in the letter. It is the responsibility of the superintendent or the head-clerk to see that the letter is complete before he puts his initials. Otherwise the incomplete letters which go out will earn a bad-name for the organisation.

Letters are also of many types according to the importance of the contents. Ordinary letters, acknowledgement letters, form letters, price lists, etc., are signed by the superintendent/head-clerk. The letters containing important messages or information should be signed by the executive or manager or secretary. The letters are signed according to the office procedure laid down in each organisation.

After the signature, just below it, the designation of the person signing it must be indicated. In some cases, after the signature, name and designation of the person are indicated. If any power of attorney has been issued in favour of any executive, then, after the signature, but before the name of the firm "per pro", or PP., will be mentioned.

Signature should be affixed in ink or with a ball-pen. At least two copies of the letter should be taken. The original is to be sent to the addressee and the other (carbon copy) to be retained in the office. The office copy must be initialled by the person who signs the original. It is the responsibility of the superintendent or head-clerk to do corrections, if any, in both the copies. If corrections are done in the original, but not in the office copy, it may create complications in future. For circulars the facsimile or the signature of the executive with rubber stamp need be affixed.

In order to distinguish different letters that are despatched generally numbers are assigned to each letter. When the recipient sends the reply against a letter, it will be easy to find out the copy of the letter sent to him.

Now all the letters are received by the mailing department that in turn, does the following jobs.

(A) All outgoing letters are to be recorded in the mailing section, as shown below :

OUTWARD MAIL REGISTER

Date	S. No.	Ref.	Name and Address	Subject matter	Encl. if any	Stamp used	Re-marks
1	2	3	4	5	6	7	8
1.12.2009	849	Sales	M/s.Ram &Co., Agra	Special Price list	Price lists and Cata-logue	5.00	–

By maintaining such a register, it is possible :

(a) to find out the exact number of letters sent out, on daily record basis.

(b) to keep a proper account of the stamps used.

(c) to have an evidence of outgoing letters.

(d) to maintain daily balancing of stamp account.

The stamp account is maintained as in the petty cash-book. If it is difficult to maintain such a register, then a stamp book/postage book is maintained, mainly to record the stamps consumed. This work depends upon the volume of outward mail of an organisation.

(B) After assigning the serial Number (Despatch Number) to the letters, they are placed in a tray. Then they are sorted out in two trays–local letters and outstation letters. All the local letters, which are to be sent through the messenger should be marked on the envelope as 'By Hand'. Then such local letters are again recorded in a delivery book or local letter book and handed over to the peon, who delivers them to the addressees and obtains their signatures. The form is as follows.

LOCAL DAY BOOK

Date	Name of Addressee	Contents	Through (name of peon)	Signature
1.3.2009	M/s Gopinath & Co. New Delhi-110010	Drafts for Rs. 450/-	Ramesh	

The out station letters, along with the enclosures are properly folded and inserted in the envelopes. If the letter is not folded properly, it will have a bad appearance. Letters must be folded according to the size of the envelope. The folded letter must fit in the cover to have a nice appearance. The address of the letter and the address on the cover must tally. If there are enclosures in any letter a red flag (1" 2 or 3) may be pinned to attract the attention of the despatch clerk. When the letter is placed in the cover, the despatch clerk must remove the flag. The address need not be typed on the envelope, if window envelope is used. This saves time. The comparison of the address is also not required. But care should be taken to fold the letters in such a way that the address is shown through the window. Certain types of messages are printed in such a way that they look like envelopes when folded. Such letters need be stapled.

(C) The despatch clerk has to weigh the letters so as to know the value of postage stamps required for each letter. If the despatch clerk is careless, it is likely that the stamps affixed are more than or less than the required value. There is the possibility of letter being posted without any postage stamp at all. By all these, the firm earns a bad name. Addressees of letters without postage stamps as well as those that do not have stamp to the required value will have to pay a penalty of double the deficiency in cash to the postman who delivers them. The addressee has the right to refuse to accept such letters. If the addressee has to pay penalty, he may stop further contact. Returning of important, but unstamped or under-stamped letters will cause loss to the organisation. So care should be taken to fix postage stamps according to the weight. It will be safe to keep up to date circulars of the postal rates and other rules with the despatch clerk.

(D) When the letter is placed in the cover, it is sealed properly. After sealing, it is weighed. Then required stamps will be indicated with pencil on the cover (where stamps are to be fixed). After that the required stamps are affixed. There may be rubber stamps-"REGISTERED", "BOOK-POST", "V.P.P.", "PRINTED MATTER", etc. According to the nature of the letter, the stamps are affixed, on covers. If there are many letters, the postage stamps are affixed by the means of a franking machine or stamping machine (see Office Machines-Chapter 8).

(E) After all the above jobs are over, the letters are handed over to the peon, who will carry them in a bag and post them. If the letters are to be registered, receipts are obtained and pasted in the Despatch Register. If there is a decentralised system of correspondence, then one peon goes to all the departments, collects the letters at a fixed time and gives them to the Mailing department.

MAILING MACHINES

The mailing department staff has to engage in many repetitive and monotonous activities in the course of the performance of their functions. In large organisations, the handling and disposal of mail calls for speed and accuracy of the mailing services. Many mechanical aids have been devised for the use in mailing department. Some of the devices which may be profitably used in the mailing department are:

1. **Letter Opening Machine :** This is used for opening envelopes of different sizes at great speed. This machine can be operated manually or electrically and can be adjusted to open envelopes of any standard size.

2. **Date and Time Recording Machine :** This machine is used to record the time and date of receipt or despatch of mail. When envelopes are inserted in it, the machine print the time and date on it.

3. **Addressing Machine :** This is used to print addresses on letters, envelopes etc. which are sent to regular correspondents.

4. **Folding Machine :** This machine is used to fold a large number of letters of identical size at a high speed.

5. **Sealing Machine :** This machine is automatically mositen and seal the flaps of envelopes.

6. **Inserting Machine :** This is used to insert folded letters into envelopes at a great speed.

7. **Tape Moistening Machine :** This is used to seal bulky packets and parcels etc. It takes a roll of strongly gummed tough paper tape and moisten it before affixing it.

8. **Franking Machine :** (Stamping machine) It is used in large offices for affixing postage stamps on envelopes. In large offices, where thousands of outgoing envelopes have to be stamped each day, these machines are very useful. The machine not only marks the envelopes with the required denominations of the postage stamps but also prints the balance on hand. This machine gets locked automatically after the value of stamps, for which payment has been made to the post office, has been printed.

9. **Mailing Scale :** This is weighing machine which weigh letters, envelopes and packets to ascertain the correct postage to be affixed on them.

10. **Sealing-cum-Stamping Machine :** It is an electrically operated machine which not only seals the envelopes but also franks and count them.

QUESTIONS

1. Explain the merits and demerits of centralised correspondence.   (B. Com., M.S.)
2. State the advantages of written communications.   (B. Com., Punjab)
3. State the merits and demerits of decentralised correspondence. (B. Com., Kerala)
4. How you handle with incoming letters of a concern where you are secretary ?
                                                                      (B. Com., Chennai)
5. What is the use of registration of incoming mail ?
6. What are the methods by which incoming letters can be replied ? (B. Com., M.S.)
7. State the merits and demerits of typing pool with departmental typing.
                                                        (B. Com., Kerala, M.S. Madurai)

8. How do you eliminate the time-waste at typist's work ?
9. Write short notes on :
   Franking machine, Outward mail register.
10. Mention the merits of adopting dictaphone in a concern.
11. Describe how departmental correspondence is superior to centralised correspondence. *(B. Com., Madurai, Chennai)*
12. What is mailing service? State how would you plan mailing service ? *(B. Com., M.S., Madurai)*
13. Centralisation of correspondence is better than its decentralisation". Discuss. *(B. Com., Chennai)*
14. Describe the procedure for maintaining incoming and outgoing mail of an office. *(B. Com., Bangalore, Punjab)*
15. What is meant by office correspondence ? How would you organise correspondence in the office ? *(B. Com., Madurai)*

8

Record Administration

INTRODUCTION

Records are very important in modern business. The office is responsible for maintaining the records for future reference. A good and systematic preservation and maintenance of letters and records received and copies of outgoing correspondence, for future reference is known as filing. Filing is nothing but systematic record keeping. Filing is concerned with the work of arranging and preserving the records or copies of records kept in an organisation so that they are readily available when required. All the office communications are done orally or through correspondence. Information received in the office may be in the form of enquiries, orders, invoices, complaints, contracts of business, etc., and includes the internal accounts, payments, progress reports, stock records, sales, purchases etc. All the information so received is to be processed and arranged in the form of statistical statement, financial statement, returns etc. And these are to be preserved for future reference. All stages leading to the transactions are evidenced by written documents. Thus records management and filing is an important thing for an efficient office management.

Office work is basically concerned with the records of organisation. The value of any record in business depends upon the speed and accuracy with which it can be made available and put to use.

In the words of *Little field* and *Peterson*, "Records management can be described as the management control of records."

In the words of *Denyer*, "Modern records management involves much more than the methods of filing or the systems of classification, important of these are—indexing, central filing, records retention, follow up and micro-photography, all these receive attention in the present day office."

OBJECTS (Purpose) OF RECORDS MANAGEMENT

Past records of the business are maintained. The purpose or objects in maintaining these records are as follows :

1. **Accounts of progress kept in an orderly way :** If a patient approaches a doctor, it is usual that the patient's past history is needed to diagnose the disease properly. In the same way, to measure the progress of the concern or to find out certain other facts, a history of the firm is needed. And the past records, history of the business, recount the dealings.

2. **Proper study of the position of the firm :** Records of past transactions are the basis on which further study can be made. The preserved records are the contributory factors, without which a good and proper study of the position of the firm cannot be made and a statement cannot be prepared.

3. **Comparison of business (periodwise/statewise) :** Past records make it easy and possible to compare the performance of one period with that of another period, one place with another, one result with another, etc. By comparison, one can know whether there is progress or not.

4. **In case of disputes :** The need for referring to these records or documents often arises for the settlement of disputes in transaction. All information cannot be remembered.

5. **Policy making :** Past records, events, progress, etc., are very necessary to decide future policies and plans. In the absence of records, the policies and plans may not be successful.

6. **Legal requirements :** Certain records are to be kept for a number of years from the legal point of view.

7. **Evidence :** Records are good evidence in the court of law, in the case of suits.

8. **General use :** Some customers may simply refer to the previous correspondence by quoting the number and date. In such case, if the letters have been filed properly, it is easy to comply with the needs of the customers. Otherwise, there is a wastage of time and money.

9. **Facilitate to detect errors and wastes :** Past records help in locating the errors and identifying the wastes occurring in the organisation. Thus the management can eliminate the errors or wastes.

The past records are just like tools in the hands of a technician. They enable the management to promote the business by making a thorough study of them. Filing is one of the main functions of a concern and the filed records must be readily available when needed. There are no hard and fast rules by which the documents are to be filed. The system and method of filing will generally depend upon the size of the office. The importance of a good filing system cannot be exaggerated in the modern days, when there is stiff competition among the firms. Filing is the systematic arrangement of keeping business correspondence and records which enable quick reference whenever needed in the future.

Records are written data that are made for possible future use. The records may be classified into :

1. Personnel records.
2. Correspondence records.
3. Accounting records.
4. Legal records.
5. Other business records.

PRINCIPLES OF RECORD MANAGEMENT

In order to be successful, the records management must be based on the following principles :

1. **Verification :** Records can be verified whenever needed.
2. **Justification :** Records must be maintained with some justifiable purpose. Otherwise, it will be a waste of money, space and time.
3. **Classification :** Records must be classified according to their use. It may be classified according to time or chronology or subjects.
4. **Information :** The required information must be available whenever needed.
5. **Elasticity :** The record system must be elastic in capacity so that expansion or contraction of records is possible.
6. **Reasonable cost :** The cost of record management must be a reasonable one. For more important records larger amount may be spent and for less important records only smaller amount should be spent.

Record management must be simple, accurate, economic and useful for the organisation.

Records Management : In the words of *Zane K. Quible*, "Record management refers to the activities designed to control the life cycle of a record for its creation to its ultimate disposition." Accordingly the life cycle of records involves the following stages :

1. **Creation Stage :** The first stage involves design and control of office forms. Data should be recorded in the forms accurately and completely. The time period for which the records are to be kept should also be determined properly.
2. **Storage Stage :** Under this stage, records are properly classified and put into appropriate file covers. The records should be stored at an accessible location and arrangements should be made for their protection.
3. **Retrieval Stage :** The purpose of maintaining records is to make them available for future reference. Therefore, an efficient filing procedure should be designed to retrieve the records in time. There should be a proper procedure for the issue of files.
4. **Disposition Stage:** This stage is concerned with disposition of obsolete and unnecessary records. Valuable documents are preserved in water-proof and fire-proof cabinets. The documents which are no longer required should be destroyed. Less important records which are not in current use should be transferred from high cost storage area to low cost storage area.

ESSENTIALS OF RECORDS MANAGEMENT SYSTEM

In order to achieve the above mentioned objectives, record keeping must have the following essentials :

1. **Simplicity :** There should be simplicity in record-keeping. Records should be maintained according to the requirements of the organisation so as to facilitate comprehension.

2. **Accuracy :** Records should be preserved accurately so as to reduce the chances of errors and frauds.

3. **Economy :** The cost of maintaining and providing records is also an important factor which the office manager has to keep in mind.

4. **Usefulness :** Record should be useful for better management of the affairs of the business. Record-keeping should avoid retention of papers not needed.

ANALYSING RECORD KEEPING

All the records should be carefully examined and analysed with reference to the following questions:

1. Are the records necessary ? Do they accomplish the purpose desired ? Is that purpose justified ?

2. Are the records used ? The fact that a record is not used does not necessarily mean that it is useless. It may be an indication that its value is not appreciated; it may, of course, also mean that it is actually useless.

3. Are the records so made as to avoid unnecessary writing ? It should be remembered that carefully chosen abbreviations reduce labour and that there are many forms of abbreviating or symbolizing.

4. Is unnecessary copying avoided ? This may involve copying either the whole of a record or part of it.

5. Are the forms used the best for the purpose ?

6. Is the equipment - binder, cabinet or desk-the best for the purpose ?

7. Are the tools used the best for the purpose ?

8. Can the record be co-ordinated or combined with another already in existence ?

FILING

According to *Neuner and Keeling*, "Filing is the systematic arrangement and keeping of business correspondence and records so that they may be found and delivered when needed for future reference." According to *Zone K Quible* filing is "One of the activities in the records management programme which involves systematically classifying, coding, arranging and placing of records in storage." It is a form of record keeping.

It is the process of arranging and storing records so that they can be easily available when required. It is also the systematic arrangement and preservation of business correspondence in such a way that they can be found and used quickly whenever required for future reference. Proper filing is essential to handle a large number of papers and documents systematically.

In the words *of George R. Terry,* "Filing is the placing of documents and papers in acceptable containers according to some predetermined arrangement so that any of these when required, may be located quickly and conveniently."

Importance of Filing : In the modern organisation the importance of filing has increased because of growing correspondence and documents. These cannot be preserved without proper arrangement. Previous letters and documents are necessary for reference. So a systematic preservation of various types of records is possible only by a good filing system.

Functions of Filing

Functions of filing system can be classified into :

1. **Information function :** Records are protected and maintained to supply information.
2. **Administrative function :** Files help the executive in framing business policies. For this previous records are maintained.
3. **Library function :** The records are stored for future reference. Thus it performs the library function.
4. **Historical function :** Files preserve important records of the progress of the business in a systematic manner. Thus it performs the historical function.

Proper arrangement of filing is necessary for a large number of papers and documents. In an office filing is an important activity. Records are maintained by the management for future planning. Records of correspondence with the suppliers and customers are necessary for reference in the future. It provides documentary evidence in the event of any dispute. Good filing system is the preservation of various types of information for various purposes. Systematic filing system helps in taking prompt action and increases the efficiency of the organisation. Correspondence can be handled carefully and quickly. Thus it increases the goodwill of the firm.

Advantages of Filing

An efficient filing system claims the following advantages:

1. Often customers refer to their past letters or orders by writing only the date and in such cases filing serves the purpose of ready reference.
2. When past records are maintained through a good filing system, they save time and also increase efficiency.
3. A proper filing system safeguards the documents against loss.
4. Old or past records serve as a reliable basis for future planning and action.
5. Past records are good evidence in case of disputes.
6. Certain documents have to be kept in order to fulfil legal obligations.
7. A proper control is facilitated. According to the importance of letters, they can be disposed of quickly.

Objects of Filing

1. It keeps the records, protects letters and documents.
2. It makes past records easily accessible.
3. It provides suitable storage function.
4. Proper filing leads to economy in space.
5. It improves the appearance of the office considerably.
6. It is less expensive and consumes less time to take out the records.

ESSENTIALS OF A GOOD FILING SYSTEM

An efficient filing system should have the following essentials:

1. **Simplicity :** It must be simple in operations, so that every staff of the office can easily understand the filing system. The filing system should not be overelaborated or complicated. But it should not be sacrificed for sake of simplicity.

2. **Suitability :** The filing system should be completely applicable to the firm concerned, and suit the nature and requirements of the business for which it is introduced.

3. **Adaptability :** The system must be adaptable to the changes that occur in business. For example, a book dealer, in course of time, starts publishing books. In such a case the original filing system cannot be overthrown to adopt a new system. The existing system must have room for expansion in its newer form ; otherwise it will be a waste. Modern tendency of business is that it grows from time to time and accepts a new and complex form by carrying many transactions or opening new branches or creating new departments. Therefore an easy system is to be adopted to the needs of a growing trade.

4. **Economy :** Cheap system of filing is to be adopted. The cost incurred by the system must be proportionate to the results obtained. The desired result must be obtained by using minimum finance, time, clerks, etc.

5. **Protection (Safety) :** The filed documents must be available to the person, who needs them. They are easily available when they are filed properly and securely. Documents should not be damaged by dust, insects, thefts, mishandling, fire, rain etc. Certain documents have to be kept for a longer time or for the life-time of the concern. They must be housed in suitable equipment.

6. **Less Space :** Economy of space is of great importance in all concerns, because of high rent. So it is necessary to see that the system requires minimum floor space. For this, dead papers can be removed, older files which are not at all needed should also be removed. A regular removal of such documents and files can save space.

7. **Accessibility :** The files should be so arranged that the required letter or document for reference be picked up without loss of time. Of course it is possible through a good index system.

8. **Cross Reference :** When the same letter is to be kept in more than one file, a cross reference should be filed in other file. It enables the filing clerk to know that the cross reference letter is in a certain file. That is the most relevant file housing the letter and a cross reference in sheet or card is placed in the appropriate place in others files (unimportant files).

9. **Co-ordination and Control :** A good practicable system of filing cannot be separated from the whole problem of an organisation. Different departments may be there under an organisation. A good system of filing must permit constant co-ordination among all departments and to have an effective control over the organisation.

10. **The Guide :** Whenever a file or document is taken out, an indicator should be placed at the same place, if possible with the signature of the recipient, to show the file or document has been removed. When it is returned, the indicator will be removed.

11. **Flexibility:** If there is any expansion of work in the business concern, then the filing system can be expanded. So it must be flexible.

PLANNING OF FILING SYSTEM

The mode of filing system should be formulated on the basis of objects and nature of records. The following points will help to plan the system of filing, apart from the above :

The filing system should be planned with due regard to the objects of filing and nature of records. When one prepares a system for filing, the first job is to make out a list of records and documents to be stored. The following steps may be considered while planning a filing system.

1. **Period of Storage :** After deciding the records and documents to be listed, the period of storage should be determined with the consultation of various departmental heads of the organisation. All documents are not needed for a long time while others may be needed for a considerable time.

2. **Storage Space :** Nature of the organisation and availability of funds are the basis to layout a storage plan. Arrangements should also be made to protect the records from losses or damages.

3. **Arrangements in Storage :** Storing arrangement should be kept in view of the frequency of use of the documents and departmental heads who will need the records.

4. **Determining Equipments Need :** Various types of filing equipments should be procured to store the records. Availability of funds and importance of records decide the choice of filing equipment. Fire proof equipment must be preferred.

5. **System of Classification :** A proper system of classification of records to be adopted is to be selected. The system should be simple, economical and efficient.

6. **Training:** Proper arrangements should be made to train the staff who handle the files. The filing procedure should be designed to fit the needs of the organisation.

ORGANISATION OF FILING

The filing function should be organised in such a way that it helps in proper maintenance of records. It is important to note that the records should be made available whenever required. The office manager has to decide whether the filing should be centralised or decentralised - Centralised Filing and Decentralised Filing both have their own merits and demerits.

1. Centralised Filing System :

It is a system where all records relating to the various departments of a concern are filed at one place or in the central office. In other words, individual departments or sections of an organisation do not do the filing of records.

Merits of Centralised Filing System

1. It is put under the control of specialists and this facilitates more efficiency.
2. Space available is used economically.
3. There will be an effective control over them.
4. There will be no duplication of filing equipment and work (as in decentralised system) and as such there is economy in filing.
5. There is uniform standard to file the papers and to take them out. This enables speedy location of documents.
6. People, who do the same work again and again become specialists in their work. This adds to greater efficiency.
7. Papers will be filed the same day.
8. The location of missing files or papers is easily known (by the proper use of indicator).

Demerits of Centralised Filing System

1. When a departmental head is in urgent need of any letter, it will not reach him in time because of the long procedure. This is a main drawback.
2. Errors may creep in.
3. Much time is consumed if the filing department is located in distant rooms.
4. Rigid rules are there in giving and returning files. The rules become more important than the dealings.
5. Secrecy cannot be maintained.

2. Decentralised Filing System

Under this system, filing is done by different departments independently and not centrally in one place. Every department instals separate equipment and appoints staff to look after the filing work. This system is also known as departmental filing system.

Merits of Decentralised Filing System

1. Suitable, simple and easy methods can be adopted according to the convenience of the department.
2. The files are easily and quickly available.
3. Quick availability of file facilitates more efficiency.
4. Secrecy can be maintained.
5. Receiving clerk will file the letters without mistakes, because he has to deal with a few letters only.

Demerits of Decentralised Filing System

1. In one organisation, in different departments, different methods of filing will be followed. As such no standard system will prevail.
2. The filing clerk has many other jobs; he cannot become a specialist in filing system.
3. Inter-department transfer of clerks will fail to understand the filing system of other departments.
4. If one document relates to two or more departments, there will be difficulty in filing the document.
5. Filing will be done at the convenience of a clerk, who has many other jobs to do along with the filing. As such he may misplace the letters or keep them in other registers or leave them unnoticed.

METHODS OF FILING

Various methods of filing are based on the different type of equipments in use. Each method has its own merits and demerits. A system which is suitable for one business may be totally useless for another. Therefore, the methods can be classified into two broad categories: (1) Old (Conventional) method and (2) Modern method.

Old (Conventional) Methods

In the good olden days, when there were a few transactions, it was easy to keep and maintain files. Some of these methods, still used in small organisations, are discussed below:

1. Guard Books

The method of guard books is often used for recording minutes of voluntary associations, companies, Government committees etc. In this method, all the letters are pasted in the guard book in chronological order to avoid the possibility of misplacement of any paper. The method is not common.

2. Spike or Pillar File

A spike is lifted on a wooden disc which may be kept on the table or hung against the wall. The papers are punched into a metal spike and made to rest on the disc. This is the cheapest method of filing. But the method is not suitable where frequent reference to the documents has to be made.

3. Press Copy Book

All outgoing letters are copied out in a book, either in geographical or alphabetical order. It is good evidence of letters sent out. It is not good for big concerns.

Spike or Pillar File

4. Pigeon-Hole Method

A cupboard is divided into a number of tiny compartments and each compartment is allotted to letters alphabetically. The letters are folded and a brief description is made on the outside fold. As soon as the transaction is concluded, the letters are cleared to some corner of the room, for small offices it is practicable, but for a big concern it is impracticable.

5. Metal Holders

These are used for holding the papers together. The papers are placed in metal holders in chronological order. This method is inconvenient and does not serve the real purpose of filing if the number of papers are large.

Pigeon Hole Cabinet

6. Box File

Generally cardboard boxes are used for filing papers. The box contains clips to hold the papers. The box consists of a set of manila sheets or folders, in which the letters are sorted out alphabetically. The box file will not last long.

With the development of communication and the development of civilisation, transactions have increased tremendously. As such the number of incoming and outgoing letters has also increased. When the movements of papers have increased, the prevailing filing system has also gone out of the date. So, new methods of filing have to be adopted in place of the old one. From the point of view of the large concerns, the old method has been found useless. Therefore, to meet the requirements, the system of filing has been revised.

MODERN FILING METHODS

The conventional filing methods and equipment are obsolete and useless from the standpoint of a large-scale organisation. The modern methods of filings are broadly classified into two categories: (*i*) Flat or Horizontal Filing and (*ii*) Vertical or upright Filing.

1. Flat or Horizontal Filing

Under horizontal filing, the papers are inserted in files or folders which are kept in drawers in horizontal position, that is one upon the other. The papers are filed in the folders in chronological order. As files are placed one above the other, there may be some difficulty in tracing the files whenever required. To avoid this, each file is allotted a number and an index prepared. When a file is removed for reference, a guide card about its movement is kept in its place.

This method is simple and flexible. It facilitates easy reference to current documents since they are filed in the chronological order. The main defect of horizontal filing is that reference to previous records would be inconvenient because in order to refer to any old letter, other letters which are filed above it have to be taken out. Moreover, insertion and withdrawal of papers take much time.

The important files used for keeping the papers under horizontal filing are :

(A) Flat Files

These are cover of cardboard or thick papers, fitted with metal hinges with which to fasten the papers together. A separate cover (file) is allotted to each customer or subject, and all the correspondence and documents relating to the customer or subject is placed in that cover in a chronological order. If a letter of paper related to more than one file, copies are made of it and placed in different covers. The paper to be filed is punched with a punching machine and is inserted in the file through the metal hinges. The files are placed horizontally one upon another. An index of files is generally prepared for quick reference. This index is displayed outside the almirah or drawer in which the files are kept.

(B) Arch Lever Files

It is a very popular type of horizontal file. It can be described as a strong cardboard folder which contains strong metal arches which can be opened with the help of a lever. Records to be filed are punched with two holes with the help of the punching machine either at the top or on the left-hand side of the forms, are then filed on the metal uprights, after the arch has been opened by the lever. The arch lever file facilitates alphabetical division which is done by inserting thick card at suitable places. The greatest advantage of this file is that papers can be inserted or taken out with great ease without disturbing the order of other papers in the file. The file also offers the advantage of proper preservation of papers from mutilation and dust, if the files are stored properly in the almirahs.

Advantages of Horizontal Filing :

1. It is simple to operate. It is easy to file documents.
2. It facilitates easy references of documents as they are filed in chronological (date-wise) order.
3. It is a flexible system.
4. It can keep all letters in proper order with the help of spring fastening device.
5. The letters can be referred without removing them from the file. Thus, risk of being lost is maintained.

Disadvantages of Horizontal Filing :

1. It is unsuitable where volume of records is very high.
2. To take out any paper, other papers have to be dislocated as the papers are kept in the order in which they are received.

3. When a large number of papers are stored in one file, their location becomes some what difficult.

4. This system is less flexible and takes more time as compared to vertical system.

2. Vertical or Upright Filing

This is the most modern system of filing. It has grown essentially out of the drawbacks and defects of the horizontal method under which papers are so arranged that it is impossible to refer to them at short notice. Because of its outright superiority to the horizontal method, vertical

Arch Lever File

filing has come to be adopted by most of the modern offices aiming at efficiency in record keeping. Under this method, the papers and the files containing them are placed vertically or in a standing upright position. Hence, the name vertical file.

To put vertical filing into operation, the following equipments are needed :

Vertical Filing Drawer

(A) Folder: Folders are the basic of vertical filing. They are made of manila paper or some other strong paper and are used to hold papers and documents. The back of the folder is slightly higher than the front. The extended back is used to write the contents and necessary details about the subject. When the folders are placed in the cabinet, the extended edges are visible in a sequence so that contents can be easily read.

(B) Filing Cabinet : Folders are kept vertically in a wooden or steel cabinet which consists of a number of drawers. The drawers are deep enough to permit folders to be placed in a vertical position. Each drawer is fitted with slider which pushes it backward or pulls it forward. There is also a mechanism fitted in the drawer for holding the folders together. In order to divide the drawer into convenient sections, guide cards are inserted at appropriate places. Generally a cabinet has four drawers and each standard size drawer can accommodate about 240 folders.

Advantages of Vertical Filing

1. Vertical filing allows ready reference of papers and documents. The heading of each folder is visible from the extended edge of the back-sheet.

2. It is really adoptable. The folders can be arranged according to any classification such as alphabetical, numerical and subject-wise.

3. It is economical as compared to the horizontal equipment as it can accommodate more papers.

4. It provides ample scope for expansion while installing this type of equipment, adequate provision for expansion of the number of folders can be made in the drawers.

Disadvantages of Vertical Filing

1. Vertical filing is not as fast as the other methods of filing such as visible card filing and rotary card filing.

2. There is always a possibility of folders slipping down the drawers. This may lead to unnecessary wear and tears of various folder.

Suspension Filing

Suspended filing involves the use of special cabinets whose drawers are fitted with rectangular metal frames to support the suspension folders. These folders are fitted with metal bars to enable them to remain in suspended position. The top metal bar of each folder carries a movable index-title tab. Thus, the system serves the purpose of visible indexing also. The main advantage of this system is that sagging of files in the drawers is avoided. The folders can be moved freely backward and forward since they do not lie on the bottom. Though the equipment is quite costly, it is very useful in locating the records easily. The records are not spoiled as mishandling is avoided.

Flat-topped Suspension Filing.

Lateral Filing System

Lateral filing is also a kind of vertical filing as files are placed vertically across the width of the cupboard with four or five shelves. Papers are put in folders which have hooks. The folders are hung on the railings of the shelves in the same manner as clothes hangers are hung in wardrobes. The lateral filing equipment facilitates the placing of files side by side. The tops of the folder are fitted with title indicators which can be adjusted for the required angle of vision. Ordinary almirahs can be used for lateral filing. Lateral filing equipment has been developed to save floor space, to give greater visibility and to facilitate easy reference. All the files housed in the cupboard are simultaneously exposed to view. Lateral filing is more suitable where space for filing is limited because no space is needed for opening the drawers and leaning over them.

Open Shelf Filing

Open shelf filing is not a new method, but has been in use in India for a long time. It is a method of filing in which open shelves are used in the library for storing folders. Under this method open shelves or wooden or steel racks are utilised for keeping files and papers. In open shelves, filing may be done horizontally or vertically, and any method of classification may be adopted. This method of filing is especially used where papers are kept in enveloped of packets or some other covered jackets.

Open shelf filing offers mostly the same advantages which are offered by lateral filing. This method of filing is more economical because shelves are cheaper and they accommodate more files. Open shelves may be made upto the height of ceiling. Open

Open Shelf Filing

shelf filing is commonly used in libraries for placing books in open shelves. This method of filing is used in banks, insurance etc. It requires more space and a dust-free area for the protection of documents.

Visible Card Filing

Visible card filing is gaining popularity with the big industrial enterprises. This equipment can be used for retaining records such as accounts receivable and personal data in a fairly permanent position for frequent reference. But this equipment is costlier as compared to the other filing equipment discussed above. However, the speed in which the cards can be located and necessary entries made justifies the use and cost of visible card filing equipment. This equipment has been developed on the principle "Look at the record, not for it". The main characteristic of visible filing is that the main reference on each card is visible at all times. Generally, the cards are laid in a flat shallow tray or in a metal hinge. The cards are put in transparent covers before arranging them in trays. Each card is so arranged into a metal hinge that it overlaps the one before it is such a way that a narrow strip at the bottom containing the name, telephone number of the subject remain visible. This facilitates reference at a great speed. Visible filing also allows to insert new information in the file cards without wasting much time.

CLASSIFICATION OF FILES

The problem is not in filing records, but in finding them. The object of classification is to enable the managers to select any one paper from among all the papers stored in the office, without loss of time and at the least cost. In order to make files promptly available, it is necessary that they should be given proper titles and classified or grouped according to some fixed basis. Classification is the process of selecting headings under which documents are grouped or classified on the basis of common characteristics before filing takes place. The following are the chief methods of classification of files.

1. Alphabetical Classification

Under this system letters are filed in the alphabetical order of the names of parties. This classification is the most commonly followed of all. The telephone directory is an example, which requires no explanation. This is good when the headings of files can be expressed in one word, name of people or products, etc. Files containing letters are arranged according to the alphabetical order. The first set of files may contain the papers of customers whose names begin with A; those having their names beginning with B, in another file and so on.

If there are more names under A, dictionary method will be followed :

e.g., Mahesh, Mohan, etc.

Advantages of Alphabetical Classification

(1) Training is not needed for the clerks to perform the filing.
(2) It is easy and convenient to group papers by names of persons, firm, products, etc.
(3) Direct filing is possible without the help of an index. It is self-index.
(4) Files can be located immediately.
(5) Number of files can be reduced or introduced without disturbing the classification.

Disadvantages of Alphabetical Classification

(1) Mistakes creep in under common names, *i.e.*, when there are several persons having the same name.

(2) There is also difficulty if the names are mis-spelt.

2. Numerical Classification

In this system a number is allotted to each customer and the same number is put on all papers or documents relating to transactions with him. The file is also numbered and the papers are filed on the basis of numbers. Thus, the number allocated to each correspondent becomes his file number. If one file contains records of more persons, decimal system may be used *e.g.*, 21.1 denotes one person; 21.2 denotes another and so on. And these are file No. 21. To locate a particular file, it is necessary to refer to an index. Therefore index cards are prepared and the file numbers are written on them and arranged in alphabetical order in a safe place or drawer. Whenever a file is needed, one will consult the index card, obtain the number of the files and then take out the file required.

Merits of Numerical Classification

(1) Accuracy in filing system is greater.

(2) Reference is made by numbers.

(3) Expansion facilities are there.

(4) It is simple to understand.

(5) If files are misplaced, it can be noticed promptly.

(6) It is easy to operate; numbered files can easily be located and arranged serially in comparison to alphabetical index.

Demerits of Numerical Classification

(1) A separate index is a must.

(2) More time is required to locate a file. One has to refer to index and then search for the files.

(3) Transposition of figures causes mis-filing.

The system of classification is useful for mail order houses, banks, advertising agencies, departmental stores etc.

Out of many variants of the numerical classification, three systems are worthy-noting. (A) Consecutive Classification, (B) The Dowey Classification System and (C) Terminal Digit System.

3. The Alphabetical–Numerical or Alpha–Numerical Classification

Now a days this system is very popular. It has the advantages of both the above said systems. It is a combination of the alphabetical system and the numerical system. In this system each letter or sub-letter is given its own number and an index card is placed behind the guide card for each alphabetical section. The names and numbers of all the folders are mentioned in numerical order behind each card. The coloured guide cards are used to sub-divide for folders into groups to facilitate their speedy location.

For instance, all files are arranged alphabetically and the first group is Aa-Ag. The folders of ABC firm, Agra book stores are first and second in order within this group; the first folder will bear the number A/1 and the second folder will bear the number A/2 and so on.

Merits of above Classification

1.   It has all the advantages of the alphabetical and numerical classification.
2.   It is an elastic classification.
3.   It facilitates quick reference.

4. Geographical Classification

Geographical filing is an arrangement of countries, towns, other areas in an alphabetical order. It is convenient to use the geographical system for major groupings and then introduction of alphabetical order. This is a good system and is being adopted by the concerns. The area over which the activities of a firm are spread may be divided into a number of regions and the papers are filed on the basis of locality. This is a good system, when a firm has many branches or business throughout a country. The files which contain the correspondence of one locality are arranged statewise, citywise, etc. This system is generally profitably used by banks, insurance, departmental stores, etc.

Merits of Geographical Classification

(1)   Statistical data can be collected easily.
(2)   It is simple to operate.

Demerits of Geographical Classification

(1)   Geographical location must be known.
(2)   Addresses of the persons must be known.
(3)   Clerks must be trained.
(4)   Index is required.

5. Subjectwise Classification

In this, records are filed according to the nature of their subjects or contents. This system can be profitably adopted by a concern which may classify correspondence into well-defined groups. Papers are first arranged subjectwise and then in alphabetical order. There may be order file, invoice file, complaint file, etc. Papers on a particular subject are arranged and put together, rearranged alphabetically or numerically and filed accordingly. This system is more important where subject-matter will be given more weight than the name of the correspondence.

For examples:

Main subjects classified:

Purchase

Sales

Promotion

Sub-division of classified subjects:

Sales   —   Cycle Parts

Sales   —   Scooter Parts

Sales   —   Motor Parts

6. Chronological Classification

Various records are identified and arranged in strict date order and sometimes even according to the time of the day. For examples, newspapers, current prices, market reports etc. It is a useful system if dates are known.

INDEXING

Index means to guide something. Some further information can be had through index. An index is an indicator, indicating any subject-matter. In filing, index helps the location of any letter, record, files, etc. Thus it provides quick reference, which is essential of a good filing system. An index can be seen in almost all books, in last pages. There, the index will indicate the page number, where the particular subject is dealt with. In the same way, in filing system the index is much helpful to locate the files needed. In a concern, various files are maintained for different departments and different topics. Therefore, to locate the files, the index as an indicator is inevitable.

Classification and indexing are not the same. Classification is a method of filing and the manner in which the files of different subjects are arranged. Indexing is a method of making reference to the files. "An index is a finding tool. It furnishes the key as to how the materials are arranged.

Importance of Indexing

(1) Indexing is an essential part of a good filing system as it is a guide.

(2) It provides a ready reference.

(3) It facilitates easy location of files.

(4) Even if the files are arranged in self-indexing method, index will further speed the work.

(5) It possesses minimum information.

Essentials of a Good System of Indexing

A good system of indexing should possess the following essentials :

1. It must be simple to operate and use.
2. It must be economical in terms of money, space and effort.
3. It should be flexible to allow for expansion.
4. It should allow for speed.
5. It should be suitable for the particular business.
6. It should have locking arrangement.

Methods of Indexing

The following are the important type of indexing:

1. Bound Book Index

This system normally consists of a bound book, each page of which is allotted to one letter or more letters of the alphabet. Each page of this book has a tab which indicates the letter or letters of alphabet allotted to it, for example, if it is desired to see the number of the page in which the account of Mr. Anil is kept, the page marked 'A' will be seen or against the name of Anil will appear page number, that is, page number on which Anil's account appears.

Such an index may take the form of a separate book or an index in the front or at the back of a book. A bound

Bound Book Index.

book index is a very simple method of indexing. No special training is required for office clerks to operate it. The pages cannot be lost as they are bound.

2. Vowel Index

When the number of correspondence is very large, the alphabetical indexing described above is further classified according to vowels. Here each letter of the alphabet is sub-divided into six divisions according to five vowels, that is A, E, I, O, U and Y.

If there are many names begining with the same alphabet, they can be again sub-divided on the basis of vowels. For example, Ram's name will be written on the page of the register marked "Ra". The Rekha will be written on the page of the register "Re" and so on. If this system is adopted, it will be easy to locate the page number of respective persons. This is an improved system of book index, and can therefore be called vowel index. This type of index can be used for small and medium size concerns.

Merits of Vowel Index

(1) It is a permanent record.

(2) It is safe, because it will not be lost.

(3) It is always in the Register itself and no time is spent in searching the index.

Demerits of Vowel Index

(1) In the book index, the names of persons are written, as and when occurred. So it takes much time to search a name. There are many pages allotted to the same letter. But vowel index is an advantage.

(2) The system is inelastic.

(3) The names of the persons, who are not dealing with the firm have to be struck off.

3. Loose Leaf Index

This is another form of book index. Loose leaf is a sheet ruled like the pages of ordinary index.

The sheets are inserted in or taken out from metal hinges or screws, as and when required. It is arranged as the library card index system. Each person (correspondent) is allotted a card on which the name of the person, the address, the file number, etc., are entered. The loose indices are kept in a drawer.

Merits of Loose Leaf Index

(1) Index of dead files can easily be removed.

(2) The system is elastic.

(3) Complete information can be had.

(4) Additional information can be written or typed easily.

(5) It saves time and material.

(6) It is very economical.

(7) The despatch of monthly statements and trade circulars is easy.

Demerits of Loose Leaf Index

(1) It is possible that cards are torn quickly by constant use.

(2) Equipments are needed to keep the cards ; therefore this system is expensive.

(3) There is the possibility of the cards being misplaced, when they are inserted or taken out.

(4) For small firms it is a mere waste.

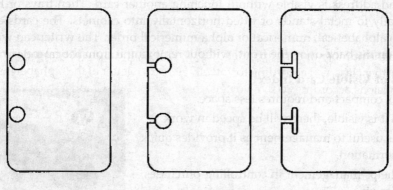

Loose Leaf Index

4. Card Index

Card index is another method of preparing index. The index is prepared in cards, each card is allotted for one information : *e.g.* customers, firms, etc. The details of the reference are shown on cards. Cards of equal and uniform size are used. The cards may be of different colours for getting a good appearance or for distinguishing one group of cards from another. The card may be generally smaller than a postcard 5" x 3". The card bears the number of file and the names of references along with particulars. These cards are placed in drawers, which are specially made for them. The cards are arranged in the dictionary order. For example, if the file of Rama Medical is to be taken out, first we have to look for the card, in the index drawer under Ra section indicated by the guide card, Ra. After a look at the index, the file number of Rama Medicals can be known. Then find out the file from the filing cabinet.

The cards are kept in drawers. A rod is put through them to hold the cards. So the chance of misplacement is reduced. The cards may be placed vertically or horizontally.

Merits of Card Index

(1) Any type of ruling can be adopted for the cards.

(2) Insertion or removal of cards is easy.

(3) It is capable of being expanded.

(4) Location of cards is easy.

(5) Rearrangement of cards is possible.

(6) The system ensures quick and accurate references.

(7) It is simple in operation.

(8) Foldable card can also be used.

Demerits of Card Index

(1) It is complex and elaborate.

(2) There is the danger of the cards being lost or misplaced.

(3) It is not suitable for small firms.

(4) It requires special equipment and specialised clerks.

5. Visible Card Index

The defects of the card system are removed by this system. A large number of cards cannot be seen at one sight. But in visible card index method the cards are placed flat in transparent covers in a shallow tray or metal frame. It is so placed into a metal hinge that the name and address is visible without touching another card. Then trays or frames are fitted vertically to metal stands or fitted horizontally into cabinets. The cards are placed according to alphabetical, numerical or alpha numerical order. The writer can write on the card (either on the back or on the front) without removing it from the frame.

Advantages of Visible Card Index

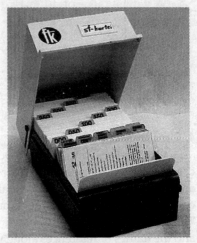

(1) It is compact and requires less space.

(2) As it is visible, there will be speed in work.

(3) It is useful to management as it provides quick information.

(4) It helps management in controlling purchases, sales etc.

(5) It gives a list of customers easily visible to the eyes on the frame and requires less expense and minimum effort.

6. Wheel Index

To increase the speed of reference further, the latest development of indexing is used—wheel index. It is a system according to which cards are mounted round the hub of a wheel. The wheel moves or rotates on ball

Visible Card Index

bearings. When a particular file is needed, the wheel is rotated and the required card is referred to. This system is economical as well as flexible.

Wheel Index

7. Strip Index

This system consists of strips of cards or thick paper fitted in a frame in such a way that the strips can be taken out or inserted. The frames are fixed in a shelf or in a book form. Dead strips can be removed and new strips can be inserted.

Selection of a suitable Indexing System

Every system of indexing has its own merits and demerits. Some methods are rigid while others are flexible though expensive. The installation of a suitable indexing system depends mainly on the following :

1. The type and the extent of information needed.

2. Cost of equipment in each system.

3. Cost of labour in each system.

4.   The requirement of space required for each system.

5.   The frequency of adding or deleting.

6.   The purpose of keeping an index.

FILING ROUTINE

Establishment of a filing routine is essential to avoid misfiling and misplacement of files. It is also essential for any organisation because a large number of papers bearing the record cannot be handled and preserved without any proper arrangement. Filing routine refer to receiving papers and documents and placing them in files. It also refers to issuing files for reference and use.

Following are the steps in filing routine :

(1) **Instruction for Filing :** Some responsible officer should issue an instruction for filing the papers. The authorised officer should write 'file' on the paper along with his signature and date. No document should be filed unless this procedure has been followed.

(2) **Classifying :** The responsibility for deciding the heading under which any document should be filed must be clearly defined. This task may be done by the senior filing clerk or by the executive himself.

(3) **Indexing :** The documents to be filed are then coded. The code is written on them and then they are indexed.

(4) **Cross Reference :** Sometimes certain documents relate to more than one file. They are to be filed under the most appropriate heading but a cross-reference card is inserted in every other relevant file for easy referencing.

(5) **Filing :** After the papers have been classified, indexed and codified, they may be filed in the appropriate files or folders in the chronological order.

(6) **Follow up :** Certain documents or papers require a follow-up action, like a letter. The concerned executive put on the follow-up instructions and filing clerk prepares a follow-up slip to act as a reminder. The follow-up document slip is filed in a follow-up file along with the copy of the paper and the original document is filed. The filing clerk sends the needed document to the concerned officer on the specified date.

(7) **Issue of file for reference:** Whenever a paper or a file is needed by an executive, he should send a requisition slip, on the receipt of which the filing clerk will prepare a 'Charge Out' slip. He will also prepare an 'Out Slip' which indicates the whereabouts of the file and is kept in the place vacated by the file issued. The out slip should be taken out only when the file has been returned to its place.

(8) **Disposal of Dead Files :** In office the filing department should transfer the inactive files into the central store room. But when the paper has become dead, it should be destroyed according to the instructions of the officer responsible for retention of records.

QUESTIONS

1. Distinguish between horizontal and vertical methods of filing. What are the main advantages of the vertical method ?   (*B. Com., M.S*)
2. What characteristics would you look for a good filing system ?
                                                         (*B. Com., Punjab, Madurai*)
3. What are the main purposes of indexing ? State the merits and demerits of loose leaf index as compared with bound book and card index.   (*B. Com., M.S*)
4. What is card index ? What are its merits and what are the uses to which it can be put ?   (*B. Com., Punjab*)
5. Describe the most important methods of classification of files. State the advantages of each method.   (*B. Com., Delhi*)
6. What are the characteristics of an efficient filing system ?   (*B. Com., Delhi*)
7. State in general terms the fundamental requirements which should be fulfilled by a good filing system?   (*B. Com., Chennai*)
8. What are the main purposes of filing ?   (*B. Com., Delhi*)
9. State the respective merits of centralised and departmental filing system.
                                                                 (*B. Com., Jabalpur*)
10. Compare the advantages of central filing system with that of departmental filing system.   (*B. Com., Jabalpur*)
11. What is meant by centralised filing ? Discuss its merits and demerits.
                                                                  (*B. Com., Mumbai*)
12. What are the main uses of card index? How is it superior to loose leaf index?
                                                                 (*B. Com., Madurai*)
13. What do you understand by indexing? What are its objects?
                                                         (*B. Com., Punjab, Madurai*)
14. What is 'Record Management'? How far this may be taken as the key to efficient office administration?   (*B. Com., Punjab*)

CHAPTER 9

Office Stationery and Forms

STATIONERY

Every modern office whether big or small requires a large variety of stationery and other articles in connection with its day-to-day work. These are often known as 'Office Supplies'.

Office work cannot be performed without the use of stationery. Therefore, stationery is a must for office work. In olden days, the expenditure to meet the cost of stationery was a meagre figure. But in modern office age, the amount of stationery increases year after year. Office stationery includes paper, envelope, rubber, ribbon, stencil, correcting fluid, printed form, ink, pencil, stamp pad, paper weight, pin, tag, sealing wax, folders, file boxes, ball-pens, refills, cellotapes, dilutor, letter pad, writing pad etc. Each of the items is manufactured by different firms, in different qualities. According to *Terry*, "The lack of a typewriter ribbon, order pad, envelopes and letterheads might cause serious delays in getting out serious office work. The importance of stationery articles is recognised only when they are not available in time. Want of office supplies and stationery will reduce the efficiency of the clerical workers, waste their valuable time; even the submission of records and returns in time are not possible. Bad planning will seriously jeopardies the work of the office. In a small business, stationery does not create such a problem as it does in large concerns."

SIGNIFICANCE

There is hardly any office which is doing office works without stationery and supplies. Efficiency in office operations would not have been achieved, but for the use of supplies'. Office supplies have become an integral part of any office organisation. These are next to personnel in terms of cost of running the office. Accountant's Handbook (Wixon Edition) defined office supplies as those expandable items which are necessary for and consumed in the daily operations, but do not generally enter into the finished product. This is a broad definition in the term 'office supplies'. It includes all types of stationery forms and other items used in day-to-day operations of modern offices.

Stationery and supplies are in demand by both executive and clerks in daily transactions. In the words of *Robert H.A. Davis*," A ream of your letterhead stationery represents 500 contracts. Your stationery is you to your customers and business associates. Select it with as much consideration as you would use to decorate your reception office or select your business attire. As an office buyer, if you have the responsibility of selecting the stationery for your firm, remember that you have a great influence over the effect, the letters have on your company's clients, the labour cost of preparing office paper work, and the basic costs of paper consumption ."Like office machines and furniture, stationery and supplies are valuable, and enable the office staff to perform their work efficiently and effectively.

Selection and Quality of Items

The selection and qualities of stationery materials depend upon the financial position and status of the firm. The main points are as follows:

1. The stationery articles must be well-suited for the purpose for which they are purchased.
2. The letters must give a good impression to the recipient, by the very quality of the stationery used. They create a goodwill for the firm.
3. It is better to use stationery of good quality, because stationery of cheaper quality will have a shorter life, *e.g.,* carbon paper, typewriter-ribbon, etc. Cheaper quality can be used only for a few times. Therefore items of superior quality will be cheaper in the long run, because of their recurring use.
4. When letters are sent out to the customers, they are to be typed out in duplicate. The original goes to the addressee and the carbon copy is retained in the file. So, the paper of the original copy will be of the best quality so as to be attractive and the second copy of the letter must be more durable than attractive.
5. Cost of the articles may also be considered when selecting stationery.
6. Those, who go for more economy purpose, may sometimes waste money, because cheaper carbon, ribbon, etc., can be used for a short time. If superior quality is purchased, it may go for double the time; and when the expenditure is compared, the stationery of superior quality will be profitable.
7. When a particular brand gives satisfaction, the same brand is continued to be used. If the brand in use is defective, then only it has to be substituted by another brand.

Control of Office Stationery

The office workers should be provided with the best stationery items in order to produce the best work. As such, office supplies are important for efficient performance of office operations. Therefore, it is essential to control office stationery. The following points are to be borne in mind :

1. **Cost :** The cost of the stationery not only includes the price paid but also includes the interest on capital tied up, labour cost of keeping the items, depreciation of storage equipments, etc. Therefore, a proper control is essential to keep down the cost to the minimum.

2. **Avoidance of wastage :** Wastage in stationery may happen because of careless handling, deterioration of items, poor quality, over-stocking etc. All these are to be avoided. Proper control of office stationery must be followed by proper issue control.

3. **Standard :** Standard items alone should be purchased. Substandard items bought have less life and go waste soon. The envelope and letter, if of poor quality will repel the readers.

Management of Office Supplies

In order to achieve effectiveness and efficiency in office operations, proper management of supplies is a must. Over-stocking or under-stocking of supplies have their own demerits. If they are purchased in abundance (over-stocking), the demerits are :

(1) Bigger amount of capital is blocked, (2) extra storage space is needed and (3) risk of obsolescence etc. On the other hand, short supply of supplies will create numerous difficulties in performing the office work.

For smooth and efficient handling of office work it is essential that the selection, procurement, storage and use of stationery should be organised and regulated in a systematic manner. It is only thus that continuous supply of the right type and quality of supplies can be ensured and the cost of supplies minimised. In the words of *L.H. Brigham*, "The plan of purchase, stocking, distribution and control of use determines whether or not a company is exercising all reasonable economy concerning necessary stationery and office supplies."

J.C. Denyer lists the following essential requirements for a good system of dealing stationery :

1. Efficient buying in the right quantities.
2. The maintenance of as little stock as possible, but sufficient to ensure economical buying.
3. The storing of stationery should be in the best way possible so as to prevent deterioration, and to save space, lighting and heating charges.
4. The issuing system should be so planned that wasteful consumption is checked.
5. Office management should exercise a proper control and use of stationery.

The essential requirements of a good system of controlling office stationery and supplies are :

   I.   Selection of supplies,
   II. Purchase of stationery supplies.
   III. Storage of supplies.
   IV. Issue of supplies, and
   V.   Control over use of supplies.

I. Selection of Supplies

Selection is the process of choosing the right type of supplies which suit the purpose for which they are meant. What kind of stationery and supplies should be selected may depend upon the type of business concerned and its financial position. In the selection of office supplies due attention must be paid to its quality. Any item of stationery and supplies required should be determined keeping in view the purpose for which the item is to be used. The good qualities of various items available in market should be tested to select the sample which will best suit the purpose.

Supplies may be classified in two main categories: (1) Standard Branded Products and (2) Non-Standard Products. Standard products of reputed firms are generally 25-30% more costly than Non-Standard products. The difference is usually in quality. But, in practice, there is no economy in getting cheap supplies. For instance, cheaper quality of carbon papers can be used only a few times. But the superior quality of carbon papers can be used many more times. Similarly, inferior quality of duplicating paper may be good for cyclostyling only on one side of the sheet. When a standard duplicating paper which is about 25% more costly, may be used on both sides. Thus there is no economy in getting cheap and unbranded items. These may be made up of inferior materials and this prove to be more expensive in the long run.

(A) Paper : Generally more papers are used in an office work than any other single item of stationery. The following points should be considered when selecting paper for office stationery:

(a) How long can it be kept ?

(b) How often will it be referred to after filing ?

(c) How many copies are needed ?

(d) Are stocks of different colours necessary ?

(e) What kind of office machine operations are involved ?

(f) Which duplicating process is used in making copies ?
    Carbons, mimeograph, offset or any other copying method ?

(g) How will the paper be filed; in binders, filing cabinets, envelopes ?

(h) What is the annual consumption ?

(i) Which sizes can be cut without waste from the basic sizes produced by mills ?

(j) How and where will the paper be stored ?

(B) Carbon : A good quality of carbon paper would yield better quality copies, and in the long run, costs no more than a cheaper one.

(C) Typewriter Ribbon : One way to cut down on the cost of the purchase of carbon paper and ribbons is to buy from one reliable source and contract with this course for a quantity that will be used in a period of one year. This will result in the lowest possible price.

Standardisation implies fixing the requirements or specifications as to the quality of the items of the office supplies for various purposes. The standards have to be revised from time to time to cope up with the changing requirements of the office and the changes in the technology. Different grades of items of different brands should be tried to determine which brand is more suitable.

The use of many items– ink, glue, paste, rubber, pins, clips, tags, sealing wax, adhesive tape, etc. should be standardised. Items of very good quality should be purchased because they prove economical in use even though costly in price.

II. Purchase of Stationery Supplies

In small concerns, it is generally seen that the office manager purchases stationery. If there is a separate department for purchases, then all the stationery will be purchased by it.

The department head must have a good knowledge of making purchases of durable and standard stationery in an economical way. Stationery may be stored and reserved on the basis of consumption. Large firms usually adopt the following ways to purchase the items.

(a) By Tender

The office manager or the authorised person first decides the quantity of items to be purchased. After having decided the items, he must advertise in newspapers inviting tenders for certain quality and quantity. The last date for submitting tenders will also be published. By seeing the advertisements, suppliers will quote the prices, sometimes along with samples. After receiving the tenders, the concerned person opens them, compares the prices of different suppliers and usually accepts the lowest tender. Order will be placed with the firm, which has quoted the lowest rate. Orders may be placed for the whole quantity or in parts. This is being done on the basis of agreement.

Advantages of Tender System

1. Time is saved by ordering the required quantity in bulk otherwise, every time enquiry has to be made as to the price and quality. Thus, time is saved.
2. Generally, prices go up. Moreover, there is a tendency to accept the lowest tender. Hence suppliers quote their lowest price, and the supply of items may be lasting for a year or for a contracted period. Therefore the contract price is generally lower than the rate prevalent in the market. Moreover, money can be saved on such a purchase.
3. In tender system, even one can order for items in instalment supply, so as to get fresh items.
4. Supplier will generally stick to the customers by supplying standard items. Supply of bad quality will be an obstacle for long standing relationship.
5. Fraudulent practices are minimised, because no officer can show any undue favour to a particular supplier.

Disadvantages of Tender System

1. If the rates go down within the contracted period, the firm cannot place the order with outsiders. Thus even if the prices go down, the agreed prices will have to be paid.
2. The best quality of items may not always be available in the tender system, because the lowest price means the lowest standard.

(b) By Quotations

The system is similar to that of tender. In quotation system of purchase, the officer writes to different firms (suppliers) instead of advertising it in the newspapers. Suppliers will be informed of the quality and approximate quantity of items to be purchased. Sometimes, samples will also be sent for clear understanding. In this system also, orders may be placed with the firm that quotes the lowest rates. The merits and demerits of quotation system are similar to those of tender system.

(c) Through Salesmen or from Manufacturers

There are many occasions when sales representatives or salesmen approach customers to book orders. Such people will also carry samples to show and literature of full information. A particular manufacturing firm may produce a particular brand. It is very difficult to compare its cost with the cost of similar items produced by different firms as qualities may differ. It is likely that in many cases the supply of items will not be of the same standard as the samples shown at the time of placing the order. But purchase can be made through representatives or salesmen of standard supplier, otherwise it will be a waste.

(d) From Single Supplier

Certain firms do not purchase stationery items by calling quotations or tenders. They simply send orders to a particular supplier, who will supply the required items. Orders will be placed on the condition that the supplier will supply standard articles and will charge only reasonable prices. In the field of business, blind belief is always not safe, because, it is possible that supplier will charge higher rate than the rate prevalent in the market. Therefore periodical check up is essential to measure the honesty of the suppliers. But, if the firm is a standard one usually reasonable prices are charged, sometimes lower than the market rates, in order to attract the customers. This type of purchase is allowed only for urgent needs and for a small amount. If the amount is heavy, quotation system or tender system is to be followed.

Merits of Single Supplier

(1) An intimacy is created; thereby a goodwill is created.
(2) Customers will be given priority in time of scarcity.
(3) Generally, since all the purchase is made from one supplier, normal prices will be charged by supplying standard items; otherwise business may be affected.
(4) The supplier takes the responsibility of supplying stationery items of good quality at a cheaper rate.

Demerits of Single Supplier

(1) The position can be exploited if the purchasing officer is self-interested.
(2) If the single firm fails to supply the required items, it may be difficult to purchase them from outsiders.

Purchasing System in Firms

Different departments of the concern intimate their requisition to the purchasing officer. The purchasing officer goes through all the requirements and makes out a complete list of items to be purchased. He will also keep constant touch with the departmental heads to know the opinion about stationery items issued to them. If the report is favourable, he proceeds further. He makes out a list of all items required and invites tenders or quotations. Specifications of items will be given to the suppliers. A few days after the prices are known, the firm accepts the lowest quotation by taking into account the quality required. If the terms and conditions are agreed upon, order may be placed with the firm, stipulating the mode of delivery period, payment, etc. On receipt of all the articles, at the store, entries are made in the stock register.

CENTRALISED VERSUS DECENTRALISED PURCHASING

Centralised Purchasing

In big concerns, generally the purchasing of stationery and store keeping are centralised. The centralised purchase means collecting the requirements, deciding the quality, enquiring, ordering, maintenance of records and issuing them properly to the departments that need the stationery items. Purchase is the responsibility of the centralised department.

Decentralised Purchasing

Decentralised purchasing is an arrangement in which processes of purchasing are decentralised. Each department or section of the organisation has to make its own arrangement for the purchase of supplies. That is, the authority and responsibility for purchasing have been decentralised.

The decision to centralise or decentralise purchasing of stationery and supplies depend upon the benefits and drawback of centralised and decentralised purchasing.

Benefits of Centralised Purchasing

(1) Stores are in one department, and so better supervision and control can be excercised.
(2) Layout of stores can be arranged in a better way.
(3) Greater specialisation in purchase is possible.
(4) Discount, credit facility etc., can be had on huge purchase.
(5) Better utilisation of store equipment and store space, is possible.
(6) Standardisation of stationery in all departments can be drawn up.

Drawbacks of Centralised Purchasing

1. Separate staff have to be appointed to look after the work which involves cost of maintenance of the records and issue of stationery. This is added to the overhead cost.
2. It is experienced that delay is likely to happen in the supply from the centralised store, because of procedures to be followed before getting the stationery.

Benefits of Decentralised Purchasing

1. The purchasing procedure can be shortened.
2. It has flexibility and cuts delay.
3. Purchasing can be made according to exact specifications.
4. Overhead cost of centralised system is eliminated.

Drawbacks of Decentralised Purchasing

1. Standardisation cannot be practised.
2. The benefits of buying in bulk cannot be enjoyed.
3. Specialisation in purchase is not possible.

Purchase Procedure of Stationery
1. Purchase requisition
2. Calling quotations
3. Selecting suppliers
4. Placing orders
5. Receipt of items
6. Maintenance of accounts
7. Storage
8. Safeguarding

PURCHASE PROCEDURE

Whether the purchasing is centralised or decentralised, it is essential to have a scientific procedure for the purchase of stationery and supplies in the office. The following procedure may be followed:

(*a*) **Purchase Requisition :** Purchase requisition is a printed form which is generally used as a formal request to the purchasing department. The purchase department receives purchase requisitions from various departments of the organisation. Purchasing requisition may be written in duplicate, the original being sent to the purchasing person and other being retained by the person initiating the request.

(*b*) **How much to Order :** The purchase in-charge should decide the quantity of order very carefully. No doubt, large orders bring trade discount and cash discount. But sometimes, they result in heavy waste because of over buying as there are certain articles which deteriorate when they are held in stock for too long a period. For example stamp pads, carbon papers, typing, ribbons etc. dry out. The purchasing authority should determine the quantity to be ordered at one time after taking in view the following factors :

(*i*) Usual consumption during a period.

(*ii*) Storage space available.

(*iii*) Finance available.

(*iv*) Cost of storage and capital investment.

(*v*) Quantity of safety stock.

(*vi*) Risk of obsolescence.

(*vii*) Minimum and maximum quantities to be held in stock.

(*viii*) Savings to be effected on bulk purchase.

(*ix*) Time needed to get supplies.

(*c*) **Obtaining Quotations :** After the receipt of purchase requisition, the source of stationery and supplies is to be selected. Generally, the purchasing department keeps a list of suppliers for all needed items. The quotation will be called for by keeping in view the benefits to the concern—lowest price, better quality, quick delivery, reliable supplies according to specifications etc. After receiving the quotations, they are opened at the time prescribed and a comparative statement is prepared.

Terms and conditions of supply are negotiate with one or more suppliers on a scrutiny of the price lists and examination of samples.

(*d*) **Placing the Order :** After comparing quotations and terms of delivery the actual order is placed with the selected firm in a prescribed form. The order indicates all particulars of the various items, quantity required, the price agreed upon, terms of payment, mode of delivery and delivery date. The order should be signed by the officer of the purchasing section or office manager.

(*e*) **Follow up :** Once an order has been placed, it would be proper to follow it up so that supplies are received in time. If there is any irregularity or delay in delivery, reminders must be issued to the supplier. The name of defaulting suppliers should be struck off from the list of suppliers.

(*f*) **Receipt of Stationery :** In large concerns, items are supplied along with the delivery note in duplicate to the customers. As soon as the items are received, the clerk concerned verifies the items with the delivery note. After that one copy of the delivery note is returned to the supplier. Credit bill will also be received either along with the delivery of items or after a day or two. When the bill is received, it will be tallied with the items. If the entries relating to the items are correct, then entries are made out in the records in respective pages. If all the items are satisfactory, the bill duly signed by the purchasing officer is sent to the accounts department for further action. Sometimes, goods received notes are prepared by the store-keeper instead of passing the bills.

STANDARDISATION OF OFFICE SUPPLIES

Standardisation of office stationery and supplies means securing uniformity in the specification of articles. The process of standardisation involves laying down the exact size, dimensions, quality and other specifications relating to each item of supply to be required. Procurement of various items of office supplies involves a consideration of the purpose for which they are to be used.

Benefits : Standardisation has the following advantages:
1. It helps the purchase officer to know the exact requirements of various departments of the firm.
2. It ensures efficiency in office operations by increasing the speed of work.
3. It brings economy in purchasing by buying in bulk and reducing the number of purchase orders.
4. It avoids lose which may be caused by the purchase of sub-standard supplies.
5. It ensures uniformity in the specification of various items.

III. Storage of Supplies

Stationery and supplies are an important item of cost of office work. Therefore, proper attention should be paid to their storage.

Proper Store Keeping:
1. All stationery items will be handled carefully and kept in dry places.
2. All stores will be arranged in an orderly and systematical way to avoid piling up.
3. Location of store house should be as far as possible within the easy reach of the various departments, so that no time is lost in getting the items.
4. Proper storing will facilitate easy stock taking, prompt supply, prompt purchases etc.
5. Each and every item should be carefully classified, and kept in separate places of the shelves. The often needed articles should be kept at the front of the shelves.
6. All packages of items should be marked with identification marks or sample should be fixed in the front.
7. Similar materials should be placed together or in near-by places.
8. Articles carelessly stored, will cause many inconveniences and much loss.

Bin Card

Overstocking or understocking of stationery must be avoided. Therefore, proper records have to be maintained, mainly bin cards. A bin card is maintained for each item of stores. The bin card is debited with the quantity of stores received and credited with the quantity of stores issued to different departments. A balance is also drawn up at every receipt or issue of store, so that the balance at any time can readily be seen. This card is entered and kept by the store-keeper, who is responsible for any difference between the balance of the bin card and the physical stock. This means, the balance on the basis of bin cards and the physical stock must be equal. The bin card contains proper columns apart from the maximum and minimum quantity level. The specimen of the bin card is given next :

BIN CARD

Bin No.
Name of Material :   Maximum Limit...............
Material Code :   Minimum Limit...............
Store Ledger Folio No.   Ordering Level...............
                                                    Ordering Quantity...............
                                                    Unit...............

Date	Receipt		Issues		Balance	Checked	
	GRN No.	Quantity	RNNo.	Quantity	Quantity	Date	Initial

GRN No. : Good Received Note No.
RN No. : Requisition Note No.

However, there is a difference between the bin card and the ledger. They are :

Bin card	Stores ledger
(1) Only the quantity of the stationery is entered.	In ledger, both quantity and value are entered.
(2) Each transaction is individually posted.	Summarised or periodical postings may be done.
(3) Bin card is kept within the store.	Stores ledger may be kept outside the store.

Stock Verification

Stationery stock in the store must be verified, by comparing the bin cards from time to time, say, monthly, fortnightly, quarterly, etc. Stock in hand (balance) must be equal to the bin card balance. If the shortage is high, enquiry may be made to find out the actual cause. Damaged or old items, which are not usable, must be written off by the officer-in-charge.

IV. Issue of Supplies

Any department that needs stationery must fill in the requisition form. After filling the requisition form (slip), it will be signed by the user-departmental head. This requisition form is given to the store. The store-keeper, after making entries in the bin cards issues the items mentioned in the requisition form. It is an internal arrangement for the firm to fix the day for issue of stationery to different departments. The issue must be made in specified units, e.g., pencils in dozen, papers in reams, carbon in packets, etc. Such small items may be kept in convenient unit packets, so as to be issued immediately and counted without difficulty. As soon as the minimum stock level is reached, the store-keeper prepares purchase requisitions to make purchases of the item.

A good system of issuing stationery should be based on the following principles :
1. Issue of stationery should be made in specified quantities or units.

2. The issue of stationery should be made on specified days preferably once or twice each week.

3. Each issue should be recorded in issue register.

V. Control of Consumption

There are many items of stationery which can be put into personal use. It is also found that clerks have a tendency to overstock items. Under these circumstances the following measures may be noted:

1. The responsibility of proper use must be with the person, who signs the requisition.

2. Department wise cost of the stationery consumed be maintained and comparison may be made with other departments.

3. Small items of stationery may be kept packed in small quantities, e.g., clips, pins, rubber bands, tags, etc.

4. Requisition slip will be accepted for issue on confirmation that the issued stationery has been exhausted.

It is also seen that in some cases the store-keeper is empowered to cut down the quantities mentioned in requisition slip if he feels so. In every case it may not be possible, because sometimes the requisition slip may be signed by high officials and the store-keeper may be below their rank. Therefore, there will be a separate official to see to such work, and he will control the issue of stationery and watch over the consumption. Store-keeper or purchasing officer must take proper care in purchasing standard stationery. Overstocking will reduce the value-by drying out, by changing colour, by shrinkage, by change of fashion, etc.

5. Two-colour typewriter, ribbons, (half black and half red) may be issued to every third or fourth machine. When the typewriter fitted with the two-colour ribbon is needed, it can be put into use because the black of the ribbon will wear out earlier than the red half.

6. Before issuing the items, the store-keeper makes sure of the purpose for which they are needed, so that he can issue proper article, which can be put to right use.

FORMS

When a student seeks admission to a college, or a university or borrows a book from a library or applies for a bus concession ticket, a form has to be filled in. What are office forms ? According to Leffingwell, "Forms are printed sheets of paper or card-board used to collect and transmit information". In the words of *Denyer*, "A form is a printed piece of paper or card on which entries are usually made against marked headings." In other words, a form is a standardised record used to accumulate and transmit information for reference purposes. They are the basic tools of all office work. Examples of forms are the factory orders, requisition, bills, quotations, orders, etc. An office form bears the fixed or constant data and provides spaces for variable data or information. That is, the information which is already in the form is known as fixed or static data and the information which will be filled in the form is known as variable data. The fixed information is printed on the form. The person using the form need not write the fixed data again and again, but he has to fill the variable data in the form. Since office work constitutes various routine operations, the use of forms reduces the monotony of repeatdly writing various items already printed on the forms. Thus clerical staff find it easy in filling the required information in appropriate columns, instead of writing down the whole matter. Therefore, a form can be defined as a printed piece of paper, where entries (filling) are made for a predetermined purpose. Generally, the form is printed or cyclostyled for future use. It may be filled in ink or with a typewriter.

Importance

Forms are the raw materials of office. Forms are tools for all types of office work. An office can work more efficiently and easily by getting the information, recording it and transmitting it in a well and systematic manner through forms. By using the forms in the office work, much time can be saved. Had it not been for the forms the whole matter would have been written by the clerks. As such time and energy can be saved. Therefore, the printed forms have become an essential part of the official procedure, without which no office work can be done efficiently. According to *Wylie and Brech*, "Office forms are the vehicles by which various statistics are brought together either by accumulation from many points or by individual recording at a single point for the purpose of analysis, establishment of records, or uniformity of procedure."

Forms serve as the vehicles by which various data are collected and brought together for use by the management. That is why, they are also described as the basic tools of the office. *Frank Knox* said, "Nothing happens in an office except to, or by means of pieces of paper." Forms are the medium to bear the record of the enterprise and serve as the basis of records management. Information can be collected, processed and supplied in a systematic way with the help of office forms. Forms increase the efficiency of office work and help in achieving economy in office operations.

Significance of Office forms

1. Clerical work becomes easy.
2. Output can be increased.
3. Unnecessary information means waste of time. This can be avoided by adopting printed form, with necessary queries.
4. Collection and compilation of statistical data become easier to study from the information form than from a letter.
5. In a printed form, the writer has to fill in all the columns, so as to furnish information without suppression.
6. The writer or the typist can be at ease in filling the forms in the appropriate place, by writing a few words.
7. Understanding and transmission of information from the forms are quick and clear.
8. They help to identify records and facilitate easy filing for future reference.
9. Data entry, processing and reference becomes easy.
10. They facilitate rapid processing of data since information appears in a standard form and at fixed places.

Advantages of Forms

1. Only the necessary information can be had through the forms. If the form had not been introduced, the information may be in a letter form, without all the requisite information. So, through forms, necessary information can be had and irrelevant information can be avoided.
2. The work of the writer or the typist who is to write or type the information in few

words is made easy. It is easy for him to fill in the required information correctly.

3. There will be no difficulty in analysing the data collected through the forms. If it is in a letter form, there will be much difficulty in analysing and understanding the data collected.

4. The presentation of the information will be uniform which accelerates the clerical job.

5. Forms reduce the cost of the operation work in the office.

6. Forms are helpful to fix the responsibility of the work done. (Forms are duly signed by the writer).

7. Transmission of information, which is based on the forms will also be correct.

8. Forms make for uniformity in appearance and format. They facilitate identification of records and simplify filing and sorting operations.

9. Forms make clear what information should be gathered. Thus, office forms simplify office systems and routine.

10. Since forms preserve records, they aid the organisation in better planning.

To make the forms more effective:

1. Forms should be properly designed and drawn up, to avoid confusion in the mind of the writer.

2. Forms should be predetermined with all necessary columns, to avoid waste of energy and time.

3. Forms must be simple and easy to understand; otherwise it will be tedious to fill in.

Types of Forms

Forms may be classified as follows:

1. **On the basis of operation** or function performed by the form, as for instance, purchase form, material requisition form, application form etc.

2. On the basis of use of form :
    (a) **Internal office forms,** which are received or used by the employee of the business, for examples, accounting form, application form, memorandum form, requisition form etc.
    (b) **External contract forms,** which are sent to customers, creditors, etc. for examples, order form, purchase order etc.

3. On the basis of copy :
    (a) **Single copy forms,** which are complete in themselves and often become the source documents.
    (b) **Multiple copies forms,** which are made in duplicate or more copies and which may be used to transmit information or serve the function of providing additional records.

Forms Designing

The designing of forms is an important function of office management. Since forms are the basic tools of office systems and routine, it is necessary that they should be well designed and complete in all respects. *J.C. Denyer* lists the following disadvantages of a badly designed form over a well designed form:

1. Forms are basic tools of office work, *i.e.,* for recording and communicating information. A badly designed form impeeds this function most seriously and jeopardise the working of the entire organisation.

2. Badly designed forms inherits mistakes in clerical work. Sometimes a single error may cost the company many times more than the cost of printing and forms put together.

3. A badly designed form is bound to increase the manual labour required to process it and impair efficiency.

4. A badly designed form may also have an adverse impact on the goodwill and reputation which the organisation enjoys.

5. A badly designed form may have a psychological effect on people using it. It may lead to frustration among people using it.

6. Office forms are related to systems of the organisation. A well designed system may be ruined by badly designed forms.

Principles of Form Designing

Forms must be properly designed to serve the purpose already stated. In designing the forms it is necessary to observe certain principles. They are summarised as follows :

(1) Principles of purpose

A form should be brought into existence only if there is a purposeful need for the use of that form. The basic purpose of a form is to make clerical work easier, speedy and accurate. Where a plain sheet of paper can serve the purpose, there is no need to introduce a form. The form designer should consider the answers to the following questions, before introducing a new form :

(a) What is the purpose of the form ?

(b) If the form has more than one purpose, which is the most important ?

(c) Is the purpose justifiable ?

(d) Will the purpose of the form be fully accomplished by its use ?

(e) Is there any another form, for the same, or a similar purpose, now in use elsewhere in the office?

A form should be used :

(a) If something is to be recorded as a matter of necessity.

(b) When certain data are to be recorded repeatedly. These data can be pre-printed on every copy of the form in order to save time in forms preparation.

(c) If it is necessary to have all information recorded in the same place on each copy of the form. This arrangement helps to serve as a check on the completeness of the record,

(d) Where it is desirable to fix responsibility for the work done by providing spaces for signatures of persons who did the work.

(2) Principles of Standardisation

In order to reduce costs and avoid confusion it is necessary that all forms should be standardised. Standardisation affects mainly their physical arrangement like size, colour, quality of paper used and printing style. No form should be larger in size than is necessary. While determining the size, it should be ensured that the form is capable of being properly handled. Different colours may be used for different forms to make identification of forms easier. The title of the form should be brief but clearly descriptive.

(3) Principles of Centralised Control

The process of designing, use, replacement, elimination etc. of the forms should be centrally controlled. This will help to achieve proper co-ordination and efficiency in forms management. In some organisations new forms get added while old outdated forms may remain in existence. This problem may be solved by having centralised control of the forms under one office manager, who is responsible for designing.

(4) Principle of Economy

The size of the form, the quantity of paper used, the number of copies printed and the method of producing forms should be so chosen that there is economy in procurement of forms. Forms should be so designed that their handling costs are also minimum.

Guidelines in Form Design

Forms are Printed or Cyclostyled on ordinary sheets or thick sheets or paper to collect information. In office, collection of information is being done through the forms. Forms are sent to those who have to put the information on the forms. Then, the filled in forms are gone through in order to understand and collect the information. After that they may be filled or destroyed on the basis of office procedure. In view of these facts, it is essential that careful attention be given to the correct design of the form, so as to put it into proper use and speedy action. In order to attain the merits and objective of the forms, proper design is needed according to the office system. Bad design of the forms will be a waste as it will not attain the desired object. Therefore, before designing and printing the forms the following points may be noted.

(*a*) **Purpose :** The foremost point in designing the form is to study the purpose and aim of the form. One of the aims may be to reduce the labour of the clerks and the other may be to get a clear and full idea of the information needed. If there are no advantages in getting a special form, the idea of having form can well be given up. The designer of the form must draw a complete picture of the form in his mind with the aim for which he designs the form. The manner of the information may be studied in relation to the sources to be followed.

(*b*) **Size :** The form is to be according to the size of the file, or cabinet. It must be of convenient size to be inserted in the typewriter, if the information is to be typed. Blank space should not be left out on the form, as it will be a waste. The form should neither be too small nor very big because sufficient space should be given in order to write the information legibly and neatly. The width of each column should be on the basis of information to be given neither more nor less. The forms may be filled in either by hand or with a typewriter. If it is to be filled in by hand, more space may be provided with lines and if it is to be typed out, less space is sufficient without lines. The size of the forms must be convenient to the staff. Apart from these, the size must be decided by considering the size of paper available, so that the waste will be minimised, while cutting the paper to the size needed.

(*c*) **Simplicity :** Simplicity makes the work of the user easy. It will be easy for the writer to fill in a simple form. The name and the number of the form should be placed at the top of the form so that they are easily visible. If any instructions are to be followed in filling the form, they must be given at the bottom of the form. Over-elaboration should be avoided.

(*d*) **Name and Number :** Every form must have a name and number. Name is easier to remember than the numbers. The name should be short. It must be self-explanatory. The number of the form is printed to simplify the work of record-keeping.

(*e*) **Appearance :** The appearance of the form is based upon the quality of the paper. It is usually seen that the form of invoices, debit note, credit note, etc. is of high quality and has attractive colours. Good quality paper brings goodwill and respect.

(*f*) **Proper Quality of Paper :** Ink should not spread while writing on the paper. Even when pencil is used the form should not be torn by the pressure of the pencil. If the forms have to be preserved for a long period, durable paper must be used. The paper should be of good quality and durability, if the form has to be handled often or if they are to be sent to high officers. If carbon copies have to be obtained, thin paper will be convenient. On the basis of purpose and period, the quality of the paper must be decided. In the end, the cost of the paper will also be considered for economy. Different coloured paper can be used for different forms, *e.g.*, credit notes and debit notes.

By keeping in mind the above considerations, a form can be designed in the following ways:

1. Name of the form (at the top of the form) will be self – explanatory.
2. Number is to be given to the form.
3. The matter is printed in the proper order.
4. Sufficient space is provided for the writer, who has to give the information.
5. Instructions or guidances to the writer may be in different colour print.
6. Wordings in the form must be clear, so as to raise no doubts in the mind of informant.
7. Ruled lines may be provided to fill in if written by hand.
8. The matter must be printed in good type of letters.
9. The sequence should be in such an order that the questions asked must have connection with each other.
10. Longer the preservation period and more frequent handling of forms, require better paper.

Form Control

In modern business, forms are the basic tools of all types of office work. The forms are linked with efficiency in office work because they save time by eliminating the need of writing and standard information every time. But very often too much stress is placed on the use of forms for every type of work and far too many kinds of forms are used than are necessary. In the words of *Littlefield*, "Forms control is a means of exercising management control over the costs of producing and processing forms." In the words of *J.C. Denyer*, "Forms are important in any organisation, therefore, there should be proper management control of them to ensure that they are efficient and economical in design as well as in use."

In a concern, there may be many forms in use. Therefore all specimens of the form must be held centrally at one place. Forms are the basic tools for an office work, office systems and procedures. If there are many forms, the importance and advantages are lost. Therefore, it has become essential to have control over the forms in order to have effectiveness in use. There may be a committee or a form supervisor, who has specialised knowledge in forms. He is vested with the authority of design, printing, issue, etc. He keeps a Form Book or Form Register. A copy of each form is pasted in the Form Book. Whenever any change or alteration, is suggested, it will be noted in the copy of the form in the Form Book. When a revised form arrives, it will be placed or tipped in over the old form.

Objects of Form Control

The following are the objects of form control, in brief:

1. To ensure regular supply of various forms;
2. To economical use of forms for the firm;

3. To reduce the clerical work;

4. To minimise the use of number of forms;

5. To make necessary changes in the existing forms if they are not satisfactory;

6. To make reviews, whenever needed;

7. To introduce new forms which are really necessary;

8. To retain and use only those forms that are necessary for office systems;

9. To study whether the introduction of new forms or revision of old forms, is essential;

10. To evaluate forms design on the basis of time required to use them;

11. To review periodically all forms in use to find out their current utility;

12. To eliminate obsolete and irrelevant forms, to consolidate different forms doing the same thing and to introduce only such forms that are really necessary.

The form no longer required, should be disposed of. After obtaining proper approval of the officer concerned, the approval will be pasted on the form, in the Form book, marked as "dead", if possible along with date.

Steps in Forms Control

Forms control implies a proper designing, printing, economical use and supply of forms so that office work may be efficiently and effectively performed. The following steps may be suggested a proper forms control :

1. Establishment of Centralised Authority

The first step in forms control is to set up a centralised authority for it. In big organisations, a forms Control Department may be set up and headed by a Forms Control Supervisor. Alternatively, a committee of individuals possessing adequate knowledge of forms may be constituted. The important functions of Forms Control Department or Committee are :

1. Introduction of new forms

2. Modification of existing forms

3. Elimination of unnecessary forms

4. Combination of two or more forms

5. Deciding and contents of forms

6. Designing and production of forms

7. Storing and issue of forms.

2. Preparation of Forms Register

The centralised forms control authority should collect at least two copies of each and every office form in use and paste them into a Forms Register or Forms Book. A separate list or index of all the forms in the Forms Book should also be made.

3. Listing of Office Routine

The designing and use of forms are closely linked with office procedure and routine. Therefore, it is necessary to prepare a list of all office procedures which may need the use of forms. The relevant forms may be then be classified, marked and numbered according to the procedure or department using them.

4. Analysis of Forms

All forms should be analysed periodically to determine whether any of them can be eliminated, combined with other forms or improved. At this stage, requisitions for new forms or redesigning of existing forms, along with suggestions, may also be obtained from departments. After this, the Form Control Supervisor determine the elimination of unnecessary forms or consolidation of forms or modification of forms or introduction of forms.

5. Design and Production

Since office forms are the basic tools of all office work, they should be so designed that they result in economy and efficiency of operations. After designing, the decision shall be taken regarding the number of copies of each form which can be produced economically. The Forms Control Supervisor will determine the method of reproduction of forms with the help of a duplicator or to get it printed from outside agency.

6. Disposal of Obsolete Forms

Before disposing of any form, the head of the department using such form should be asked to give in writing that the form is 'dead'. Then the form should be submitted to the office manager, who will also recommend and sign with date. Thus, the form no longer required, should be disposed of. After obtaining proper approval of the officer concerned, the approval will be pasted on the form, in the Form Book, marked as 'dead', if possible along with date.

Form Sets

It is convenient to use sets of form when more than one copy of any document is required. It is always convenient to use sets of form so that multiple copies can be made out by a single writing method. There are various methods. The use of form sets saves time and labour involved in writing the same information. Different type of form sets are discussed below :

(A) Sets of Loose Sheets

This is simplest and most commonly used method of making form sets. Loose sheets may be put together to form a set. It is very easy to assemble and jog the forms and carbon paper in between the forms before writing or typing. But this method is not economical because the clerk intending to use such sets has to make the set himself every time.

The system has the following drawbacks:

(i) Only a limited number of copies can be made.

(ii) It is time consuming as it requires the operator (typist) to do the preparatory work for making the form sets.

(iii) If carbon paper is not placed properly, the matter may not be recorded except in the first copy.

(iv) If carbon papers are over-used, the copies may be dim.

(B) Sets in Pads

Forms of the same kind or different forms collected into sets, can be padded in such a way that all copies are perfectly aligned together. Carbon paper for such pads is usually inserted at the time of use. The forms in pad are normally glued on the top or side edge and the sheets are removed as used. The forms should be in pad rather than bound in books as the record copies look untidy after removal of the original sheets. Besides the 'used' books take more space. If the forms are in pads, the record copies can be put in a lever file and got bound as and when necessary.

(C) Sets in Gangs

The term gang refers to group of two or more identical forms printed on a single sheet which are separated by perforation. Gang sets may be in a loose form, but they are often bound into pads or collated and glued into unit sets. All the sheets may be collated and perforated into gangs, or the record copies may not be perforated and used as a register.

(D) Unit sets

Under this method, variable lengths and widths of the respective sheets in the sets are used. Units sets may be constructed in two ways, (i) Unit blocked sets can be made of sheets of the same size or unequal size, (ii) The other alternative method is the snap sets method. Under this method sets are prepared by having a perforated stub portion holding the sheets together.

(E) Continuous Sets

This type of form set is also known as Continuous Stationery and is described below in detail.

CONTINUOUS STATIONERY

In business concerns, invoices, bills, price-lists, quotations, etc., are to be sent out and copies of such correspondence have to be kept or sent to different departments. In such cases, the typists have to take four or five printed forms from the pad, insert them in the typewriter, interleave them with carbon, thus making the document ready for signature. If these processes are continuous at every stage, much time is wasted, specially in inserting forms, setting carbons, etc. To avoid such waste of time, continuous stationery has come into use. Continuous stationery means the printed forms are automatically produced in a continuous strip and departed from one another by perforations. The preliminary operations which have to be undergone by the typist can be avoided by using continuous stationery. The forms either in rolls or flat packs attached to the machines, are fed in an automatically come into the typing position.

Denyer has defined continuous stationery as "A device whereby office forms are produced in a continuous strip and where the separate forms are usually divided from one another by perforations; and where several copies are usually detained by the use of various copying methods." Continuous stationery is labour saving device which comprises various forms such as invoices, accounting form etc. printed in continuous strips, made up of a series that comes in multiple copies set separated from one another by perforation. With continuous stationery, several copies are obtained by the use of copying methods without going through the process of tearing off forms and inserting carbon papers.

Advantages of Continuous Stationery

1. It is a laborious job for the typist to set the carbons between the forms, insert them in the machine, take out typed matter and separate the carbon. All these involve waste of time. In the continuous stationery system, the waste of time can be avoided.
2. By handling carbon, the fingers as well as the forms may get dirty. By using continuous stationery, neatness can be maintained.
3. It is also possible that the carbons may not be inserted or inserted carbon may be folded or inserted reversely. This waste can be avoided.

Disadvantages of Continuous Stationery

1. It is more expensive than ordinary forms.

2. Mistakes cannot easily be corrected. Therefore efficient typists have to be appointed, and this will increase the salary bill.

3. Bottom copies of the set may be faint and there may be confusion in respect of figures.

TYPES OF CONTINUOUS STATIONERY

(1) Roll Stationery

In roll stationery the forms in set are in continuous roll (just like stationery in teleprinters). There will be no perforations. The typed forms are separated or cut by metal blade, by pressing a lever attached. Continuous rolls are interleaved with carbon. Thus, the paper is set in the typewriter only once; and the typist need not waste his time in taking out printed forms, interleaving them with carbon, setting them in the machine, etc. The roll is adjusted at the back of the machine. As soon as the matter has been typed, it is separated by pressing a lever which cuts it. The next set automatically comes in.

(2) Inter Fold Stationery (Flat Packs)

It is further development made on the above. In this the forms are in folded flat type instead of rolls. The edges are perforated. It is also interleaved with carbon. After typing, the carbon sheets are thrown out. It is also known as concerting fashion.

In the above methods carbon can be used only once. After the use, it is thrown away, because very thin and cheap carbon is used to interleave. Thus more time of the typist can be saved. In another method, the back of the form which is chemically processed will give impression over the next form below. Therefore, no carbons are required to type out the sets. But, the typist has to take care while typing, because erasing is not possible. The first form gives an impression on the second form, the second form gives an impression on the third form and so on.

(2) Fan Fold

Where copies of the forms are joined together on all sides and folded fan wise, it is known as fan fold stationery.

Sometimes the forms interleaved with carbon may get misplaced in the typewriter or get misplaced at the friction of the machine at work. If the forms have not been set correctly, the impression may not fall in the appropriate columns of the successive copies. If so the typist has to type again. To remove this difficulty, the stationery possesses holes on both sides which are held up on the sprockets (wheels with protruding pins). The typewriter is fitted with sprockets and the sprockets hold up the stationery at the correct place, while the stationery moves, so that typing can be done in the proper places ; otherwise, in the subsequent copies, the impression may be in wrong columns.

QUESTIONS

1. Discuss the need for and importance of stationery and supplies in office work.
(B. Com., Madurai)
2. Explain the purchasing system of stationery.
3. What is a bin card and distinguish it from a ledger. (B. Com., Madurai)
4. How does one regulate the consumption of stationery in office?
5. Describe the complete plan of stationery control. (B. Com., Kerala)

6. Why is the study of printed forms important?
7. Describe the principles of form design. *(B. Com., M.S)*
8. "Forms are the basic tools of all office work." Discuss the statement.
(B. Com., Delhi)
9. "Forms are the foundations of clerical system." Explain.
10. What is the purpose of a printed form ? What are the points to be considered before designing a form ? *(B. Com, Kerala, Chennai)*
11. Why is control of forms desirable ? *(B. Com., Punjab)*
12. What are the advantages to be derived from the use of office forms ?
13. What is the purpose of a form book ? *(B. Com., M.S)*
14. What do you understand by continuous stationery ? What are the advantages in using such stationery in modern office ? *(B. Com., Jabalpur)*
15. Explain the main considerations involved in designing office forms.
(B. Com., Madurai)
16. What is mean by "Forms Control" ? *(B. Com., Madurai)*

CHAPTER

Office Appliances

INTRODUCTION

The office machines have become indispensable for the speedy, accurate and efficient performance of office operations. They affect great saving in cost of office management by increasing the output of work and reducing the requirement of staff. There are a large number of machines and appliances which may be used for different operations in the office. Office equipments and machines have become an integral part of a modern office. "While the human material can be described as brain behind all office activity, adequate and proper equipment and machines are the tools with which office work is carried out. Office mechanisation refers to a process whereby office machines and equipments are introduced in the office with a view to aid administrative process. Office mechanisation may take over some of the functions performed by office staff.

Modern offices prefer mechanisation to improve performance to achieve saving in time and clerical cost, to ensure accuracy and to provide a safeguard against fraud, Work done by machines is neat and clean and results are quickly obtained* The machines are not installed merely to tackle the volume of work but also to bring distinctive improvement in results. Since machines can operate more quickly and accurately than human brain, use of office machines increases the output of work and at the same time ensures efficiency and accuracy. At the same time, machines also help the management in keeping the employees happy and contented by relieving them of the pressure and monotony of work.

In the modern age, an increased use of machinery can be seen in every business concern. The current century is a period of mechanisation. If there is a factory, there must be an office. In the factory manual labour is done and in the office mental labour is done. In factory machines have substituted manual labour, because of many advantages. In the same way, in office also, machines are of very great importance. In office, when doing a job again and again clerks feel monotonous. They also tend to commit errors. The machines are not so liable to errors. Labour-saving devices are substituted for manual labour. In almost all the concerns, some kind of labour-saving method is used.

About half a century ago, all the letters were hand-written. All the calculation work was done by human beings. But now that stage has gone. More and more easy and speedy time-saving machines have been invented .

IMPORTANCE OF MECHANISATION

1. Office work can be done quickly and effectively through the means of office machines. To err is human, but machines seldom err. Therefore, to promote accuracy of work, machines are employed.
2. A single machine may substitute two or three persons; *e.g.,* typewriter. Thus, labour cost can be reduced.
3. Speedy work is possible, in addition to economy. Thus much time can be saved.
4. Machine operations relieve manual drudgery and reduce the monotony of work and fatigue and to that extent machines improve the morale of the employees.
5. Mass of information can be secured at ease. At present, business concerns need detailed information. For this many clerks may be required. But through machines, the cost of the information can be reduced and at the same time more result is gained at ease and economy.

ADVANTAGES OF MECHANISATION

Mechanisation has become an important part of modern office administrative process. It offers many advantages, chief of which are as follows:

1. It is an accepted fact that the office work performed through labour-saving devices is done at a greater speed than the same work done by clerks.
2. It is also seen that not only speedy work is possible, but also greater accuracy with more economy.
3. The initial cost to introduce machines may be high. But in the long run the machine work will prove to be cheaper.
4. Standardisation, simplification and uniformity of work can be maintained.
5. The machine information is clear, complete, concise and correct. Mechanisation ensures accuracy of work.
6. Only few persons are required, if the office is mechanised; hence the labour cost is reduced and space is also saved.
7. When the office is mechanised, a greater amount of overtime is also reduced.
8. When the office expenses are reduced, the amount thus saved can be utilised for greater production.
9. From the management point of view, greater control is possible and much more information is available.

10. By dealing with the customers correctly and punctually, the firm earns their goodwill.
11. To a certain extent, fraud can be reduced.
12. Mechanisation reduces the monotony of carrying out repetitive process which are boring and time consuming.

DISADVANTAGES OF MECHANISATION

1. The initial cost of a machine is high. An idle machine is a waste. This wastage is greater, if the machine is costly.
2. Adoption of certain machines will lead to unemployment.
3. If the operator, who works on the machine is not an expert, then its result will be useless. In the same way, if he has been trained to operate it and if he is absent, the machine will lie idle and any substitution of hand will cause additional expenses. Thus there is an increase in cost.
4. Clerks can more easily be trained in new methods and systems. In case of machines for specialised jobs, if the systems are changed, it is difficult to make use of them in the new system.
5. Machines are subject to break-down and lie idle when electricity fails (if it is electrically operated).
6. Depreciation charges are high; this will reduce the profit.
7. Certain types of machines may become obsolete within a short span of time.

Advantages of Mechanisation

1. Ensures greater accuracy	2. Guarantees better quality of work
3. Relieves monotony	4. Reduces fraud
5. Facilitates control	6. Saves labour time
7. Improves efficiency	8. Reduces operating cost
9. Standardisation of work and	10. Guarantees greater speed.

FACTORS IN SELECTING OFFICE MACHINES

The decision to buy a particular type of machine should be based upon the requirements of organisation. Machines should not be purchased just because they are being purchased by other organisations.

1. **Simple in Operation:** Easy operation of the machine, less fatigue to the operators and good results are required. Operators may be trained effectively at less expense.
2. **Flexibility:** The machine must have flexibility to adopt for multiple purposes, when the cost of the machine is high.
3. **Durability:** There are different people to work under different conditions and therefore the machines must be strong and durable. Breakdown of the machine means investment is waste.
4. **Portability:** In modern times, the size of the machine is reduced into portable size. When the machines are small it is convenient to handle and easy to move from one place to another.
5. **Benefit:** When manual labour is replaced by machine, greater accuracy and better result

must be produced. There must be a qualitative change in the office when a machine is introduced.

6. **Service:** Quick repairs and proper maintenance are essential for continuous performance of the machines. Service facility is an essential to be looked upon.

7. **Operating Cost:** When the machine is in operation, its operating cost must be minimum. Cost of additional machines, if any, and supplies must be minimum.

8. **Suppliers:** When one goes to purchase a machine, the integrity and reputation of the manufacturer may be carefully considered. The machine must be good at mechanical qualities and guarantee over its performance.

9. **Style :** Pleasing design and colour is preferred. When one looks at the machine, it must be attractive, apart from satisfactory operation.

10. **Cost:** Generally when the cost increases, the performance will be better. Costs of the machine are comparable in terms of savings in labour, lower cost of repairs and maintenance etc.

The following questions are to be considered when one goes in for mechanisation.
1. Is it absolutely necessary for the operation ?
2. Is it profitable for the operation ?
3. Can it save human labour and time ?
4. Is the machine flexible in operation ?
5. Is it portable and durable ?
6. Will the operation cost be reduced ?
7. Can the machine offer good output ?
8. Can it give continuous and reliable services ?
9. Is the machine easy to operate and maintain ?
10. Whether service men are readily available ?
11. How much space is needed to house it ?

Following are the important labour-saving appliances found in the modern offices.

ADMINISTRATION AND CORRESPONDENCE

1. Telephone

It is an important instrument of modern office communication.

It facilitates speedy exchange of information. The customers and the firm can get into touch with one another and talk directly. This is an external system which connects the business house with the outside world such as, customers, suppliers etc.

In big offices where a large number of telephone messages are received, there will be a telephone controlling room. Telephone messages are received by a telephone clerk. The managers or the business executives can get useful information and give necessary directions to other offices over the phone.

2. Dictaphone

There are four types of dictating machines (a) The Electronic Belt type, (b) Electronic disc type, (c) Electronic cylinder type, (d) Acoustic cylinder type. In these types three machines are required : (i) Dictating machine, (ii) Transcribing machine and (iii) Shaving machine.

The businessman dictates letters or reports in the dictating machine at any time at any place. It records it in a special record. Then it is sent to the typist. The typist places the record in the transcriber. He makes the necessary adjustments with regard to volume and speed and then types the matter. The shaver is used to remove the record from the above said belt or disc or cylinder. Thus the belt or disc or cylinder can be reused by the dictator any number of times.

Advantages of Dictaphone

(1) The dictator can dictate matters at any time.

(2) It ensures speed and accuracy and saves time.

(3) The typist can type well without knowing short-hand.

(4) It increases accuracy and efficiency.

(5) Telephone dictation can also be recorded in dictaphone.

(6) It is portable, and like a book, can be carried anywhere.

3. Combination of Telephone Plus Dictating Machine:

It is a new machine. The conversation of both the parties can be recorded on the dictating machine. By the use of twin cylinders continuous conversation can be recorded and can be used for future reference. It is useful in newspaper offices.

4. Ipsophone :

It is used in Switzerland, it records telephone messages and speaks for its owner and repeats the messages when required. When the telephone rings, the ipsophone will start its work, by speaking its number and asking for messages to be recorded. Thus all the messages and calls are recorded in the machine.

5. Auto Abstract :

It is an electronic machine, mainly used in USA. This machine reads lengthy reports, letters etc. and writes abstracts or precis version of them. The entire article is transcribed by the machine and is understood by electronic brain. The precis form of the article is printed on paper. These types of machines are much useful to company secretaries, managers etc.

6. Typewriter :

This is the most common machine used by every modern commercial office. This is so familiar to everyone, that it need not be explained. The typewriter has superseded the pen. The execution of work through a typewriter is accurate, legible and fast. Typewritten letters are more attractive than handwritten letter. The following are the types of typewriters generally used in firms.

(a) Portable machine

This type of machine is good for personal use. It is extremely light. It is compact and is only three or four inches height. It can be kept in the drawer of a table. During travels, it can be put in a small carrying case. This type of machine is invaluable for professional people, who travel much.

(b) Standard and silent (noiseless) machine

Silent machines are quicker in action than the standard typewriter. Standard machines are usually with Roman type or any other type of specified letter. The standard machines are further developed as noise proof at action. Such noiseless machines are invaluable as the typist can do the work in the same room where the executive officer is also seated. But when the ordinary typewriter is at operation, telephonic conversation becomes impossible. In these machines, more copies can be taken out than in portable machines.

(c) Variable type machine

Typewriters which have different variety of style and size of types are so adjusted that according to the requirements, the type of letters can be changed—italic type, small type, etc. Big size (bold type) types are used when the correspondence is little and small type is used when the correspondence is lengthy. This is useful particularly in preparing reports where different styles of types can be used to distinguish one set from another.

(d) Electric type machine

This type is now in general use. The expense is more. But there are many advantages. The operator will have less fatigue. In one operation 20 or 25 copies can be obtained against 6 on standard typewriters. The operator need not exert himself much. The typist can type faster.

(e) Automatic electric type machine

It is an American invention. This type of typewriter is used when there is much circular correspondence. The automatic typewriters are controlled by coded instructions punched in paper tape or card recorded magnetically. The typist prepares original record. This is done on a special machine and holes are cut on paper tape and instead of letters, by the typist. These tapes are played back, through a recorder attached to the typewriter. In a single roll 50 or 60 letters or as many paragraphs can be recorded. By the operation of a push-button the particular letters or paragraphs are preselected and the letters are typed automatically. At the predetermined point, the machine can be stopped, if any additional paragraphs are to be inserted by the typist. The machine can also stop at any point in the letter; and date, address, amount etc., can be typed out in their proper place. Three or four machines can be operated at the same time by one operator. This system is good when many circular or standard letters of personal touch are to be sent out. If mistakes are made in the original record, they can be corrected by sticking a slip on the wrong holes and retype to correct them.

Points to be considered when buying a Typewriter

1. First the volume of the work is a prime factor on which basis portable or standard size may be purchased.
2. If the typist has to work in executive's room, then it should not produce sounds. For this silent or noiseless machine is good.
3. A typist must be consulted to know the touch and working condition.
4. Machines which have simplified operation may be preferred.

7. Stenographic Machine

The common practice is that shorthand typist takes dictation in his note-book and transcribes it in letters. The officer sits along with his stenographer and dictates the letters; the latter after taking them down types in letter pads, making the letters ready for signature. The new invention of dictation machines has come into use. These types of machines make it possible for the officers to dictate letters at their convenience. Then the recorded tape is sent to the typist, who fixes the recorded tape on a reproducing machine and types it by hearing the recorded dictation. The speed of the playback can be adjusted to the speed of the typist through controls.

There are many methods of making outward correspondence ready. They are (a) giving dictation to a stenographer (b) dictating directly to a typist, who types out at the same time (c) dictation to a stenographic machine (d) recording a dictation in a dictation machine.

Dictating machines have become very popular nowadays. Replies to correspondence can be made through the machines. The officer gives the dictation through a mouthpiece, which is connected to the machine, and the message is impressed, on a cylinder or disc. The disc or cylinder is placed on another machine; and through an earphone the dictated portion is reproduced; and the typist types out the letter. The dictated message can be erased and the disc can be reused. The speed can also be regulated according to the speed of the typist.

Merits of Stenographic Machine

1. The executive can dictate or give reply even if the stenographer is absent.
2. When the executive is in the mood to dictate, he can do so even if his steno is absent.
3. The number of clerks can be reduced.
4. Salary to stenographers is paid high and salary to typist, is low. Instead of appointing stenographers, typists can be appointed. It is more economical.
5. All stenographers may not be able to take dictation at a high speed. If the stenographic machine is available, the executive can dictate the reply at any speed. When the typist types, the speed of the tape or disc can be regulated.
6. It is usual that visitors may come often and often during the dictation and waste the time of the stenographer. Such waste of time can be avoided.

Demerits of Stenographic Machine

1. Personal contact is neglected.
2. It is very difficult to make correction in dictaphone.
3. Since tape or disc is used again and again, original records cannot be maintained.
4. For efficient operation of the machine, the executive must be a good dictator.

The stenographic machine is portable and noiseless. The keyboard on the machine is pressed down by the stenographer, when a word is heard. The machine is operated at a good speed by a trained operator. The tapes are passed on to the typist, who is trained to read and type from these tapes. This machine is very useful for recording at meetings, reporting, etc.

8. Duplicating Machine

The type-writers can produce only a few copies of documents. Sometimes, the office requires many copies of certain documents. There are many processes of copying out records. The duplicating machines are used when several copies of documents are required. Duplicating machines produce fewer copies than the printing press. The various types of duplicating machines are as follows : Spirit Duplicating

It is also known as hectograph. The method is very simple. The master copy is prepared on art paper by means of a hectograph carbon paper. A reverse image is obtained on the back of the master copy. The master copy is fitted round the drum on the machine, exposing the carbon image to the outside. The papers pass first under a pad dampened with spirit. It is then passed against the master copy. The spirit on the paper dissolves a very little of the carbon on the master copy and thus gives an impression on the copying paper. The spirit on the paper dries very quickly, leaving the image on the paper. It can be operated by hand or by electricity.

Stencil Duplicators (Mimeograph)

It is a common method of taking out copies of letters. In this system, a stencil is cut on a typewriter or by hand (if by hand, a type of pencil known as stylus is used.) The typed matter will be within the frame marked in the stencil. Also, when a stencil is cut, the ribbon is so adjusted that the typist will cut the stencil directly with the letters (the ribbon should not be in between the stencil and the letter or the ribbon is removed). Any error, if happens, can be erased by using correcting fluid. The correcting fluid will dry soon, and after that the correct letter or word can be typed on it. The cut stencil is placed in a duplicating machine. The cylinder of the machine is inked with a special type ink. The machine is rotated till the ink is spread over the rollers. There may be two trays on each side. The tray on the one side carries papers of the correct size and the tray on the other side receives the printed papers. When machine is switched on, the machine feeds papers automatically, and after that leaves the printed paper on the other tray. In the latest models, simply switching on the button gives the required number of copies of the letter, as the copies produced are also counted automatically in the machine itself. The stencil is removed and kept for reuse. This type of duplicators is inexpensive and is a good system.

Photostat (Photographic duplicator)

This method can also be used whenever an exact copy of any document is required. In this, photography of the documents is first taken out through camera. No dark room is required for this. The produced copies are soon developed and when dried are ready for use; copies of larger or smaller size than the original document can be taken in any colour.

There are two processes. The contact process and the camera process. In the former case, a box containing a frosted glass screen is used. The light and sensitized paper are placed behind the screen with the document to be copied, placed face downwards on it. The box is then closed, the light switched on for necessary exposure. Thus the negative copy is produced. From this, the positive can be reproduced in the same way. In the camera process, by use of camera document can be copied by using sensitized paper to produce negative and also to produce positive copies.

J.C. Denyer lays down the different factors, which should be considered in choosing a particular duplicating process :
1. Number of copies needed.
2. Frequency of demand, that is, how often the machine is to be used ?
3. Speed of reproduction.
4. Type of copy paper, to be used. Sometimes a good writing surface is required.
5. Economy in operation *i.e.* the cost of materials and operator.
6. What kind of image is needed ? Is it to be in halftone, or a line drawing or text ?
7. Change in size, that is, whether it is desired to enlarge or reduce the size of the original document.
8. Number of colour, needed.
9. Durability of the master and image.
10. Is necessary to have variable details on pre-cut forms ?
11. Type of appearance, that is whether type-written appearance is desired or printed type set appearance is preferred.

9. Addressing Machine

Addressing machine is generally used to print the address on envelopes, labels, wrappers etc. In big concerns frequently letters have to be sent to the same customers. For example, electric company, gas company, insurance company etc., have to send bills, premium notices, etc., monthly to their customers. In such cases, it is a tedious job to write or type out thousands of addresses. The addressing machine overcomes this difficulty. It is a great time saver.

The addresses are stencilled or embossed on metal plates. When addresses are to be written, these stencils, or plates are placed on the machine and allowed to pass through the machine with the help of a lever, envelopes are fed one by one and the required addresses are printed. The speed of the operation and the printing of correct address are remarkable.

10. Letter Opening Machine

It is a machine having a revolving knife edge which will slice a very thin part from one edge of the envelope. The contents of the envelopes should be shaken to the other side, so that contents may not be cut. The opening of the early morning letters becomes easy by this machine; hundreds of envelopes can be opened within minutes.

11. Folding Machine

The letters after being signed, reach the despatch section which sends them out, by placing or housing them in envelopes. If a large number of letters are there, this machine can be used to fold letters in one or two or three parallel folds with additional cross folds at a greater speed.

12. Envelope Sealing Machine

This is a machine which automatically seals the envelopes. It will dampen the gummed flaps of the envelopes; thus sealing of the envelopes becomes very easy.

13. Stamping Machine

In small concerns, this type of machine is used. Rolls of stamps are purchased from the post office. The stamps are placed in the machine. Water is kept in a part of the machine. The stamps are automatically moistened and affixed on the envelopes as required.

14. Franking Machine

It is a machine, advantageously used in the despatch department. The machine is licensed by the post office. The payment of postage is made to the post office, in advance for an agreed total of postage. The purchasing company has to be registered in the post office and a number is allotted. After receiving payment, the franking machine is issued. It has a metre, which reads out the amount of stamps, which the machine can print. It has adjustments within to print the postage stamps required. When cards and letters are fed into it, the required stamps (along with date, name of the company and registration number) are printed on the post cards, envelopes, wrappers etc. When the credited amount is exhausted, the machine automatically locks itself. Then further an advance remittance is made to the post office to reset the machine for further use.

Merits

1. Much time is saved. It is claimed that 2,000 letters can be franked by hand-operated machine while 15,000 letters can be franked by electrical machine.

2. The maintenance of postage account can be avoided.

3. If envelopes are wrongly franked, the amount can be refunded from the post office.

4. The firm need not purchase stamps of different denominations and keep the stocks.

5. The postal department also saves time and stationery, because there is no need to print the stamps.

When using franking machine, the correct amount of franking will be done in order to avoid overstamping and understamping. Moreover, the post book is avoided; thus there will be no recording of despatched letters. However, firms using the machine will have to keep in reserve some postage stamps for emergency use.

(15) Dating Machine :

Dates are written on the letters by this machine. It is mostly used in offices where a large number of letters are written everyday.

ACCOUNTING

1. Calculating Machine

Calculating machine replaces the human labour in operations of adding, subtracting, multiplying and dividing of arithmetical figures. To err is human. Mistakes may occur, when dealing with figures. The chances of these mistakes are completely removed by the calculating machines. These machines are also used for calculation including interest, commission, discount, exchange, etc. These machines can perform four or five times the work done by a man.

2. Adding-listing Machine

Simple adding machines will show the result of adding operation, whereas adding-listing machine will give a printed record in the adding operation. There are three kinds-full rank type, half keyboard type and simplified keyboard. In non-listing machines, the result appears in the metre and it will not give printed answers.

In all types, the figures of the keyboard are pressed and the result is known then a particular key is pressed to clear off the metre.

The following are the general types :

1. Printing calculators

2. Key-driven calculators

3. Automatic calculators

4. Rotary calculators

5. Electronic calculators

6. Electronic printing calculators etc.

Printing calculator is like an adding machine which gives the result in printed form.

Key-driven calculator is a non-listing machine, which gives the result on the metre. Automatic calculator is run electrically and gives the result on the metre.

Rotary calculator is a machine which does all the functions of arithmetic.

Electronic calculator is the latest development. This machine will perform calculations in a thousand part of a second and some machines will display the result on a small screen, as in a television set. Electronic printing machine in addition to the above, will also give printed result.

Chief Advantages of Accounting Machine

1. Errors in operation are minimised.
2. Working time is saved.
3. Mental strain is reduced.
4. Machines are handy-portable.
5. They are simple in operation.
6. They give quick result.
7. They give accurate result.
8. The labour cost is reduced.

Even though the machines are costly, they simplify the work and save time. In the long run it is a great advantage. Almost all big concerns use these calculating machines with great advantage. The general types of machines are comptometers, duplex adding, calculating machine, etc.

3. Calculators

A variety of calculators are available in the market. They contribute to efficiency and remove the tedium of calculations. Hence calculators have become very popular. They are useful for multiplication, division, addition and subtraction; calculation of discount, interest, wages etc. The calculators help to reduce human labour in arithmetical calculations. To err is human. Mistakes may occur, when dealing with figures. The chances of these mistakes are completely removed by the calculators. These machines are quick in action.

4. Accounting Machine

The accounting machine is similar to a typewriting machine. These machines have become popular in use. These machines are used for posting of accounts. Ledger posting, journals, cash receipts, records of invoice, payments, cash book etc. can be made by these appliances. These accounting machines are able to perform different sets of accounting operation. These machines are a combination of typewriter and calculating machine. They give not only printed records, but also do automatic calculation. At one operation, this machine can make a number of copies of a document by means of carbons.

Advantages of Machines

1. Greater speed is possible than in human operation.
2. The accounting result is more accurate, neat and reliable than that of manual accounting.
3. They have human labour.
4. Ledgers are automatically balanced.
5. Monotony of human work is eliminated.
6. Work is up-to-date and posting of personal accounts is done in time. Therefore collection of dues can be done in time and thus bad debts can be reduced.
7. Overtime work to the staff can be reduced.
8. They give reliable data.
9. Junior clerks, after a little training, can work on the machines.
10. Mental strain in calculation is reduced.

Disadvantages of Machines

1. Cost of machines is high.
2. Repairing charges are high.
3. Electricity failure will bring to a standstill the work of accounting department.
4. When human labour is cheap, the machines are not popular.
5. It is possible that loose leaves of accounting documents are stolen or misplaced.

5. Recorder Machine

It is useful in modern accounting and record keeping. The photographic method is used and it is known as microphotograph. It is accurate and has not very high speed. It can take 2,500 copies at a time, here a camera is used inside the machine.

6. Book Keeping Machine

Entries in the accounts books are made and ledgers are prepared and quick preparation of final account is possible. There will be no mistakes.

7. Time Recording Clock

This is a machine, which is used advantageously in big concerns, where hundreds of thousands of workers are employed. They are just like clocks. Each worker will be given a card which contains his name, address, section where he is attached, etc. When the worker enters the factory or leaves the factory, he inserts his card in the clock, which prints the time and date on the card. Thus it will help to show the arrival time as well as departure time from the factory. This card can be treated as attendance of the employees. On the basis of the cards, wages can be calculated.

8. Card Punching Machines

This is a machine usually used in factories and workshops. Separate cards have been used for each piece of information. The machine will record the information by means of punched holes on the cards. Each hole has a code number indicating the significance of the punch. Each card, at the top, is printed with date, department, value, quantity, etc. The punching is done either by hand or electric power. Special arrangement of cards is designed for each job.

The advantages are :

1. Permanent and unaltered record.
2. Accurate record etc.

9. Cash Register

It is a mechanical appliance for recording and checking cash receipts. It can be much useful in a concern where many payments are received, as in the case of a retail shop. The amount paid by the customers is shown on the dial and it is also at once printed on a sheet. Some of the latest cash registers will issue receipts to the customers and at the same time total the amount received. The chief cashier will be at ease to check the cash with the cash receipts and the management will have effective control over the cash receipts. This mechanical device simplifies the jobs of a cashier to a great extent and also reduces the errors and defalcation.

10. Small Coin Counting Machine

Small coins can be counted by this machine. It is like a box and there are many trays according to the types of coins. In the first or the top tray there is only one hole. By this hole all the small coins will go down. Big coins remain at the top. The trays are arranged one below the other. Thus the coin sorter is a device which sorts out coins of different denominations, in different trays, meant for them. Coin counter will count the changes. Both these help the cashier and ease his job. These are usefully adopted in banks, railways and other big concerns where cash dealings are numerous. Coin changing machine will automatically tender the changes correctly to parties or customers.

11. Cheque Writing Machine

In large concerns, where numerous cheque have to be issued, the cheque writing machine is of great help and safety–safety in the respect that there is protection against fraud, because hand-written and type-written cheque are exposed to possible fraud, contents of the cheque and crossing of the cheques, if in ink, are possible to be erased and the encashment is highly possible. Therefore protection against misuse or forgery is essential. For this purpose, cheque writing machine is used. This machine only writes on the surface of the cheque, but it shreds into fibres of the cheque paper, the shreds being formed under pressure and being then filled with acid proof ink. Such a machine saves time and protects the drawers. Cheque writing machine is also known as cheque protector. When there are hundreds of cheques to be signed the cheque signing machine can profitably be used.

12. Electronic Computer

Electronic computers are the latest addition to the long list of office machines. These are general purpose machines capable of performing most clerical operations at high speed. They can handle whole systems of operations change automatically from one operations to another in a desired sequence and even select alternative courses of action on the basis of the data received and the results of previous operations. It is an electronic device by which data is processed electronically at great speed. It is used to solve business problems through decision-making techniques. It is an electronic device to process data and communicate the results.

Uses of Computer

A computer is a giant mechanical brain which can process, analyse, store or supply information instantaneously. It can perform the following functions:

1. To receive one or more programmes of instructions, store them and obey them as and when required.
2. To take new information through one or more input channels and store it for reference as required by any of the programmes.
3. To perform any arithmetical calculation, which may be repetitive in nature, as required by the programme.
4. To select and carry out alternative courses of action, according to the information it produces.
5. To apply checks to the data it receives or produces and, if a test indicates a failure, produce a record or signal to procure human intervention.
6. To store the data produced for future reference.
7. To select information from the store, arrange it in any sequence, and discharge it through one or more output channels to be printed for human use, or to be recorded for subsequent computer use.

In fact, it is difficult to list the uses to which a computer may be put. For instance, it can be used for the preparation of payrolls, stock control, sales and purchase accounting records, costing, budgetary control, production control, hire-purchase accounting etc.

Advantages of Computer

1. It possesses a high speed in operation.
2. Many staff members can be substituted with a computer. Thus, operation costs are reduced.
3. There is a greater accuracy of work.
4. Since information is correct, sound future policy can be drawn.
5. Monotonous jobs of the staff can be removed by computers.
6. Any type of complicated calculation can be solved with advantages.

Disadvantages of Computer

1. Initial cost is very high.
2. If installed, maintenance cost is very high.
3. Trained, experienced and capable staff are very rare if available, high salary is to be paid.
4. Breakdown is very common.
5. If errors happen, it is very difficult to correct them.

Choosing an Office Machine

1. One should first consider the advantages before a machine is purchased. By purchasing any machine there must be some saving of labour and time. The life of the machine, its cost and the work to be done by the machine must be considered before obtaining it.
2. The questions whether the proposed machine is essential for the smooth running of the office work and whether the machine will be fully utilised for the work are to be considered. If the machine is kept idle, then it is a waste of capital investment.
3. It should be seen whether operators of the proposed machine are available on normal remuneration. If the cost is high and the remuneration of the operator is also high in relation to the work to be done, then there will not be much benefit in getting it.
4. Other questions to be considered are whether the machine gives greater accuracy than a human agent and whether it removes the monotony of the worker. Accuracy is more important for figure work.
5. By purchasing the machines, frauds through operations must be reduced to zero.

AUTOMATION IN OFFICE

Automation refers to the use of devices for saving human labour. That is, automation means complete mechanisation of a process or operation thereby elimination of manual labour. It involves not only substitution of machinery for human efforts, but also a system of mechanical feedback in scientific manner. The terms 'automation' and 'mechanisation' are not synonymous. Mechanisation means use of machines to replace human labour. The mental work has to be done by the human mind. But in automation, mental work is also done by machines. Thus, automation is the next stage after mechanisation. Feedback is inherent in automation. In case of automatic machinery, the machine is able to sense, feel, detect and correct errors and mistakes while they are occurring.

There is generally resistance by the employees to any scheme of automation. Trade unionists also oppose it as it will create unemployment. This is of course true in the short-run, but in the long run this is not really true. Although the manpower requirement in direct production will be reduced in industries introducing automation, more skilled indirect labour force will be required to operate the machines and provide for their maintenance. Production increases with automation leading to increased requirements for skilled labour. Hence automation does not necessarily lead to unemployment. In developed countries having 'full employment', automation is essential, otherwise the available resources will not be fully utilised and standard of living will not be improved.

The following principles should be borne in mind when selecting an office machine :
1. Principle of cost
2. Principle of equality
3. Principle of suitability
4. Principle of durability
5. Principle of adequacy
6. Principle of least space occupancy
7. Principle of multiple use
8. Principle of standardisation
9. Principle of fullest use
10. Principle of safety.

Through processes of automation the production increases. With more production, the overhead expenses go down leading to reduction in cost per unit. Consequently, the prices go down and prices also go down because of more goods being available against demand. Further competition is also a reason for low price. However, the sellers can make more profits by selling more quantities at lower prices. Thus, automation helps both the consumers as well as the manufacturers by keeping down the price level.

QUESTIONS

1. What factors would you take into account in deciding whether to go in for the purchase of labour-saving devices for office ?   (*B. Com., Chennai*)
2. State the advantages of postal-franking machine ?   (*B. Com., MS*)
3. Describe the important labour-saving devices for smooth running of the office work.   (*B. Com., Madurai*)
4. Describe the duplicating machines.   (*B. Com., Mumbai*)
5. Define (*a*) Cheque protector (*b*) Typewriter (*c*) Addressing machine.(*B. Com., Punjab*)
6. What are the objects of introducing office machine ? State the relative advantages.
                    (*B. Com., Madurai*)
7. Briefly describe the functions and working of three labour-saving machines commonly used in modern offices.   (*B. Com., M.S*)

8. In selecting a machine, what are the points to be considered ?   *(B. Com., Punjab)*
9. Comment on (1) folding machine (2) stamping machine.
10. What are the main functions of the adding-listing machine ?   *(B. Com., Madurai)*
11. What are the uses of teleprinters ?   *(B. Com., Madurai)*
12. Explain the principal considerations in mechanisation of office procedures.
                                                                          (B. Com., Madurai)
13. What are the objects of introducing office machines ?Point out the advantages of introducing office machines.   *(B.Com., Bangalore)*
14. State the criteria for the selection of office machines ?   *(B.Com., Bangalore)*
15. What are the uses and functions of computer ?   *(B.Com., Bangalore)*

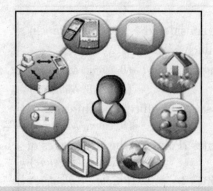

CHAPTER

Office Communication

INTRODUCTION

The term 'communication' is derived from the Latin word 'communis' which means common. Therefore, communication may be defined as an exchange of facts, ideas, opinions or emotions to create mutual understanding. It refers to various means of transmitting information from one person to another or from one place to another. Communication is one of the fundamental aspects of all human interaction. The ability to communicate effectively has enabled human beings to build organisations, societies and other social groups that make for survival and better living. "No business can exist without communication." Communication is a management skill and it is an indispensable part of any management. Communication plays the same role in a business organisation as the nervous system in a human body.

Communication is one of the fundamental and basic functions of an office. Communication is a must for all types of business. It promotes office function. Business cannot be performed without communication. It is a process of conveyance of information from one person to another. The term communication is used in a wider sense. Communications means not only letters, telegrams, telephone messages, but also transmission of reports, estimates instructions, invoices, order etc. Communication systems can be divided into written, oral and mechanical. The selection of communication system is essential to be considered before discussing the systems.

According to *Louis A Allen*, "Communication is the sum of all the things one person does when he wants to create understanding in the mind of another. It is a bridge of meaning. It involves a systematic and continuous process of telling, listening and understanding."

According to *Haiman*, "Communication means the process of passing information and understanding from one person to another. Communication, fundamental and vital to all managerial functions, is the process of imparting ideas and making oneself understood by others."

FEATURE OF COMMUNICATION

The above definitions reveals the following characteristics of communication:

1. Communication is a two-way process.
2. It involves at least two persons–Sender (communicator) and Receiver.
3. It must convey a message.
4. It is a continuous process.
5. It may be verbal, written or gestural.
6. It may be formal or informal.
7. It aims to motivate a response.

PROCESS OF COMMUNICATION

The communication process consists of the following elements:

1. **Sender :** Sender or communicator is the person who sends a message or an idea.
2. **Message :** Message is what is conveyed by the sender.
3. **Encoding :** Sender translates the message into words, symbols or gesture, known to both the parties.
4. **Channel :** It is the medium or route through which the message is passed from the sender to the receiver.
5. **Receiver :** The person who receives the message is known as receiver.
6. **Feedback :** The effectiveness of communication is measured through feedback. When the sender receives the feedback, the process of communication is said to be complete.

SELECTION OF A COMMUNICATION SYSTEM

Office manager should be familiar with the various devices of communication and the different factors which should be considered before adopting a particular communication system. In order to get a good decision over the means of communication, the following factors may be considered:

1. Quickness/Speed

There are many types of transactions conducted during the business hours. One must speed up the transmission of message on the basis of importance and urgency of transaction. If the party is available in the transacted place, oral communication is enough. If the party is residing in the same city, telephonic message is good: if outside the city, message through Subscribers' Trunk Dialing (STD). If much distance is there, then telegram can also be sent. If the matter is not urgent, a mere letter will be sufficient.

2. Accuracy

If the accuracy of the message is the prime motive, a letter will serve the purpose. Telephonic conversation might be misheard by the other party. Even telegrams, sometimes lead to wrong conclusion. Therefore, success can be reaped by a letter, provided the letter is properly written. Therefore, the communication medium which is selected should ensure accuracy in the transmission of messages.

3. Safety

There is always risk when valuables are sent by post. Therefore, for safety purposes, important documents may be sent by registered post; for further safety by registered and insured post.

4. Secrecy

In business field, certain transactions have to be kept confidential. When one aims at secrecy, letter will achieve the aim. In other communication systems, secrecy may leak out to unwanted persons.

5. Record

Record of the message is essential and is possible only if it is in writing. For this purpose, duplicate copies of the letters can be preserved and they are good proof against disputes, relating to the transaction, in future. There is no record for oral communication.

6. Cost

The cost of communication is also important. Before adopting any system, the expenses in different means may also be considered. The material cost (stationery) and labour cost in preparing the letter will also be considered.

7. Distance

Distance between the persons who are parties to communication is an important factor. If distance is too short, face to face communication is suitable. If there is distance, message can be transmitted through phone or telegram or letter.

IMPORTANCE OF OFFICE COMMUNICATION

Communication is a vital tool of management. Communication is not a one way traffic. The process starts from the sender and proceeds to the receiver. But the effectiveness of communication process is further enhanced if the reaction of the 'receiver' to the communication moves in a reverse flow and reaches the 'sender'. This is known as 'feedback' process. It is said that the success of an organisation depends on the adequacy of communication. The importance of communication is as follows:

1. Effective Functioning of the Organisation

The efficient functioning of the organisation totally depends on the effective communication system. A business organisation consists of people and network of decision affecting them. Managing an organisation is getting things done through others. Communication serves the management and makes everyone aware of what the organisation wants to achieve.

2. Smooth Running of the Organisation

A smooth running of an organisation greatly depends on the effective system of communication. It is only through a good and effective office communication system that effective leadership, good human relations, high morale and motivation in the organisation can be maintained to ensure success of management objectives.

3. Proper Planning and Co-ordination

Plans and decisions must be effectively conveyed to those who translate them into action. Effective communication is essential for quick and successful implementation of the management decisions. Good communications are essential to co-ordination. Effective communication is a pre-requisite for solving managerial problems.

4. Exchange of Information

Communication helps executives to acquire more knowledge. It also facilitates executives to share the acquired knowledge with their subordinates which results to increase in the overall managerial skill of people in the organisation. It also helps in understanding the problems and offering solutions to them.

5. Human Relations

Most of the conflicts arise due to misunderstood motives and ignorance of facts. Proper communication helps to minimise friction and maximise mutual understanding, co-operation and goodwill. A good relation can be created with the help of an effective method of communication.

Communication Barriers to Communication : Communication is most effective when it moves speedily and smoothly in an uninterrupted flow. Communication is the nerve system of an enterprise. It serves as the lubricant, fostering for the smooth operations of the management process. Despite the development of high speed electronic devices, communications are not successful in many cases. All messages are not effectively transmitted or received. Several obstructions, blockades, hurdles, stoppages or bottlenecks, called barriers to communication, distort the message and make communication ineffective. Some of the barriers or obstacles to effective communication are given below:

1. Language Barriers

Words and symbols used to communicate facts and feelings may mean different things to different persons. This may act as a barrier to effective communication. The meaning intended by the sender may be quite different from the meaning followed by the receiver. The language of the sender may be very technical or incomprehensible to the receiver.

2. Inattention Barriers

When the receiver does not pay complete attention to the message, communication becomes ineffective. The efforts to communicate with someone not listening will fail. Generally, people are found paying half attention to what is being communicated orally.

3. Organisational Barriers

The classical organisation structure with a scalar chain of command restricts free and frequent communications. These days the organisation structure of most big enterprises is complex involving several layers of supervision, and long communication lines. Too many levels intervene causing delay in transmission and distortion in the message. When the message has to pass through several hands, there is filtering.

4. Status Barriers

Every organisation has some kind of status system. Some individuals have higher status than others. A superior may give only selected information to his subordinates so as to maintain status differences. Subordinates, usually, tend to convey only those things which the superiors would appreciate. Such selective communication is also known as filtering, A subordinate may also feel reluctant to report his shortcomings or may not seek clarification on instructions which are subject to different interpretations for fear of loss of prestige in the eyes of superior.

5. Premature Evaluation

Some people have the tendency to form a judgement before listening to the entire message. This is known as premature evaluation. "Half listening is like racing your engine with the gears in neutral." Premature evaluation and response tend to stop the transfer of information.

6. Perpetual Barriers

Every individual has specific areas of interest. So, he may hear, read or see only that part of the message which is valuable to him. There may be deliberate filtering of the message by the sender.

7. Emotional Reaction

Barriers may also arise due to emotional attitude because when emotions are strong, it is difficult to know the frame of mind of other persons. Emotional attitudes of both, the sender as well as the receiver, obstruct free flow of transmission and understanding of messages.

8. Channel Distortions

Physical or mechanical barriers may also cause distortion of communication. A communication is a two-way process, distance between the sender and the receiver of the message is an important barrier to communication. Many people talking simultaneously, inaudible telephone lines, electronic disturbances, wrong transcriptions in telex messages, noise etc. are examples of channels distortion.

OVERCOMING BARRIER TO COMMUNICATION

Communication is a major function of an office. The success of an organisation depends to a very large extent upon its ability to communicate effectively with its employees and customers. Effective communication takes place when a thing is understood in the sense in which it has been communicated. Effective communication is a good business and very essential for the success of an organisation. It is a two-way process. It may not be possible to achieve perfect communication. The following are some of the measures which may be adopted by the management to overcome the barriers and maintain the effectiveness of communication.

1. Proper Language

The message should be expressed in simple, brief and clear language. Use of technical terms should be minimised. The words or symbols selected for conveying the message must be appropriate to the reference and understanding of the receiver.

2. Clarity and Completeness

Clarity of thought is the first essential of good communication. The language used should be simple and precise which the receiver can understand easily. Technical jargons and high sounding words should be avoided. The contents of the communication should be adequate and complete. Incomplete message creates misunderstanding and delays in action. The message should be adequate and appropriate to the purpose of communication. The purpose of communication itself should be clearly defined.

3. Brevity

All communications should be brief. Unnecessary repetition and over elaboration should be avoided. The message should be concise and concrete. The communication must be well-planned and well-constructed. It is very essential for the management to maintain an efficient flow of communication in all directions. The flow of information should be regulated to avoid information overloaded.

4. Attention

Careful listening is essential for effective communication. The receiver should pay complete attention to the message so that communication becomes effective. The communicator should convey the message in such a way that the emotions and sentiments of the receiver are not hurt. Proper listening and open mind are necessary for this purpose.

5. Integrity

The message sent must be consistent with the objectives, policies and programmes of the organisation. Communication will be more effective if it is consistent than when it is varied. It is easier to follow consistent messages. To avoid credibility gap, management must ensure that their actions and deeds are in accordance with their communication.

6. Feedback

The effectiveness of communication is measured through feedback. Communication is a two-way process. The communication is complete when the receiver understands the message. In case of face to face communication, immediate feedback by seeing the emotions and expressions on the face of the listener can be of great help to the communicator. There should be a follow up action to ensure that the message is rightly understood. All communications should be followed up to generate feedback.

7. Media

The method of communication to be adopted should be in conformity with the nature and purpose of the message to be conveyed. The medium and method of communication should be chosen carefully to suit the particular communication needs. The equipment and mechanical devices to be used should be carefully selected and well maintained to prevent breakdowns.

8. Avoid Premature Evaluation

To communicate effectively, one should be a good listener. Superiors should develop a habit of patient listening and avoid premature evaluation of communication from their subordinates. This will encourage free flow of upward communication.

9. Developing Relations

Business requires joint efforts for accomplishing its goals. The need is, therefore, to develop proper relations among people working in the office. This will automatically reduce or eliminate behavioural barriers to communication by encouraging co-operation. An office manager should respect dignity and authority of his subordinates and be kind to them. Subordinates should also trust their superiors.

10. Gestures And Action

The way you say something is also very important along with the message for gestures such as a twinkle of an eye, a smile or a handshake etc. convey sometimes more meaning than even words spoken or written. The main reason is that action and deeds often speak louder and clear than words.

TYPES OF OFFICE COMMUNICATION

Office communication may be broadly classified into two types : (1) Internal Communication and (2) External Communication.

1. Internal Communication

Internal communication plays a vital role in the efficient performance of office operations. It refers to exchange of information and messages between persons and departments of the organisation. It is the responsibility of the office manager to see that the function of exchange of information and messages is facilitated through a proper system of communication. Internal communication may be divided into two:

(1) Oral Communication and (2) Written Communication.

2. External Communication

External communication involves exchange of messages or information with outsiders, *i.e.* customers, creditors, dealers, government, suppliers etc. It is important to note that external communication may be regarded as the backbone of modern business.

INTERNAL COMMUNICATION

Effective internal communication is fundamental to the existence of any office. Internal communication, also known as inter-communication, is a major function of an office. In a small firm having 10 or 15 staff, there may be no problem of internal communication, for these employees can easily communicate with each other. However as the organisation grows and the number of employees increases, the problem of effective communication becomes more difficult. Thus in a big organisation having a number of departments or sections, internal communication may be:

(i)   Inter-departmental, *i.e.,* communication among the employees of the same department; or

(ii) Intra-department, *i.e.,* communication among different departments of the organisation. Further, communication may be either downward or upward.

(a) Downward Communication :

It means the flow of communication from the top management downward to the operating level. It may also be called a communication from a superior to a subordinate. It follows the line of authority from the top to the bottom of the organisation hierarchy. Downward communication consists of plans, instructions, orders, rules etc.

(b) Upward Communication :

Upward communication means the flow of information from the lower levels of the organisation to the higher levels of authority. It passes from subordinate to superior, for example, from worker to foreman from foreman to manager, from manager to general manager, etc. Communication of this type includes ideas, suggestions, complaints, appeal, reports etc. Upward communication is very important as it serves as the feedback on the effectiveness of downward communication. On the basis of upward communication, the management revises its plans and policies etc. and makes further planning,

Internal communication may be :

(a) Oral

(b) Written

(c) Mechanical

ORAL COMMUNICATION

Oral communication may take place in face to face conversation or through mechanical devices.

1. Face to Face Conversation:

This is the most natural way of transmitting the message. Face to face communication is more successful because the communicator can make the listener to understand his message not only by the spoken words but also by the gestures he takes. Face to face conversation occurs in committee meetings, lectures, conferences, social gathering, interviews, personnel-counselling, etc.

Advantages

The advantages of face to face communication are:

1. It is a time and money saving device.
2. It is more effective than any other method.
3. It is quicker.
4. It is more easy to measure the effect of communication.
5. It is the only way out during periods of emergency.
6. It is more flexible.
7. It leads to greater understanding.
8. Doubts can be removed then and there.
9. It fosters a friendly and co-operative spirit.
10. Response of the receiver can be easily evaluated.

Disadvantages

The disadvantages of a face-to-face communication are :

1. It is less reliable.
2. It provides no record for future reference.
3. It is unsuitable for lengthy messages.
4. It may be less accurate.
5. It may have less weight.
6. It does not provide sufficient time for thinking before conveying the message.

2. Mechanical Devices :

Mechanical devices which are commonly used for oral communication are listed below:

(1) Telephones

The services of telephone are superior to telegram in respect of direct and detailed talk. Moreover, telephonic messages reach quickly. In telegrams, words have to be shortened, because charges are according to the number of words. Telephone conversation is of two kinds, internal and external. By means of internal telephone (intercom) the persons, who are in the same office building can talk to each other on telephone. By means of external telephone one can talk with outsiders, who have their own telephones and have subscribed to the Post and Telegraphs Department.

Direct exchange is a system where direct contact through phone is possible, especially in the same city. But for different cities one has to contact the telephone operator for the connection of the desired number. But at present Subscriber Trunk Dialing (STD) is available for all trunk calls. Under the STD, a telephone subscriber may dial any number directly, without reference to the local exchange, in another town or city connected under the STD service. Caller must first dial the Code Number of the area, before connecting the desired number.

Direct exchange line may be with extensions. When the business grows; extension may be necessary. The extension is given not from the exchange but from the existing telephone. A device is attached to the telephone by which direct contact from the telephone exchange can be had. When a call is received, it is attended to by the office superintendent, and if the caller wishes to talk with the executive, the superintendent presses a button on the "extension" device and thus passes on the call to the executive and the caller talks directly with the executive.

One of the key factors which sustain the pace of modern life style is telecommunications. It plays a very vital role in the commercial, industrial and economic activities of mankind and has helped to shrink the world into a global village. Past couple of decades have witnessed breathtaking progress marking the rapid developments in the field of telecommunications. Exchange of information, data of facts and figures including live pictures from one part of the world to any other part of earth is now routinely possible.

The early half of this century witnessed a spectacular growth of wireless communication. Wireless telegraphy and wireless telephone linked nations and continents. Ships and aeroplanes could communicate to their bases and between themselves with ease using wireless. Telecommunication became an integral part of military operations. Regular broadcast of news and features over radio became so common that it became part of modern life. This was supplemented by television in which live images could be telecast to a large number of individual viewers.

In cities, towns and other centres of population, the telephones in the individual houses, offices and other places are interconnected by overhead lines and or underground multicore cables through a central exchange which provides the switching between the various instruments automatically or manually. The cities themselves are linked by trunk telephone lines. Coaxial cables and microwave links are usually employed for this purpose as these arrangements have the added advantage that they can provide a large number of channels, so that a number of two-way telephone conversations can take place simultaneously. Such communication links can also provide telex facilities in which electric teletypewriters may be interconnected to transmit and receive printed messages. In a facsimile process, printed images on a whole page can be transferred faithfully from one place to another using fax machine.

VSAT (Very Small Aperture Terminal) service provides satellite-based network for business communication, using the cost-effective VSAT technology. All it does is to link head office of a company or a corporate house to its various locations like factories, service units and other offices, particularly those located in remote areas, using the satellite.

Telephone connections may be divided into the following categories :

(A) PRIVATE BRANCH EXCHANGE (PBX) SYSTEM

Under this system, various departments or sections can talk directly with each other. But there is no connection with the central telephone exchange. Now to over come this difficulty, the internal lines are connected with the main lines. Thus, the user is at ease to talk with the outsiders or with the other departments through PBX. There will be an operator to do this job. PBX consists of a switch board connected to the public exchanges. The operator can connect the calls to any one of the exchanges.

(B) PRIVATE AUTOMATIC BRANCH EXCHANGE (PABX)

This system is an improvement over the PBX system, mentioned above. The system is again installed with the help of the Posts and Telegraphs Department. The equipment is rented out by the department. The number of telephone connections for inter-communication would, on the one hand depend upon the equipment made available by the Posts and Telegraphs Department and, on the other, the needs of the organisation. Under this system, the need for the internal exchange is eliminated. The internal communication is possible by dialing the relevant internal phone number. The external communication is routed through the operator. However, it is also possible to have a completely private automatic branch exchange in which external telephone numbers can be obtained by first dialing a code number. This reduces the work of the operator.

(C) PRIVATE EXCHANGE SYSTEM

Such a system is available in foreign countries and to a limited extent in our country, in which 10 to 600 lines are available for inter-communication. Such a system is automatic internal exchange system in which the caller can get the desired number by just dialing the number. This system is ideal for a large organisation.

(D) INTER COMMUNICATION SYSTEM (Intercom)

This is also known as intercom. This system has become very popular in India. This system can provide quick verbal communication. In an organisation, various individuals or departments can be equipped with the speaking-talking unit, upto a maximum of 40 lines. By turning the switch or pushing the button, instant connection is obtained with anyone on the circuit and clear conversation can be done.

Intercom system offers the following advantages:

1. It can be installed as and when it is needed.

2. It has low running cost.

3. It cuts down inter-office visiting.

4. It needs no sanction of the Posts and Telegraph Department.

Computerised Intercom, popularity known as 'Intellicom, works like an intercom but thinks like a computer.

(E) RADIO TELEPHONE

Radio Telephones are now increasingly used in our country in metropolitan cities to send and receive oral messages. Some select spots and moving vehicles have wireless sets with the government allotted frequencies. The messages are passed either way. That is, from the "head quarter" to the specific vehicle and back. Radio telephones are used by the police force. In the West radio telephones are also used for business purposes.

(F) HOUSE TELEPHONE SYSTEM

This system is the same as the intercom system. Under this system, the executive and subordinates have direct access to each other. Besides, an executive may have direct and simultaneous connection with one or more points. This innovation allows a person to speak to many people at the same time as if he is in a conference. This system does not require switchboard, and the desired numbers are obtained by pressing buttons or operating keys.

2. STAFF LOCATION SYSTEM

This is a simple device. This is used to call a person with the help of call-bell, light, buzzer etc. A signal is given by the caller, indicating that a certain person is needed. The communication takes place after the arrival of the required person. It does not convey message.

3. SPEAKING TUBE

It is a device consisting of tubes, connected in different rooms. The caller can talk to other persons through the tubes. But a better method— telephone—has superseded the tubes as the tubes, beyond a limited distance will not serve any purpose.

4. DICTAPHONE

A dictaphone is a machine which is used by the executives for giving dictation to stenos. Sometimes it is also used to send messages. If an executive required to leave some message or instruction for his subordinate who is not available, he may dictate the message to the machine which records the message on the tape. The tape can be later played on by the person concerned to receive the message. They are in essence like tape-recorders.

5. ELECTRIC PAGING SYSTEM

This system provides another method of inter communication. In big organisations, like departmental stores, super bazars, insurance companies, manufacturing plants etc., the executives sometimes go around from one section to another. When some urgent matter arises it is difficult to find out the executive by telephone device. In order to overcome this problem electric paging system has been developed, which operates through telephone switchboard. Under this system each executive is allotted a number and each number sounds differently. The switchboard operator will make the electric connections for the number of the executive and as soon as he hears the sound of his number, he will call the switchboard operator from the nearest telephone and receive the message.

WRITTEN COMMUNICATION

We cannot think of any organisation functioning without its presence. As the name implies written communication is transmitted by written words. It can take the form of letters, notices, circulars, reports, memos etc. As against oral communication, written communication offer a number of advantages which are summarised below:

(A) Advantages of Written Communication

    (*i*) Written messages are accurate and exact.

    (*ii*) It carries greater weight than oral messages.

    (*iii*) It serves as a permanent reference for future.

    (*iv*) It is ideal way of sending lengthy messages.

    (*v*) It is a legal evidence in case of disputes.

    (*vi*) It has the widest possible coverage.

    (*vii*) It is often less expensive than other media.

    (*viii*) It is suited to convey messages to a large number of persons at one and the same time.

    (*ix*) It tends to be complete, clear, precise and correct.

    (*x*) It is good to send unpleasant messages.

Types of Written Communication

Written communication may be sent by a messenger or by a mechanical device :

(A) Messenger Service

Messenger service is very important for delivering important papers. The main duty of the messenger is to go from department to department and receive and deliver written messages to and from various departments. He keeps generally two bags - one for incoming and the other for outgoing papers. Messenger service is also used for sending papers to outsiders. Messenger service is very popular in commercial banks.

(B) Internal Mail Service

This is an improvement over the above system. Under this system the messenger boy or the peon collects the necessary documents, messages etc. from specified desks or departments and takes them to their destinations at specified regular intervals. Under the method "in" trays and "out" trays are provided. The papers for attention are put into the "in" tray and once they have been disposed of they are put into "out" tray from where they are picked up for further transmission to their destinations. This system operates on the lines of postal mail service.

MECHANICAL DEVICES

Although use of mechanical devices for internal communication within the same premises has not gained much importance in our country, yet they are being increasingly used to link various branches of an organisation. Some of the more important devices are discussed below:

1. Pneumatic Tubes

Pneumatic tubes are easy to instal and no special skill is required to operate them. These tubes carry papers quickly and accurately to their destination. Under this system, a cylindrical pipe connects the various offices by means of which cylinders containing papers and documents are conveyed by suction from one department to another. These can be pre-set to deliver their contents at a certain stage as required. Such systems are in great use when a messenger service is difficult to maintain and when space is limited for human messengers to move from department to department. However, this system is not popular in this country.

2. Conveyors

The conventional conveyors used for light weight goods, may be used for carrying papers and documents. The conveyors are mostly suited to convey papers and messages when the volume of work is large and fairly constant and where stations remain fixed. Under this system the multi-channel conveyors are used to transport papers between work stations along its route. The papers travel continuously in an upright position between two stationery vertical guides that are moved by a motor driven belt beneath them. There are many types of conveyors, for examples, Sandwich Belt Conveyors, Roller Conveyors, Wires Conveyors, Vertical Lift Conveyors etc.

3. Chutes

Chutes are wide channels or pipes, made of metal or wood, which run from a higher level to the lower level in a sloping fashion. In many parts of the West, they are used to drop mail or laundry. Thus papers in an office can be dropped in large bundles from a higher floor to a lower floor.

4. Lifts

When papers, folders, documents or registers etc. have to be transmitted continuously between two or more floors, a small lift may be installed. The lift may be operated eletrically or hydraulically. Such lifts are used in libraries, hotels, hospitals etc.

Electronic devices for Written Communication

Advancement in science has its offsets on the methods of communication used in the office. Electronic innovations have revolutioned the means of affecting communication. Some rare or completely unknown electronic devices brought a complete change in the means of internal and external communication. While telephone remains the most important of all links in the chain of communication, other devices have tried to play an equally important role. Some electronic devices used in modern office are discussed below:

1. Teleprinter

Teleprinter or telax is used for conveying messages from one place to another where teleprinters have been installed at both the ends. It consists of two types of equipment key board transmitter and receiver for printing the message. Any message which is typed on the type-writer key board from one centre will be simultaneously typed at the receiving centre by an automatic process. Teleprinters are most commonly used by newspaper offices, stock-brokers and commercial banks. A teleprinter may be hired from the Posts and Telegraph Department which provides the telex service. Every telex subscriber is allotted a number. The subscriber can transmit the message to any other subscriber through the central teleprinter exchange. Teleprinters are very much useful where it is required to transmit information quickly and accurately.

2. Telewriter (Tele-autograph)

This is called the electronic long-hand transmission. Under this method hand written messages are received almost simultaneously as they are written electronically. A metal plate is attached to the machine and the message is written on it and is received on the other end.

3. Telefax

This is a machine used for transmitting sketches or drawings. The chart or diagram is first drawn or sketched on a paper. This is wrapped round a cylinder in the machine which, upon switching, transmits the facsimile to the machine at the other end where it is reproduced simultaneously.

4. Television

Television is used in offices to transmit messages. The television equipment consists of a TV camera, a power unit and one or more master viewers. The television camera is focussed on the necessary records, statistical tables, important documents etc., which are to be seen or inspected. The image of these is received on the television screen placed at the receiving end. Modern bank offices can use this device for inspecting and verifying specimen signatures, documents and deeds with considerable saving in time.

5. Videophone System

A videophone enables the caller to see as well as hear the party at the other end. When the caller lifts the videophone his image appears simultaneously on one half of his screen and on one half of that of the party he has called. When the other party answers, his image appears on the remaining halves of the two screens.

Choice of Means of Internal Communication:

Internal communication should be such which maximises efficiency at minimum cost and optimum speed. In order to achieve these objectives, the communication system must have the following characteristics:

(i) Clarity is a fundamental necessity in case of communication. The system should allow clear communication.

(ii) The system should be simple to operate and need not require elaborate set up.

(iii) The communication system should be cheap to instal and to run.

(iv) It is desired that the communication must attract the full attention of the receiver immediately   on its receipt.

(v) The means of communication must also ensure safety of the message to be sent.

(vi) The system chosen for communication should be economical.

(vii) There must be speed in transmission of messages.

EXTERNAL COMMUNICATION

Communication with outsiders is known as external communication. It is essential to establish link with customers, suppliers, Government departments, financial institutions, general public etc. External communication is very vital to the existence of all types of organisations, whether small or big.

Methods of External Communication

There are two broad categories of external communication - oral communication and written communication as it is in the case of internal communication.

(A) Oral Communication

(i) Face-to-Face meet (Personal visit)

(ii) Telephones

Both these have already been discussed under Internal communication.

(B) Written External Communication

Following methods are generally used for written external communication:

(b) Postal services

A major portion of the communication is being done through the postal department. Almost all the firms usually take advantage of the service rendered by the postal department. Written communication by post is convenient, easy and clear to understand.

Letters, printed forms, post cards, etc., can be sent. If the transactions are of the general type, printed form is sufficient. If the matter is important, letter in cover may be sent in order to preserve the secrecy and goodwill of the sender (firms). The post cards or printed forms will not always create a goodwill and good impression on the recipient.

Evidence of the letters sent can also be obtained by sending the letters "Under certificate of posting", by "Recorded delivery", by "Registered post" by "Registered with A.D.", etc. Registered letters with A.D. (Acknowledgement due) sent by the sender will get an acknowledgement from the recipient through post. This is a proof that the recipient has received the particular communication. When one wants to send valuable letters or documents, through post they can be sent by registered and insured. The charges of insurance are according to the value of documents, for which insurance is effected. Proper care is being given towards such registered and insured items by the postal department. If such post has been lost in the transit then damage to the amount of insurance can be claimed from the postal authorities.

Services Rendered:

1. Post Office collects, carries and delivers the communication (letters, parcels, etc.)
2. It undertakes quick delivery of message.
3. Sellers can sell through the post office and can collect the price from customers. (V.P.P.)
4. One can remit money to any place, within India.
5. It renders the cheapest communication service.
6. For registration, insured letters and parcels, etc., the post office takes responsibility to make delivery to the right person.
7. Telephonic and telegraphic communications are of great advantage in urgent situations.
8. It works as an agent for the government.

The following services may be utilised by business offices :

(a) Letters

A post card is not called a letter. Letter means an envelope containing message. For a letter not exceeding 20 grams in weight, a stamp worth Rs. 5 has to be affixed and every additional 20 grams or fraction there of requires stamp worth Rs. 5. If letters are unstamped or insufficiently stamped the addressee has to remit to the postman double the deficiency, (minimum Rs.l)

(b) Inland letter card

An inland letter costs Rs. 2.50. Separate stationery is not required to write the message. The space is also three times as that of a post card. No enclosures are allowed.

(c) Post Card

A post card costs only 50 paise. If not stamped, it will be taxed Rupee one. The half of one side is meant for writing the address and for fixing stamps. Reply paid post card can also be purchased by paying Rupee one. In such a case, the blank post card (annexed part) will be utilised by the addressee for sending a reply.

(d) Printed Post Cards

If the communication in a post card is printed, it is a printed post card and postage payable on it is Rs. 6. The same is the case if the communication is impressed by rubber stamp. Competition post card needs stamp worth Rs. 10.

(e) Certificate of Posting

The post office on payment of small charge issues a certificate of posting as a token of a letter have been posted. For this purpose, there is a printed form, free of cost, which should be filled in and presented at the counter after fixing stamps to the value of Rs. 2 along with the letters or parcels. The fee of Rs. 2 is meant for three articles or less in number. The post office will put a seal on the stamp, thus certifying that the letter or the documents have been posted. In case of disputes, in a court of law, the certificate of posting is an evidence, in the hands of the writer.

(f) Value Payable Post (VPP)

Under this system, business people can recover the cost of articles sent to the customers through the agency of the post office. There is a form for this purpose. One has to fill in the form and hand it over to the post office along with the articles. In the form the sender must specify the sum to be remitted to himself. This system has a drawback that the buyer cannot inspect the articles, unless he pays off.

(g) Money Order (MO)

Remittance of funds can be made through the post office by means of money orders. The remitter (sender) has to fill in the money order form and present it at the post office counter along with the amount. There is a fixed rate of commission for sending money orders. The remitter also gets an acknowledgement from the payee through the post office. Maximum value of money order is Rs. 5,000. The rate of commission is Rs. one for every sum of Rs. 20 or fraction thereof.

(h) Telegraphic Money Order (TMO)

Money order can also be sent by a telegraph. System is similar to that of ordinary money orders. The telegram charges are also to be added to the commission. It is costly but the payee will get the money quickly.

(i) Indian Postal Orders

Indian postal order provides a convenient means of transmitting small sums of money by post. It is sold by the post office to the public and is encashable in any post office within India, at the option of the purchaser. It is available in different denominations, starting from Rs.10 to 100, i.e. Rs. 10, Rs. 20, Rs. 30, Rs. 40, Rs. 50, Rs. 100. The commission chargeable is:

Postal orders of Rs. 10	-	Rs. 1
Postal orders of Rs. 20	-	Rs. 2
Postal orders of Rs. 30	-	Rs. 3
Postal orders of Rs. 40	-	Rs. 4

Postal orders of Rs. 50   -   Rs. 5
Postal orders of Rs. 100   -   Rs. 10

(j) Registration

Articles can be sent to the addressee by registered post by paying a registration fee of Rs. 17. By registration, the articles will be delivered more securely. The post office has limited responsibility over the articles. When any letter is registered with acknowledgement form, the sender gets an acknowledgement signed by the addressee, by paying an additional charge of Rs. 3. It is called "Registered with A.D."

(k) Insured Post

Valuable articles - documents, cheques, demand drafts, may be sent through post office under an insured cover. Here, the post office acts as insurer and is liable for any loss or damage to the article in the course of transit, upto the value for which it was insured.

(l) Post Restante

Representatives, travellers, who are not sure of their exact addresses in a town, may receive letters addressed to the care of the postmaster of the town, and this system is called post restante. Such letters will be retained with the postmaster for a period of one month.

(m) Returned Letter Office (RLO)

Articles or letters which cannot be delivered because of wrong or, illegible addressees are opened in the Returned Letter Office. An attempt will be made to find out the addressee. If not, it will be returned to the sender. If it is also impossible, then such letters will be destroyed, after a prescribed time limit.

TELEGRAPHIC SERVICES

Telegram is a method of fast transmission of written messages. When the message is to be conveyed quickly and urgently, it can be sent by telegram. By sending a telegram, the full attention of the recipient is drawn and thereby quick action is achieved. Telegram may be written in plain language or in prescribed code of words or in combination of both. Most of the business firms, which are in the receipt of telegrams regularly, may have "telegraphic address". The telegraphic address is a code word instead of the name of the company. Instead of writing the full address in the telegram, if telegraphic address is there, the code word with the name of the place is enough. When a telegram is received, the postman by looking up the code can find out the name of the company. Telegraphic address, reduced into a code word, reduces the cost of a telegram.

Demerits

1. It is expensive.
2. Secrecy cannot be maintained.
3. Words and figures may be mutilated.
4. Detailed information cannot be sent because of high cost.

The following types of telegraphic services are available in our country :

(i) Ordinary telegram : The post office will accept the telegrams and make delivery of them during office hours; from 8.00 a.m. to 9.00 p.m. The minimum charge is Rs. 3.50 for minimum 10 words and each additional word costs Rs. 0.50.

(ii) Express telegram : The rate for the telegram is double the rate of ordinary telegrams. Such type of telegrams are delivered at the other end, when the message is received. During night time also such telegrams are delivered to the addressees.

(*iii*) **Local telegram** : This type is sent and received in the same city. The cost is the same as that for an ordinary telegram.

(*iv*) **Greeting telegram** : These are in the nature of greeting messages or congratulatory messages. Generally such greetings have code numbers. One who wants to send out such a telegram selects the phrase and writes the appropriate code number on the telegraphic form. When the form is filled in with the address of the addressees and the code number, the post office transmits it to the other end (place where the addressee lives) and the message receiving post office writes the full phrase and hands it over to the addressee. Since code number is there, the system is cheaper.

(*v*) **Phonogram** : When the sender and the receiver have telephones, the sender by calling out the operator working at the telegraph department conveys the message to him, and the operator in his turn, sends the telegram. At the other end, when the telegram is received, the telegraph department calling the particular phone number conveys the message. Thus the sender need not send anyone to the telegraph office in order to send the telegrams and at the same time the addressee also gets the message immediately on the phone. Later on the telegram is also received by the addressee on requisition by paying a prescribed fee. Thus a lot of time can be saved by both the parties. The sender's account is debited with the cost of telegram which will be paid along with the telephone bill.

(*vi*) **Reply-paid telegram** : When the sender desires to pay in advance, for the reply from the receiver of the telegram, a prepayment should be made at the post office, for a minimum of words; *i.e.*, rupees three. If the number of words in the reply is more than those for which the charges were remitted by the sender, the receiver has to remit the excess amount.

MODERN COMMUNICATION DEVICES

E-mail (Electronic Mail)

E-mail involves sending messages *via* telecommunication links. If two computer terminals, however distant from each other, are connected on network, it is possible to send messages from one to the other. The message is typed on a computer screen at one end, and is conveyed to the other end through electric impulses. The person operating the computer terminal at the receiving end is alerted by a signal that a message or mail, meant for him is in the electronic mailbox or he can occasionally see his mailbox to check for any incoming mail. Then he can get it flashed on to a screen immediately or keep it stored and attend to it at leisure.

If the computers have fax, telephone or telex facilities attached to them, E-mail can be used even to transmit telephonic messages or to fax important documents. To be able to use E-mail all that one needs is an access to a network area, a PC, a telephone, a moderm with its software and the basic knowledge of using this software, which is easy to acquire. One does not have to be a computer expert to be able to use E-mail nor does one need a separate telephone line for it.

Advantages of E-mail

1. It is the quickest means of transmitting messages.
2. It saves you from telephone tags.
3. E-mail messages are supposed to be highly secure and secret.
4. E-mail can be sent to a large number of people simultaneously.

Internet

The internet may be defined as a global collection of people computers linked together by telephone lines, radio links or satellite links. It has been introduced in India quite recently but being extremely versatile and fast its popularity increasing day by day.

Internet is a network of computers worldwide which allows its users to share information. Apart from the E-mail service of the internet, with which most people are familiar, the World Wide Web (WWW) is the latest vehicle of business now available on the internet. It is a medium in which one can represent his business, products and services to the huge and quickly increasing base of internet users all over the world.

Over millions of companies have turned to the internet as powerful yet inexpensive way to promote their companies, products and services. When an organisation links to the internet, people can reach it anytime of day or night. Potential customers can get your products information with colour photographs, leave queries or place orders. Current customers can use internet for product support to provide valuable feedback about new products.

Cellular Phone

The cellular phone or mobile phone is one of the most convenient developments of the late twentieth century. One can now make a phone call and be called almost wherever one likes and whenever one likes. It is probably the most important telecommunication break-through in recent times. Today one need never be out of touch with one's business, family or friends. Cellular phone is free from the cord which normally connects a phone to the wall, so one can move about as one pleases. Cellular phones give all the benefits of an ordinary fixed phone, but with extra flexibility, mobility, security and whole range of new services, with cellular phone, one can call anywhere and can be reached from any telephone in the world. The cellular telephone network is divided into cells, each one controlled by a radio base station. This base station transmits and receive radio signals to a centrally located mobile switching centre. This is designed on the most advanced and the most popular digital system.

Pager

Paging started a bit late in India. In India, paging and cellular services started almost at the same time. Paging is the quickest way to communicate today. Paging is a one-way wireless communication facility by which one can stay in touch with anyone - clients, office or family, when one is on the move. If someone needs to contact a subscriber urgently, all that he has to do is pick up the phone and dial the pager number of the subscriber to leave a message. The message, is instantly transmitted to the subscriber on his pager, wherever he is. Giving the subscriber instant access to the information he needs.

REVISED POSTAL TARIFF-AS ON 01-06-2002

Sl. no.	Postal Service	Item	Revised Tariff
1.	Post Cards	For a Single Post Card	0.50
		For a Reply Post Card	1.00
		For a Competition Post Card	10.00
		For a Printed Post Card	6.00
2.	Letter Cards	For an Inland Letter Card	2.50

3.	Letters	For a weight not exceeding 20 gms.	5.00
		For every additional 20 gms of fraction thereof	5.00
4.	Book, Pattern & Sample Packets	For the first 50 gms or fraction thereof	4.00
		For every additional 50 gms or fraction thereof	3.00
5.	Registered News Papers	In the case of single copy of RNP for a weight not exceeding 50 gms.	25 paise
		For a weight exceeding 50 gms but not exceeding 100 gms.	50 paise
		In the case of more than one copy of the same issue of a RNP being carried in the same packet For weight exceeding 100 gms	50 paise
		For every additional 100 gms or fraction there of of exceeding 100 gms provided that such packet shall not be delivered at any addressees residence but shall be given to a recognised agent at PO	20 paise
6.	Books Packets containing Printed Books	For the first 100 gms or fraction thereof	1.00
		For every additional 100 gms or fraction there of	1.00
7.	Book packets containing Periodicals	For the first 100 gms or fraction thereof	2.00
		For every additional 100 gms or fraction there of	3.00
8.	Parcels	For the first 500 gms or fraction thereof	16.00
		For every additional 500 gms or fraction thereof	15.00
9.	Registration	Fee for registration	17.00
10.	Concessional registration fee for Printed Books	Concessional fee for registration of VP packet containing printed book, the value of which does not exceed Rs. 50/-	2.50
11.	Acknowledgement	For an acknowledgment	3.00
12.	Insurance	Where the value of insurance does not exceed Rs. 200	10.00
13.	Money Order Form	For a Money order form	0.25
14.	Money Order	For every Rs. 20/- or part thereof	1.00
15.	Value Payable Post	For a value not exceeding Rs. 20/-	2.00
		For a value exceeding Rs. 20/- but not exceeding Rs. 50/-	3.00
		For a value exceeding Rs. 50/-	

QUESTIONS

1. "Inter-office communication is an important item in office organisation." What methods of inter-office communication are available in a modern office ?
                                                                                   (*B. Com., Delhi*)

2. What are the merits and demerits of oral communication ?

3. Discuss the mechanical devices used for office communication ?

4. Define internal communication.   (*B.A., Chennai*)

5. "Communication is a very important function of any business." Discuss the characteristics of a good system of internal communication. (*B. Com., Delhi, ICWA*)

6. Describe briefly the different types of communication services in a modern commercial firm.   (*B. Com., Madurai*)

7. Discuss the different methods of communication. Suggest measures to remove barriers to communication.   (*B. Com., Madurai, Bharathiar*)

8. Describe the services rendered by the Posts and Telegraph office to the business community.   (*ICWA*)

9. What do you understand by "Communication". What factors you would keep in mind while choosing the various media of communication for a modern.
                                                                       (*C.S., B.Com., Punjab*)

10. Explain the significance of inter-communication facilitates in a large business office. What are the different methods and mechanical devices being used in an organisation.
                                                                                         (*CS*)

11. What do you understand by inter-communication system ? Make out a case for its introduction in a modern office.   (*B.Com., Punjab*)

12. What are the characteristics of a good system of internal communication ?
                                                                                (*B.A,. Chennai*)

13. Explain the significance of inter-communication facilities in a large business office. What are the different methods of mechanical devices used for oral communication.
                                                                                    (*B.Com., MS*)

14. Mention atleast four oral communication services and explain.   (*B. Com., MS*)

15. Explain the use of the Teleprinter and Telex services in a modern office.
                                                                             (*B.Com. Madurai*)

CHAPTER

Personnel Management

INTRODUCTION

The human being as a basic factor of office management is an important element. The management of human beings is known as personnel management. There is a systematic way of organising the workers and it must aim that the workers must feel part and parcel of the organisation. As such they work to get maximum efficiency for themselves as well as for the employer. In order to achieve this, team spirit will be created in the minds of the workers. The success or failure of an organisation does not depend upon the equipments, machines and other materials, but on the will, pleasure and ability of the personnel working there. There is a task before the management to get the work done through the personnel, and therefore team spirit or co-operation will be created amongst the workers for efficient performance, and similarly a spirit of healthy competition among the workers must also be created. This will increase the production. By creating such a competition, both the workers and the employer are benefited. Personnel management does not aim at sucking the blood of the workers, but attempts to provide utilities for a common purpose, the well-being of the workers and the employer.

The scientific management aims that every selected employee works for the organisation, in the capacity for which he is selected, or finds a place where he can be put to work on the basis of his ability, for which he is best suited. This can be done through standardisation of personnel, which signifies the application of the methods of standardisation, solving problems of selecting, employing, training, managing, etc., of the personnel. When the workers are selected and employed according to some fixed system–standardisation of personnel–they naturally work to give their best effort to the management of the concern.

A few definitions of Personnel Management are given below :

1. "Personnel Management is that field of management which has to do with planning, organising and controlling various operative functions of procuring, developing, maintaining and utilising a labour force in such a way that the (a) objectives for which the company is established are attained economically and effectively; (b) objectives of all levels of personnel are served to the highest possible degree; and (c) objectives of the community are duly considered and served."*Prof. Michael Jucius*

2. "Personnel function is concerned with the procurement, development, compensation, integration and maintenance of the personnel of an organisation for the purpose of contributing towards accomplishment of the organisation's major goals of objectives. Therefore, personnel management is the planning, organising, directing and controlling of the performance of those operative functions."

Edwin B Flippe

3. "Personnel Administration is a code of the ways of organising and treating individuals at work, so that they will get the greatest possible realization of their intrinsic abilities, thus attaining maximum efficiency for themselves and their group, and thereby giving to the enterprise, of which they are a part, its determining competitive advantage and its optimum result."   *Thomas G Spates.*

4. "Personnel management may be conveniently described as that part of the management process which is primarily concerned with the human constituents of an organisation. Its object is the maintenance of human relationship on a basis which, by a consideration of the well being of the individual, enables all those engaged in the undertaking to make their maximum personal contribution to the effective working of that undertaking.   *EFL Brech*

5. "Personnel management is partly applied psychology, partly custom, partly law and partly science. It is an art, which often requires rule-of thumb methods to be developed on the spot, according to the requirements of the situation. It calls for a knowledge of the work, and the people who do the work.   *J.C. Denyer*

Personnel management is the chief function of the company management. It aims at making the workers render their best services to the firm. In all the fields of business activities, the superiors look the sub-ordinates for good results. Machines can be managed very easily; but human beings cannot be. It is difficult to manage them satisfactorily. This is the task before the personnel manager. Personnel manager is different, from the office manager, the latter improves the office efficiency, while the former maintains the quality of personnel relationship in all the groups, to say, the whole organisation.

Personnel management is that aspect of management process which deals with the development, application and evaluation of policies, procedures and programmes relating to the individuals in an organisation to optimise their contribution towards and realisation of organisational objectives. The aim of personnel management is to make the best possible use of personnel factor in the organisation. Office is the brain of the organisation. Its efficiency is dependent upon the manpower which runs it.

OBJECTIVES OF PERSONNEL MANAGEMENT

Personnel management aims at getting the 'best' out of the people by winning and maintaining their wholehearted collaboration. It is an important branch of the management of any business enterprise. The aims and objectives of Personnel management are :

1. To ensure that the organisation gets the right type of people, in right quantity, at right time and place.
2. To optimize the utilization of the organisation's manpower.
3. To create and maintain an organisational climate conducive to the development of the people.
4. To establish desirable working relationship among the members of the organisation; and
5. To maintain a high morale by ensuring the development of highly effective work group.

FUNCTIONS OF PERSONNEL MANAGEMENT

The functions of personnel management may be classified into two categories :
(A) Management Functions.
(B) Operative Functions

(A) Management Functions

Management functions of the personnel department may be as under :

(*i*) **Planning** : Planning is a fundamental function of personnel management. It involves deciding in advance what is to be done, where, how and by whom it is to be done. While planning, an office manager projects a course of action for the future aimed at achieving desired results for the organisation as a whole and each department within it. Thus merely ascertaining the future is not planning till it is followed by making provision for it. Planning then is just a rational approach to the future.

(*ii*) **Organisation** : It is used in the sense of an enterprise or a business unit. As a matter of fact, it is referred to as the social system encompassing all formal relations and yet another useful way of looking at organisation is to consider it as an essential function of personnel management. In operational sense, organisation may be considered as consisting of division of work among people and co-ordination of their activities towards some objectives.

(*iii*) **Directing** : It is the managerial function consisting of all those activities which are concerned directly with guiding, influencing and supervising the subordinates in their jobs. It is thus performance oriented. Some elements of the directing function of personnel management are :

   (*a*) Supervising the work of subordinates to ensure that their performance conforms to plan.
   (*b*) Maintaining discipline and rewarding effective performance.
   (*e*) Issuing orders and instructions.
   (*d*) Motivating the subordinates to direct their behaviour in a desired pattern.

(*iv*) **Controlling** : Controlling as a function of management means the measurement and correction of performance of activities of subordinates in order to make sure that enterprise objectives and plans devised to attain them are accomplished. Control thus consists in knowing the extent to which actions are in conformity with plans adopted and instructions issued so that errors and deviations are reported and appropriate corrective actions taken. Remedial action may result in alteration of plans, change in the organisation structure and modification in the staffing process.

(B) Operative Functions

Operative function may be discussed as under :

(i) **Procurement :** *It is concerned with the obtaining of the proper kind and number of personnel necessary to accomplish necessary organisation goals.* The function is related to subjects like the determination of manpower requirements and their recruitment, selection and placement. The manpower requirements are calculated in terms and numbers of personnel needed and their quality. Selection and placement cover different activities designed to screen and hire personnel, such as, application forms, psychological tests, interviews and induction.

(ii) **Development :** After the personnel have been obtained, it is necessary to develop them. *Development implies the increase of skill, through training, that is necessary for proper job performance.* This aspect of personnel function has acquired great importance even in our country during the last quarter of a century or so due to greater use of technology in every department of a business enterprise. Development function will be influenced by numerous factors, like induction of new machines, promotions and transfers.

(iii) **Compensation :** *This function can be defined as the adequate and equitable remuneration of personnel for their contributions to organisation objectives.* In developed countries, compensation cannot be described as a great motivating force as strong as it is in less developed countries. Compensating remains one of the basic functions of personnel management. A proper wage system takes into consideration a number of factors and subjects like job evaluation, wage policies, wage systems and wage incentive schemes.

(iv) **Integration :** *It can be defined as an attempt to effect a reasonable reconciliation of individual and organisational interests.* Integration must follow the above three functions of procurement, development and compensation. The function of integration relates to problems of communication, informal organisation and trade unions.

(v) **Maintenance :** *Maintenance refers to sustaining and improving the conditions that have been established.* This would thus include the above functions. However, it must be pointed out that it would be necessary to take care of physical well-being and mental well-being of the employees. In order to accomplish this objective, it would be desirable that research must continue in every direction so that the function of maintenance is performed properly.

°IMPORTANCE OF PERSONNEL MANAGEMENT

The importance of personnel management has been increasing day-to-day because it (Personnel management) is concerned with the procurement, development, compensation, integration and maintenance of the personnel of the organisation towards the accomplishment of its major goals. In fact, it has become a major part of every office manager's job. An office manager is always dealing with people. He can take decisions and implement them only with the help of the people working with him. It is, therefore, rightly said that the success or failure of an organisation depends not on materials, machines and equipment but on the 'will' and ability of the personnel to put in their best efforts for an efficient performance of their job. The main objective of personnel management is the accomplishment of the goals of the enterprise. According to the Indian Institute of Personnel Management, "Personnel management aims to achieve both efficiency and justice, neither of which can be pursued successfully without the other. It seeks to bring together and develop into an effective organisation, the men and women who make up an enterprise, enabling each to make his own best contribution to its success both as an individual and as a member of a working group. It seeks to provide fair terms and conditions of employment and satisfying work for those employed."

Advantages of personnel department as a separate unit

1. The management of the concern is relieved of the functions of personnel officer, and it can devote more time to important works of the firm.
2. A good relationship is created between the management and the workers through the personnel officer.
3. Since a separate unit is there, all personnel problems are dealt with promptly and remedied, and thus strikes, lockouts, etc., are reduced.
4. A good public relation can be maintained through the personnel officer.
5. The personnel officer looks after the welfare of the workers and he helps to reduce accidents, sickness, etc., with the result that more production is possible.

Personnel Manager

In most modern enterprises personnel management is regarded as a specialised task and entrusted to a separate personnel department under the charge of a specialist known as Personnel Manager, who renders staff advice and service to other departments on personnel matters. Personnel managers have a great responsibility on shoulder in promoting the optimum utilization of the human resources by providing expert professional and competent advice to management in the areas of selection of employees' training and development, job evaluation, wage and salary administration, men-boss relations, human relations etc.

A personnel manager has an advisory position in an organisation. He is a staff officer who helps the line managers to carry out their responsibilities by providing good personnel. He gives advice to the line of officers and the workers when any problem arises. He possesses no right to make out policies. But he advises the line managers, and the decision rests with them. The chief executive of an organisation is helped by the personnel manager in formulating policies and decisions. He must try to win the co-operation of the line managers, employees etc. When any problem arises in relation to the personnel management, he must try to be a source of help to the employers and the workers in solving their problems. His main aim must be to mould the human resources into an effective organisation under desirable working conditions. He must encourage mutual confidence and goodwill between the workers and the employers, as among the individual workers.

Functions

1. To give advice to the personnel under an organisation.
2. To encourage the workers by redressing their grievances providing desirable working conditions, and create a team spirit. The management may be informed of actual happenings in order to draw up future plans and policies of personnel dealings.

3. To maintain various indices relating to production, absenteeism of workers, accidents, complaints, etc. The management should be informed of this so as to draw concrete future plans in the interest of the organisation.

4. To provide personnel services—recruitment and selection of proper workers, their training and to look after the personnel working in the organisation. He must also facilitate the line officers to carry out the work more efficiently through the workers.

5. To maintain a harmonious relationship within an organisation through promotions, right incentives to workers and thus to retain the interest and loyalty of the personnel.

All the personnel matters are dealt within the department of personnel, in consultation with the chief executive. In modern times, an organisation has a separate department, where staff advice and service are rendered. The department is headed by a specialist known as Personnel Manager.

The functions of personnel administration are:
1. Placing the right man on the right job.
2. Selecting new employees for the organisation.
3. Training men for jobs that are new to them.
4. Improving job performance of each man.
5. Gaining creative co-operation and development of smooth working relationships.
6. Interpreting the company policies and procedures.
7. Controlling labour costs.
8. Developing potential abilities of each man.
9. Creating and maintaining a high level of departmental morale.
10. Protecting health and physical condition of employees.

According to *Halsey* certain principles of sound personnel management useful in building good worker morale are as below:

1. Care and skill should be exercised in the selection of employees.
2. Introduction to the job should be friendly, skilful and adequate.
3. Each employee should be made to feel that his efforts are really appreciated.
4. Careful and thoughtful consideration should be given to the probable effect of each rule, each notice, and each practice on the feelings of all concerned.
5. Employees should have a part in planning these things which affect their working conditions, whenever it is practical to do so.
6. There should be a sense of security and reasonable freedom.
7. There should be a constant and intelligent effort on the part of management to be absolutely fair in every policy and every practice.
8. Each employee should have a feeling of pride in the worthwhileness of his work and his company.
9. The organisational set up should be such that there is no confusion in anyone's mind as to his duties or responsibilities.
10. Conditions should be such that working proves to be satisfying social experience as well as a means of making a livelihood.

PERSONNEL POLICIES

Personnel policies may be defined as "guides which chart the course of an organisation and govern its activities towards the achievement of the purpose for which it was set up." Policies are not the objectives; they are merely means to an end. Policies are formulated to achieve personnel and organisation objectives. It is very important that all the supervisors must know the established personnel policies in order to assure the uniform application and results.

It is the policy :

1. To pay all employees adequately for services rendered.
2. To maintain reasonable hours of work and safe working conditions.
3. To provide continuous employment consistent with business conditions.
4. To place employees in the kind of work best suited to their abilities.
5. To help each individual to progress in the company's service.
6. To aid employees in times of need.
7. To encourage thrift.
8. To co-operate in social, athletic and other recreational activities.
9. To accord to each employee the right to discuss freely with executives any matter concerning his welfare or the company's interest.
10. To carry on the daily work in a spirit of friendliness.

PERSONNEL DEPARTMENT

The scope of personnel department is very wide and the functions performed by this department include systematic recruitment and maintenance of labour force, employee compensation, job analysis, job description, employee training, keeping personnel records, controlling labour turnover, merit rating, personnel welfare, personnel promotions, personnel transfers, dealing with office unions, personnel research, personnel counselling, employee motivation etc. These will now discussed in detail in the following pages.

Aactivities of Personal Department
They are as follows :

RECRUITMENT OF PERSONNEL

The world of trade and industry is a world of competition and if a firm wants to survive, it must reduce the cost of production by employing fewer and efficient workers. An efficient worker will naturally help to increase the production. The right person should be selected for the right job. All qualities of human beings cannot be measured. Measurable qualities inherent in human beings can be tested, and their abilities as to the suitability to a specified work can also be decided. Before the recruitment of the workers, the personnel department must have detailed information regarding the description of the job for which selection is to be done. Faulty method of selection will affect production.

Recruitment of staff involves selection of the source from which staff is to be recruited, selecting the most suitable candidates through interviews and various forms of tests and the actual appointment of the staff through letters of appointment, service agreements, etc. But before taking steps for the recruitment of staff, the office manager must obtain accurate and detailed information regarding the contents of the jobs to enable him to determine what qualities and abilities to look for in the staff to be recruited. Thus it is important to understand the meaning of the term 'job' and other connected terms. Let us discuss these various aspects.

JOB GRADING

The system of job-grading is followed both in selecting the workers and at the promotional stages. In dealing with the selection of workers it is necessary to measure the relative values of different jobs. All types of jobs are paid according to their relative difficulties and the basic purpose of job evaluation. Job evaluation is a system of which each job is rated and its relative worth determined as per the procedure laid down. When recruitment is done, the requirement of the job is thoroughly considered—educational qualifications, special training, experience, etc., laid down for the smooth functioning of the job. Arrangement of job-grading is done from the simplest job to the highest job or vice-versa. Thus jobs are graded in the ascending or descending order. This is done along with job description. Job description gives detailed information pertaining to a job.

According to *Denyer*, "Job grading consists of a scientific study of all jobs and then the placing of these jobs into broad categories called job grades. It is fundamentally a technique of determining the differences between jobs and rationalising the rates of pay in large organisations."

Job grading is the classification and analysis of each type of job being performed in an organisation. As a matter of fact, job grading can be made in various manners, such as, skilled, semi-skilled, and unskilled or Grade A, Grade B and Grade C or Grade I, Grade II and Grade III etc.

Job grading is done after undertaking job analysis, job description and job specification for each job. It is done by studying the essential characteristics of each job. These characteristics are :

1. The experience required;
2. The skill needed;
3. The initiative required;
4. The level of responsibility entailed; and
5. The level of supervision needed for the job.

Advantages of Job Grading

1. Salary can be paid on the basis of graded job, which is proper and justifiable.
2. Able worker gets the chances of promotion. Ability rather than seniority is to be given consideration.
3. Improvement in the morale of the employees and good relationship between the management and the employees can be maintained.
4. The right man can be given the right job; right salary is paid and thus wage-disputes are avoided.
5. It increases output and improves the morale of employees.
6. It reduces labour turnover.
7. It is a valuable guidance in work simplification.

The institute of Office Management, London has suggested the following grading system for office work :

Grade A : Simple tasks allotted to be done under close supervision.

Grade B : Simple copying and making entries from original documents; tasks requiring the knowledge of a limited number of well-defined rules. Simple operations requiring manual dexterity. Measure of responsibility small, work mostly checked and closely supervised.

Grade C : Work of a routine character but where the responsibility is somewhat greater than grade B. Checking Grade B Work.

Grade D : Work calling for the exercise of some initiatives. Daily routine varying. Little supervision given.

Grade E : More important clerical work with a degree of control over the sequence of jobs or over the work of small groups of staff. Work demands special knowledge or involves individual responsibility without supervision.

Grade F : Supervision of sections and responsibility for the efficient execution of a complete division of the work. Regular contact with the management and administration. Work demanding knowledge of a special character for example, legal, accounting, engineering etc.

JOB DESCRIPTION

A job description is a written statement outlining the purpose and the Principal duties and responsibilities of a job. A specimen of job description is given below :

Post	:	Clerk (in mail department)
Age	:	18 to 25 years
Sex	:	Male or female
Qualifications	:	Matriculate, preferably graduate
Salary	:	Rs. 3,000-50-5,000 plus Rs. 1800 per month
Duties	:	Sorting out letters
		handling of mail opening machine,
		handling of the opened letters to the
		section-head, writing of addresses on the
		envelopes and minor clerical jobs
Responsibility	:	Punctuality in morning hours is essential.
		Honesty is required, (for cheques, drafts, etc., are received)
Personal	:	Pleasing habit, co-operative nature, accuracy, good appearance etc.
Experience	:	Not necessary
Promotion	:	If the worker proves worthy, he may be taken in the accounts department on a higher scale

In the words of *Bethel*, "The job description is a 'boiled down' statement of the job analysis and serves to indentify the job for consideration by other job analysts." That is, it is an abstract of information gained from the job analysis report. It describes the work performed, the responsibilities involved, the skill or training required, the conditions under which the job is done, and the type of the personnel required for the job.

SOURCES OF RECRUITMENT

Personnel officer will have to take decision as to the source from where workers can be recruited. There are many sources.

1. Advertisement

The post may be advertised in local or national newspapers which have enough circulation. Advertisement, can also be done in trade journals.

Sometimes blind type of advertisement is also done by giving box number, so as to keep the firm's name unknown to the applicants. This is done so, because recommendations can be avoided. The full information of the post must be given in the advertisement, so that the applicant may not have any doubt. Through advertisement the best candidate can be selected with advantage.

2. Employment Exchange

Government has set up a department to provide the required staff to any concern. The employment exchange will be informed of all the description of the job, so that they can send proper candidates for the job. Usually it sends local persons. In such a case a proper selection is not possible. The merit is that the post can be filled in very soon, without any expenditure for advertisement. Moreover, when most of the candidates are from local area, travelling expenses need not be paid.

3. Professional Organisation

Institute of Chartered Accountants, Institute of Cost and Works Accountants, Institute of Company Secretaries, etc., can be contacted in order to get trained and qualified candidates. They recommend the names of candidates along with full particulars to the needed firm. They always keep a register having such information. There is an advantage that a qualified accountant or secretary can be selected.

4. Colleges and Universities

Generally, Universities maintain a register of employment bureaux in order to help the students. A firm that has vacancies can inform such bodies in order to get information of suitable candidates. One has to inform the bureaux along with the description of jobs. This is the easiest way of filling vacancies. But the drawback is that a good selection is not possible.

5. Ex-employees, Job-seekers, Friends, etc.

Job-seekers may sometimes apply directly. Old employee of the concern can also suggest names of candidates to be selected. The vacancy can also be informed to the friends, who may suggest candidates.

6. Appliance Companies

Office appliance companies have trained persons to operate on new machines. Such companies may be informed of the vacancy so that trained candidates can be had. One can be selected out of the batch.

7. Circular Letters

It is also seen that sometimes the management writes circular letters or places the information on the notice board of the firm, inviting applications. Through the workers of the firm, the news goes out and they bring candidates to personnel department.

INTERVIEW

After advertisement of the posts, the firm may receive applications for the required post. Generally, a formal application is called for, in order to send out prescribed application forms duly printed, and this form has to be filled in by the candidate. By sending such prescribed forms, it is easy for the management to obtain the required information of the applicant.

When the firm has received many applications, scrutiny of the applications will be done in order to select proper and qualified applicants. When the applications are rejected, the applicants may be informed of the fact with regret. There must be a good system in selecting candidates.

For the selected applicants, interview may be conducted in order to assess the personality and the ability of the applicants.

The candidates will be informed of the time and date of interview. When the candidate comes for the interview, let a personal and friendly treatment be given. Questions should not be asked just to confuse the applicant. The interview may be done in a friendly and informal manner. He will be given a cordial welcome. There must be congenial atmosphere to enable the applicant to express himself freely. The interview will be carried out in a separate room with proper seating arrangement and without any external disturbances.

TEST

Occupational test can be conducted in the case of a typist, steno, accountant, etc. Such tests must be simple to conduct and easy to evaluate. The candidates may be informed of these tests in advance, so that they may come ready for the tests.

Quality-rating tests are conducted on the basis of the description of the job after grouping the applicants in different categories in relative degree of importance. The assessment of the qualities is rated in the form of grades through numbers or average, above average, poor etc.

A candidate is selected after interview and other tests. An appointment order will be issued and the candidate has to fill in certain service agreement. Where the post is of an important nature involving secret processes, technical process, serving for fixed period; etc., the service agreement must be, in writing in order to avoid dispute in future.

TRAINING

Training follows the recruitment of workers. A job may be simplest one, but guidance is necessary in order to have efficiency in the work. That is, in all types of posts, a little training is essential, to instruct as to how a particular job is performed. Even the most simple job like telephone handling, despatch of letters etc. requires some training for its efficient performance. The basic purpose of training is to guide and direct the learning of employees so that they may perform their duties as efficiently as possible. Any good training programme lays down the procedure by which people gain knowledge and skill for a definite purpose. According to *Little field*, "Training is the process of increasing the skills and knowledge of personnel for the purpose of improving individual and organisational performance." It is the duty of the personnel department to suggest training programme for the new-comers. The skill and aptitude can be increased by training. Training is not only necessary for new entrants, but also for the old workers, whenever new technological development has been brought into work because the old workers may not possess knowledge to work upon the new technique. Therefore, training programme is a must to achieve a given aim.

Need ForTraining

1. Training makes the new employees efficient.
2. Training helps to provide mastery in new methods and new machines.
3. Training is needed to prevent industrial accidents.
4. When workers with little or no training selected, they need training for efficient performance of work.
5. Training reduce the need for supervision to the minimum.

Hints for Conducting Tests and Interviews
1. Plan a tests programme.
2. Devise tests that may be easy to value.
3. Prepare a list of candidates to be tested.
4. Decide upon the knowledge required.
5. Test must consume normal time.
6. Fix the place of Interview.
7. Inform the applicants.
8. Provide proper waiting place.
9. Fix the members of the interviewing board.
10. Decide how to make the final selection.

THE METHOD OF TRAINING

1. Oriental training

When a new man is appointed, a little training is being given to him so that he may understand the nature of the work and adjust himself to his job. He will also be informed of the rules and regulations of the firm and the working conditions in which he has to work. It has a short duration followed by lectures, film shows, tours, etc.

2. Training on the job

This method is suitable and effective as the employee is given training on the job itself—either within the organisation or outside. The worker works along with other experienced workmen, during the course of training. Generally, the newcomer will be put under an expert or a specialist, who is in care of the training—apprenticeship. The period of training may vary from firm to firm or from job to job. The advantage is that the applicant gets an adequate knowledge of his work.

3. Training in outside schools

When necessary technical education is imparted outside the firm, the trainees can be sent there to get themselves trained. The fees for the training will be paid by the firm. The existing employees can also attend it before or after the working-hours. Therefore, it is convenient for the firm to send the trainees instead of managing training programmes.

Sometimes, an organisation may run a school to impart instruction to its workers. There will be no fee to attend the classes, but the employee has to attend it. Trained teachers are appointed. The day and time of the training are fixed and the trainee has to attend it. The trainee can have a good knowledge of his job.

Benefits of Training

1. Training results in higher quantity and quality of output.
2. Training builds self-confidence in the employees.
3. Proper training reduces the accident rate.
4. Well trained employees make better use of machine and materials.
5. Trained employees show less resistance to change.
6. Rate of spoilage or wastage of materials is reduced.
7. Maintenance cost of machines is reduced and cost of production per unit is also reduced.
8. More skill and accurate work can be expected.
9. An organisation with trained personnel can introduce the latest technology in order to reduce costs of production.

10. Trained employees are self-dependent and can perform routine work independently.
11. An enterprise having a pool of trained personnel can maintain its effectiveness despite the loss of key personnel.
12. It increases the chance of promotion.
13. In the initial stage it is expensive; but in the long run cost of production can be reduced.
14. Trained workers need less supervision, thus there is economy.
15. Training gives a worker higher responsibility and his ego is satisfied.

Drawbacks of Training

1. Initial expenses are high and all the firms may not afford it.
2. If there are no chances of promotion, workers may seek for better chances elsewhere, so the amount spent on their training is a waste to the firm.
3. Temporary dislocation of work, during the period of training, will decrease the output.

JOB

Otis and *Leukart* defined a job as "A group of position involving substantially the same duties, skills, knowledge and responsibilities." The job is impersonal. The position is personal. Each job or sub-division of a job must have an unambigous name or title to avoid confusion. A job is a collection of task, duties and responsibilities which as a whole is regarded as the regular assignment to individual employees.

JOB ANALYSIS (Job Study)

According to *Harry L. Wylie*, "Job analysis deals with anatomy of the job. This is the complete study of the job (or position) embodying every known and determinable factor including the duties and responsibilities involved in its performance; the conditions under which performance is carried on, the nature of the task; the qualifications required in the worker, and the conditions of employment, such as pay, hours, opportunities and privileges." Job analysis is the process of studying and collecting information relating to the operations and responsibilities of the specific job. Job analysis is based on job description, job specification and job classification. According to *Terry*, "Job analysis is the process of critically examining the components of a job, both separately and in relation to the whole, in order to determine all the operations and duties." Job analysis has two aspects - (a) Job-aspect - description of features of the work and (b) man - aspect - consisting of the detailed description of the necessary physical, mental and personal characteristics of the worker.

JOB ANALYSIS

Job Description	Job Specification
– Statement that provides information about :	– Statement of personnel characteristics needed to perform the job :
Job Title	Education
Duties	

Machines	Experience
Materials used	Judgement
Supervision	Vision
Working condition	Communication skill
Hazards etc.	Physical skill
	Ability to work etc.

JOB SPECIFICATION

Job specification is a statement of the minimum acceptable human qualities necessary to perform a job properly. It is a product of job analysis and description. While job description describes the duties and responsibilities of a particular job, specification specifies the personnel qualities required for the performance of a job–formal education, experience, aptitude and attitude etc. That is, a job description is a study of the job, while a specification is a study of the qualities required for the performance of a job.

JOB STANDARDISATION

Job standardisation includes the establishment of specifications for tools, equipment, working conditions and methods. These specifications are arrived at by scientific analysis. Standards of performance cannot be maintained unless conditions of work, systems and personnel are standardised.

JOB CLASSIFICATION

This branch of job study refers to comparative study of jobs. It embodies the comparison of individual jobs and the determination of identical duties and qualifications so as to achieve the objective of grouping similar jobs into classes so that identical and consistent titles may be assigned.

JOB EVALUATION

Job evaluation is the rating of each job or work according to a particular procedure in order to determine its relative worth. It is the system by which each job is rated in relation to other jobs of the firm. The purpose of job evaluation is that each job is paid according to the relative difficulties in performing it. One will not accept a job when he is not satisfied with the salary offered.

In the words of *Dale Yoder*, "Job evaluation is a practice, which seeks to provide a degree of objectivity in measuring the comparative value of jobs within an organisation and among similar organisations. It is essentially a job rating process, not unlike the rating of employees."

According to *B. H. Walley*, "Job evaluation is a systematic of the value of a range of jobs, so that ultimately wages or salary payment scale is produced for them."

According to *Brech*, "Job evaluation is the method of determining the relative worth of jobs on some scale, usually by an analysis of the contents of jobs under classified headings."

The basic purpose of job evaluation is to determine the relative worth of each job so that proper remuneration can be fixed for different categories of jobs. Proper job evaluation helps in devising a wage structure which is acceptable to the workers as well as the organisation.

The salary or the wages must well compensate a worker in accordance with the expected skill and labour to be expanded on his job. Employees feel dissatisfied and discontent when the salary is low, on the other hand, if the salary is too high it will be disastrous to the firm. Therefore, a systematic salary structure should be accepted for the common well-being of both the management and the employees and it is possible only through the job evaluation methods. For a proper job evaluation the following factors are to be considered :-

1. Skill and labour required to perform a particular job.
2. Effort and responsibility to be undertaken for a job.
3. Physical requirements needed for a job.
4. Working conditions of a job.

Benefits of Job Evaluation

Job evaluation offers many advantages, more important of which are as follows :

1. Proper and rational salary and wage structure can be formulated.
2. When job evaluation is practised, wage rates can be reviewed with ease.
3. Job evaluation helps in evolving uniform standards to be applied to all jobs in the organisation.
4. Settlement of grievances and disputes regarding individual wage rates is greatly facilitated.
5. Job evaluation helps in the maintenance of harmonious relations between employer and employee.
6. Job evaluation allows for simplification of wage administration because it brings about uniformity in wage rates.
7. Job evaluation helps in the elimination of personal prejudice in establishing rates by putting the rate structure on an objective basis.

MERIT-RATING

Merit-rating is a technique applied on workers to assess their relative merit while doing their jobs in comparison with others. When the workers, who have the same qualifications and training, work on the same type of job, the quantity and quality of the output will differ because of their individual abilities and aptitudes. Therefore, it is essential for the management to evaluate their differences–abilities and qualities–in order to reward them with promotions or additional remunerations. The merit–rating system is followed in each department of a firm. For example, a supervisor may differentiate the workers who are working under him, he is able to take decision as to which employee will be recommended for promotion, or for training, or for wage increase or for demotion, etc. The worker may have interest to know his merit-rating, so that he may try to improve his standard, when compared with other workers.

Merit-rating is the name applied to the system of evaluating and recording the abilities and personal characteristics of an employee. It is the evaluation or appraisal of the relative worth to the company of a man's services on his job.

According to *J. C. Denyer,* "Merit-rating or merit grading is an assessment according to individual ability which may be rewarded by additional payments to the ordinary rates of pay for the different jobs."

According to *Edwin P. Flippe,* "Merit-rating is a systematic, periodic and, so far as humanly possible, an impartial rating of an employee's excellence in matters pertaining to his present job and to his potentialities for better job."

According to *Quible,* "Merit-rating is a formalised way of giving out merit pay increases."

Advantages of Merit-Rating

1. The system enables the supervisor to evaluate the performance of his subordinates, scientifically and systematically.
2. Wages or salaries can be paid according to merit-rating which is more justifiable.
3. A systematic promotion system can be adopted, especially confirmation from the probationary to the permanent cadre.
4. The system protects the employee in sanctioning promotion. If the system of merit-rating is absent, favouritism will play its grotesque role.
5. It encourages the weaker employees to improve themselves.
6. It serves as a systematic guide to the supervisor in planning the employee's further training.
7. It assists in locating and recording special talents and capabilities that might not be otherwise noticed.

Methods

There is no proper method of evaluating individual jobs. It is not possible to measure mathematically the qualities of individual workers. However, the following methods are used:

(A) Point Method

Under this method, the supervisor evaluates the qualities of each worker and awards marks or points for each quality in him. Due weightage will be given to the most essential qualities required of him. Then the points or marks are looked up in order to apply merit-rating.

(B) Descriptive Method

Under this method, the supervisor writes a small description giving the quality assessment of each worker. On the basis of this description, the particular worker is rated.

(C) Ranking Method

Under this method, on the basis of the performance and the abilities of each worker, he is ranked. It may be either numerically or alphabetically or on percentile basis.

(D) Field Review Method

Under this method, a trained employee from the personnel department takes down detailed notes of the interview with the supervisor, which is duly signed by the supervisor. This report is kept in the personal file of the worker.

PLACEMENT OF EMPLOYEES

After the employee has been selected and recruited, the problem of placement arises. Placement refers to the task of assigning specific job to employees. Correct placement is in no way less important than accurate selection. Even a competent employee may be inefficient and dissatisfied if put on a wrong job. Correct placement helps to improve efficiency and satisfaction of employees. It is proved by experience that placement of an employee in the right job results in improvement of morale and performance, reduces absenteeism and employee-turnover, leads to better utilization of machines, equipments and materials and keeps the employee satisfied. While placing employees on jobs, the requirements of both the organisation and the employees should be considered.

A good and effective system of follow-up helps to avoid wrong placement. That is, follow-up is a process in which the work of the employee is assessed at frequent intervals and the performance is recorded in his service record. This will help the management to locate cases of wrong placement and to take corrective action by way of transfers. Supervisors can do much in locating the wrong placements.

A proper placement of employee results in the following :

1. Better motivation resulting in better performance.
2. Lower rate of absenteeism. .
3. Lower rate of labour turnover.
4. Better utilisation of materials and machines.
5. Reduced cost of supervision.
6. Keeps the employee satisfied, etc.

PROMOTION

The word promotion means shifting a worker to higher post with more responsibilities and higher salary. There is a change in the designation and in the status. Upgrading or promotion systems are used to reward the employees for their better service. Upgrading of salary, without the corresponding changes in the post means higher grade of salary for the existing work. The annual increment is not a promotion. Promotion must involve changes in the status. Promotion means filling higher posts with the junior workers instead of taking fresh hands. And of course, it is a good system to create a healthy atmosphere in the organisation, and this every worker does his best for the promotion.

The term promotion denotes the idea of advancement of an employee to a higher job with more emoluments and prestige, higher status and higher responsibility. If higher posts are filled up by promoting the existing employees, the morale of employees will be high, they will be loyal to the concern and they can put in their best. On the other hand, if the higher posts are filled from outside sources, the employees would become dissatisfied and they get frustrated and lost all interest in the concern. The dissatisfied employee is a source of trouble to the management and he will disrupt the normal functioning of the organisation. Further, he will encourage the other workers to follow his path. Hence every concern needs a systematic programme of promotion. A sound promotion policy should, therefore, be based on both seniority and ability. It should primarily be based on the merit of the worker, due weightage being given to seniority or length of service. A happy blend of both criteria maintain employee morale; at the same time it encourages the employees to give better performance.

Basis of promotion

1. Seniority of service	:	Service period is considered.
2. Ability	:	Past record of performance is the basis of promotion.
3. Loyalty	:	There are some employees who work sincerely and for the interests of the firm.
4. Education	:	One who has higher qualification than the basic qualification should be considered for promotion.

5. Character   :   If the worker is obedient to his superiors and co-operative, he is also to be considered for promotion.

6. Punctuality   :   One who is punctual should also be given credit.

TRANSFER

Transfer refers to the movement of an employee from one job to another within the organisation without involving any significant change in the emoluments and status. Though there will not be change in the general nature of work, there may be some change in its specific nature. Transfer may be beneficial to both the employer and employees. Reasons for transfer may be :

1. Expansion or contraction of business.

2. A shortage of man with a particular skill or ability in one department or plant.

3. Improper initial placement.

4. Change in employee's interest or capacity, etc.

5. To meet contingencies of absence, leave etc.

MORALE

Morale is a mental condition or attitude of individuals and groups with determines their willingness to co-operate. It is the attitude that creates a feeling of enthusiasm and happiness during and after working hours. It is sometimes defined as moral condition of an individual as regards discipline and confidence in relation to his job. For some people, it includes the mental and emotional feeling of an individual regarding the tasks expected of him, for still others, morale may mean personal acceptance of group goals. In relation to job, morale may be defined as the extent to which an individual perceives satisfaction of his needs as they stem from his total job situation. A few definitions of the term 'morale' may be noted:

1. "Morale may be defined as the collective attitude of workers towards one another, towards their employer, the management or their work."   *J.C. Denyer*

2. "Morale has been defined as an attitude of mind which conditions how well or how badly duties are performed."   *W.H. Walley*

3. "Morale is the capacity of group of people to pull together persistently and consistently in pursuit of a common purpose."   *Dr. Leighton*

4. "Morale means the co-operative attitude or mental health of a number of people who related to each other on some basis."   *Spreigel*

5. "Morale represents the attitude of individuals and groups towards their work environment and towards their voluntary co-operation to the full extent of their ability in the best interest of the organisation."   *Keith Davis*

6. "Morale is mental condition or attitude of individuals and groups which determines their willingness to co-operate. Good morale is evidenced by employee enthusiasm, voluntary conform once with regulations and orders, and the willingness to co-operate with others in the accomplishment of organisation objectives. Poor morale is evidenced by surliness, case of insubordination, discouragement and dislike of job, company associates."   *Edwin P. Flippo*

An analysis of the above definitions clearly indicate that morale is the enthusiasm and willingness or readiness with which the individiual members of a group set out to accomplish the task given to him. Industrial morale has also be described as the "sence of feeling by an employee, of being accepted and belonging to a group, of employees through adherence to common goals and confidence in the desirability of these goals." Morale of an employee is a collection of attitude, feelings and sentiments towards his employer and also his willingness to strive for the attainment of goals of a particular group of organisation to which he belongs. High morale encourages effective work and low morale tends to poor work. High morale is associated with less industrial troubles and less complaint of disobedience, good feelings among the workers, fewer strikes and lock-out etc. They are in reverse with the low morale workers.

Prof. Jucius observes, "Definitions of morale are many, a review of them all would show that they define it in terms of what it is, what it does, where it resides and whom it affects and what affects." Thus morale is composed as follow :

1. What it is? - An attitude of mind, an esprit de corps, a state of well (or unwell) being and an emotional force.
2. What it does? - Affects output, quality, costs, discipline, enthusiasm, co-operation and other aspects of success.
3. Where it resides? - In the minds, attitudes and emotions of individuals and groups.
4. Whom it affects? - Immediately employers and executives and ultimately the customer and the community.
5. What it affects ? - Willingness to work and co-operate in the best interests of the enterprise.

Morale should be distinguished from motivation. The two concepts are inter-related but differ from each other. Morale is composite of attitudes and feelings whereas motivation is the process of inspiring people. Morale is a group phenomenon while motivation is basically an individual's willingness to work. Morale indicates predisposition towards all aspects of work but motivation is basically predisposition towards the job itself. Morale is a function of group relationships. On the other hand, motivation is a function of needs and incentives. Morale is concerned with the mobilisation of sentiments while motivation is concerned with energy mobilisation.

Morale is the indicator of the attitude of employees towards their jobs, superiors and the organisational environment. Employees with high morale like their jobs and co-operate fully with the management towards the achievement of organisational objectives. High morale is key to proper action by the employees. It keeps the office running smoothly by bringing efficiency and economy in office operations. Low morale refers to a reverse situation, that is, low morale might well lead to the following consequences :

1. Frustration of employees.
2. Excessive complaints and grievances.
3. Friction among the employees.
4. Low productivity.
5. Increased rate of absenteesim.
6. High labour turnover.
7. Waste of materials.
8. Unnecessary disputes over discipline.
9. Creation of resistance groups.
10. Failure to co-operate with management.

To improve the morale :

1. To create good feelings among the workers and a healthy atmosphere in the firm, the management must promote a high morale in workers.

2. To create harmony among the workers, weekly staff conference may be conducted and everyone will be given a chance to express his feelings,

3. Proper placement is necessary. When a man is not interested to do a particular work, he will be allowed to do the job which he likes.

4. Worker will be allowed to meet his superiors whenever he needs.

5. Workers must be protected from accidents and diseases.

6. Promotion, transfer, demotion, etc., must be dealt with properly.

7. Settling grievances, facilitating employee-management collaboration, contact with employees union ensuring the co-operation between the workers and the management etc., must be permissible.

Factors Determining Morale

Morale factors are those that affect or influence personnel interest of individuals in relation to their organisation. Any factor which tends to produce favourable attitudes among employees towards organisation and its management is a moral stimulant. On the other hand, any factor that tends to produce unfavourable attitude is a moral depressant.

Morale Stimulants: *Davis* outlines the following factors to be the most usual moral factors in any business organisation:

1. **Worthwhile Objectives** that are compatible with public interests as well as personnel interests of organisation.

2. **Good leadership** is based on a sound philosophy of managements.

3. **Homogeneity** of group characteristics and interests.

4. **Symbolism** and a degree of identity of organisation and personnel interest.

5. **Decentralization and delegation** of responsibility and authority.

6. **Good Techniques** used for handling men, including those for order giving and disciplinary action.

7. **Individual and group opportunities,** including financial and non-financial incentives.

8. A satisfactory physical **work environment**.

9. **Training, education and indoctrination.**

10. **Organisational confidence** based on equity as well as material success.

Morale Depressants : *B.H. Walley* lists out the following factors to be the morale depressants:

1. Salary :

(*a*) Low salaries compared with other departments, other companies in the same area, or other companies in the same industry.

(*b*) Disproportionate salaries for effort and responsibility.

2. Promotion prospects :

(*a*) Apparent lack of promotion prospects.

(*b*) Promotion of 'wrong' people (favouritism)

3. Supervisory problems :

(a) Dislike of supervisors.

(b) Absurd disciplinary actions for minor infringements of discipline by supervisor.

(c) Lack of leadership and decision taking.

(d) Supervisors who do not know their job.

4. The job :

(a) Muddle in handling work.

(b) General lack of efficiency in the office.

(c) Insufficient work to keep clerks busy.

(d) Wrong kind of work–clerk either over or under qualified to handle the job.

5. Working conditions :

(a) Poor office environment.

(b) Sub-standard office equipment desks, chairs, lighting etc.

6. Management and the worker :

(a) Badly organised company, dual reporting.

(b) Lack of knowledge of what is going on in the company.

(c) Feeling of isolation: sense of being ignored.

7. Personal factors :

(a) Wrong size of working group.

(b) Inability on the part of the clerk to fit into the team.

(c) Personality factors which affect others in the office.

8. General :

(a) Irritating and petty regulations.

(b) Badly introduced changes in the company.

MORALE AND PRODUCTIVITY

It is generally assumed that morale is directly related to productivity of the employees. If the morale of the employees is high, it would automatically, lead to higher productivity and conversely if the morale is low, the productivity of the employees will be less. According to *Koontz and Donnell*," There is evidence from the long experience of many managers that morale does materially influence productivity." The following suggestions may be followed in order to improve morale in the organisation:

1. Evolving of an effective system of two-way communication.

2. Keeping the employees informed about organisation policies and inviting their comments there on.

3. To provide suitable job incentives relating to job, security, working conditions, opportunity for promotion, benefits, social status etc.

4. Making provision of welfare amenities like health, recreation, housing accommodation, medical facilities etc.

5. Encouraging workers participation in management.

6. Analysing and removing the cause of workers' dissatisfaction in the organisation, if any.

7. Encouraging group activities by the employees, like sports, social get-togetherness, picnics etc.

8. Providing an effective grievance settlement machinery within the organisation, to hear, employees' complaints and to take steps to remove them.

MOTIVATION

The term motivation has been derived from the word motive. Motive is anything that initiates or sustains activity. It is an inner state that energies, activates or moves and that directs or channels behaviour towards goals. Motive is a psychological force within an individual that sets him in motion. Behind every human action there is a motive. According to *Brech*, "Motivation is a general inspirational process which gets the members of the team to pull their weight effectively, to give their loyalty to the group, to carry out properly the tasks that they have accepted and generally to play an effective part in the job that the group has undertaken."

According to *Littlefield* and *Rachel*, "Motivation is the process of being influenced to take action or accomplish a goal. In an organisation, people are motivated if they are willing to perform efficiently and effectively."

According to *Hodge* and *Johnson*, "Motivation may be defined as the willingness of an individual to respond to organisational requirements in the short run."

According to *Stanlay Vance*, "Motivation implies any emotion or desire which so conditions one's will that the individual is propelled into action.

The most important task of the management is to get the work done by the subordinates and achieve results. Getting the work depends mainly on whether a person has been motivated to do it. Motivating a worker is to create a need and a desire on the part of worker to better his present performance. This will mean to do anything beyond just what he is required to do. This can be done by creating in him a sense of responsibility and feeling of special interest in his work. Motivation concerns itself with the will to work. It seeks to know the incentives for work and tries to find out the ways and means whereby their realization can be helped and encouraged. Motivation has been defined by *Jucius* as "The act of stimulating someone or oneself to get a desired course of action, to push the right button to get a desired reaction."

How to Motivate your staff :
1. Get to know your staff individually
2. Understand their interests
3. Let them to work in good condition
4. Motivate them in and out of work
5. Share information with them
6. Provide them with increasingly challenging opportunities
7. Give them feed-back on their job performance
8. Analyse their strengths and weaknesses
9. Coach and guide them in areas where they are working
10. Tell your friends of other departments, "how well your team works.

11. Let your team gets the reward they deserve
12. Give recognition for good job performance
13. Encourage them to come up with ideas for improvement
14. Involve them in decisions and seek their views
15. Get them involve in the department budgeting
16. Help them to solve their problems, etc.

IMPORTANCE OF MOTIVATION

Studies have shown that motivation plays a crucial role in determining the level of performance of employees. If motivation is low, employees, performance will suffer as much as if ability were low. According to *Allen*, "Poorly motivated people can nullify the soundest organisation." Another view is that "Motivation is the core of management." The president of an American Corporation remarks, " you can buy a man's time, you can buy a man's physical presence at a given place but you cannot buy his enthusiasm, initiative or loyalty. "This enthusiasm or willingness to work can be created through motivation. All organisational facilities will remain useless people are motivated to utilise these facilities in a productive manner. Motivation is an integral part of management process and every manager must motivate his subordinates to create in them the will to work. High motivation provides the following benefits:

1. Motivation is an effective instrument in the hands of management to maximise efficiency of operations.
2. Motivation inspires employees to make best possible use of different factors of production.
3. Higher motivation leads to job satisfaction of workers. As a result labour absenteeism and turnover are low.
4. Increased labour productivity in turn results in higher wages for employees. This will reduce labour unrest and create better relations between management and workers.
5. An enterprise that offers abundant financial and non-financial incentives enjoys reputation in the labour market.
6. High motivation helps to reduce resistance to changes.

NEED-HIERARCHY THEORY OF MOTIVATION

Abraham H.Maslow. an eminent American psychologist, developed a general theory of motivation, known as the Need hierarchy theory, which is as follows:

1. **Physiological Needs :** Physiological needs are the basic needs of the organism and are essential for survival. These are needs for food, thirst, exercise and shelter. In organised co-operation, these needs are satisfied through adequate compensation in terms of employee needs of this kind and through job security.
2. **Safety Needs :** Safety needs are more important when a man is in a dependent relationship and fears arbitrary deprivation. Since people in the organisation stand in dependent relationships safety needs become important informal structure.
3. **Social Needs :** As a social element, it is the desire of human being to be accepted by others. Need for belonging is manifested in the form of social groups formed on informal basis.
4. **Self-Actualisation Needs :** These are needs relating to personal growth and realisations of man's full potential. The need for self-actualisation is not strong in all subordinates. At the same time, organisations usually offer limited opportunities for satisfying self-actualisation needs.

5. **Ego Needs :** These are needs relating to one's self esteem, such as self-respect, self-confidence and achievement. Ego needs relating to reputation may be satisfied through promotions and allotment of status symbols to deserving individuals in the organisation. Ego needs relating to self-esteem may be satisfied by assigning challenging and stimulating work the accomplishment of which will result in recognition.

SOUND MOTIVATIONAL SYSTEM

A sound motivational system is an essential ingredient in any organisation. Evolving a good system of motivation in an organisation, requires a good deal of care and imagination. Generally speaking, sound motivation system should have the following characteristics :

1. **Permanence :** It should be a permanent features of an organisation.
2. **Reflect the goal etc. :** It should reflect the goals, objectives and philosophy of the organisation.
3. **Simple and equitable :** The motivation system should be simple so that it is well understood by all employees. Further, it should be equitable.
4. **Relate to efforts :** It should be directly related to efforts and its operations should be evident to all.
5. **Standards :** The motivation system should be correlated to motives and needs of the employees and should be based on proper standards.
6. **Flexible :** The motivation system should be flexible, comprehensive and competitive.

MANAGEMENT OF GRIEVANCES

According to *Jucius*, "A grievance is any discontent or dissatisfaction, whether expressed or not, whether valid or not, arising out of anything connected with the company which an employee thinks, believes or even feels to be unfair, unjust or inequitable". According to *Pigors* and *Myers*, **dissatisfaction** is anything that disturbs and employee, whether he expresses it in words or not. A **complaint** is a spoken or written dissatisfaction which is brought to the notice of the management or trade union representatives. A **grievance**, on the other hand, is simply a complaint which has been ignored, over-ridden or, in the employee's opinion, dismissed without consideration ; and the employee feels that an injustice has been done, particularly when the complaint was presented in writing to a management representative or to a trade union official.

The International Labour Organisation defines a grievance as "A complaint of one or more workers in respect of wages, allowances, conditions of work and interpretation of service stipulations, covering such areas as overtime, leave, transfer, promotion, seniority, job assignment and termination of service."

CAUSES OF GRIEVANCE

In a study undertaken by *Chandra*, the following causes have been given of employee grievances: (*i*) Promotions; (*ii*) Amenities; (*iii*) Continuity of service; (*iv*) Compensation; (*v*) Disciplinary action; (*vi*) Fines; (*vii*) Increments (*viii*) Leave; (*ix*) Medical Benefits; (*x*) Nature of the job; (*xi*) Payment of wages; (*xii*) Acting promotion; (*xiii*) Recovery of dues; (*xiv*) Safety appliance; (*xv*) Superannuation; (*xvi*) Supersession; (*xvii*) Transfer; (*xviii*) Victimisation; and (*xix*) Conditions of work.

Grievances may arise from various causes related to the work and working conditions of the employees. The typical areas where causes of grievances may occur are : (a) Wage structure including bonus, incentives, overtime, leave facilities etc. (b) Seniority, job classification, promotion, transfer, lay-off and discharge; (c) Supervision and discipline, (d) Physical environment and working conditions in general (e) Welfare arrangements including health and safety; and (f) Employer's attitude towards interpretation of the service contract or collective bargaining agreement, settlement of grievances etc.

HANDLING OF GRIEVANCES

Grievances represent situations in which employees feel that they have not been treated fairly. A grievance may broadly be defined as any discontent or dissatisfaction, whether expressed or not and whether valid or not, arising out of anything related to the organisation that an employee thinks, believes or feels is unfair, unjust or inequitable. A grievance may relate to excessively long hours of work, unfair treatment in promotion, non-fulfilment of terms and conditions of service, non-implementation of the Government orders etc.

A grievance is the embryo of serious trouble to come because accumulation of minor grievances may lead to major conflicts in the organisation. Hence, prompt and effective handling of grievances is necessary for peace in the organisation. If the grievance is real and genuine, it is necessary to take corrective action; but if it is imaginary, there is need of explaining and clearing up of the matter. If the grievance is not handled properly, the employees will feel frustrated which may lead to so many troubles in the organisation. Therefore, it is advisable to develop an effective grievance procedure in the organisation.

PROCEDURE FOR HANDLING GRIEVANCE

In practice, it may not always be possible to settle the grievances internally through negotiations between the management and the employee concerned or the union representative. In such cases, the grievance or complaint may be settled through conciliation or arbitration. The procedure for referring grievances for conciliation or arbitration is as follows:

(i) **Conciliation Procedure :** Conciliation refers to the process of reconciliation of the differences between the two parties. Under this method, a third party known as the conciliator acts as a link between the two parties to bring about a compromise or settlement. This is possible when both the parties agree to submit their differences for conciliation by an agreed third party. As a neutral party, he suggests the basis of compromise or settlement which may be acceptable to both the parties.

(ii) **Arbitration :** When the process of conciliation fails to bring about agreement between the parties, the grievance of dispute may be referred to arbitration. Both the parties voluntarily agree to submit differences to a neutral third party or umpire, known as arbitrator. Both the parties, the management and the employee or union, agree beforehand that the decision of the arbitrator will be final and binding on both the parties.

Whatever may be the grievance procedure developed by an organisation, it must be simple and unambiguous. It must be developed with the co-operation of employees and must be accepted by all in the organisation. The grievance procedure should ensure the speedy redressal of the grievances and must be capable of ensuring a sense of satisfaction to the individuals concerned. As far as possible, the procedure should have a limited number of steps with the provision for at least one appeal.

STAFF WELFARE

In addition to the salaries, certain facilities may be provided to the workers for their well-being. The main aim of the arrangement is to look to the workers morale in office as well as in factory. In almost all big concerns there may 'be a specialist known as Welfare Officer, whose duty is to look after the welfare of the workers. Within the organisation, the welfare activities include the following;

1. Fixing possible hours of work.
2. Providing fair wages.
3. Maintaining cleanliness, ventilation etc., within the working place.
4. Providing medical services, recreational facilities, libraries and reading-rooms, canteens and rest-rooms etc.
5. Taking precautions against fire of explosives.
6. Making provisions for holiday, sick leave with salary.
7. Providing opportunities to workers to progress.
8. Creating a spirit of co-operation among the workers.

Outside the organisation, it aims at the following :

1. Providing housing facilities.
2. Establishing educational institutions for the children of the workers.
3. Giving free medical advice to the family members of the workers.
4. Starting sports clubs.

LABOUR TURNOVER

Labour turnover refers to the changes in working staff of a concern during a defined period. It involves the changing of employment from one concern to another. It involves not only the movement of labour from one concern, but also a corresponding number of new employees joining those places which have fallen vacant. Thus labour turnover involves accessions and separations of workers. Accessions involve the employment of new workers or the re-employment of former workers, while separation includes termination of employment on account of quits, lay-off, discharges, death etc. The following are the methods to find out the rate of labour turnover:

(a) Separation method
(b) Replacement method
(c) Flux method

Causes for Labour Turnover :

The causes can be broadly divided into two categories :

(a) Avoidable Causes :

1. Dissatisfaction with job.
2. Dissatisfaction with wages
3. Poor working conditions
4. Unsuitable working hours
5. Non-co-operative attitude
6. Lack of promotions
7. Unfair method of promotion
8. Unsympathetic attitude of management

9. Inadequate protection
10. Weakness (employee-employer relations)

(b) Unavoidable Causes :
1. Quitting the job (due to inefficiency)
2. Lack of work
3. Retirement or death
4. Accident or illness
5. Marriage
6. Disliking job
7. Personal betterment
8. Worker's roving nature
9. National service

Effect of Labour Turnover :
1. Fall in production
2. Increased in cost-selection, training etc.
3. Dislocation of even flow of production.
4. Increase of scrap, defective-work, additional supervision etc.
5. Higher accident rate
6. Mishandling of machines
7. Instability of labour and their low team spirit.

Methods of Reducing Labour Turnover :
Following measures are suggested to the management to maintain a happy and contented labour force :
1. Better working conditions may be provided to workers.
2. Selection of candidates must be made on the basis of scientific principles and workers must be placed on appropriate jobs.
3. Well organised programmes must be chalked out to increase their efficiency.
4. There must be a cordial relation between employer and employees.
5. There must be job security and opportunities for career advancement.
6. A good wage policy and incentive plans must be devised.
7. An effective grievance procedure is to be adopted.
8. Labour participation in management must be encouraged.
9. A good working condition conducive to health and efficiency should provided.
10. The personnel department must prepare a periodical report, relating to causes of labour turnover and suggest remedies.

INCENTIVE PLANS (BONUS OR PREMIUM SCHEMES)

Generally speaking, there are two basic methods of wage payment. One method relates to the hours, the employee is at work, regardless of output. This is known as time rate or day rate system. The other method is related to the production or output, regardless of the time taken for production. This is known as piece rate system. Each method has its own merits and demerits.

In order to take advantage of the merits and eliminate demerit of both time wage and piece rate systems of wage payment, a third method of wage payment was evolved which is known as incentive wage system or bonus or premium plans of wage payment. Any wage system which induces a worker to produce more is called 'Incentive Wage System'. The essence of the so-called incentive wage plans is that they adjust earnings to output or production, thus providing a special financial incentive for increasing effort while guaranteeing the minimum wages. The incentive wages are given in the form of 'premium' or 'bonus' calculated on the basis of efficiency of workers, time saved or increased production. For convenience the various methods of remuneration may be divided as under:

1. Time Rate Systems :
   (a) At ordinary levels
   (b) At high levels
   (c) Guaranteed time rates

2. Piece Rate Systems :
   (a) Straight piece rate
   (b) Piece rate with guaranteed time rate
   (c) Differential piece rates :
       (i) Taylor differential piece rate system
       (ii) Merrick differential piece rate system
       (iii) Gantt task bonus system

3. Bonus systems (Incentive wage system or premium plans)
   (a) Individual bonus systems:
       (1) Halsey Premium plan
       (2) Halsey-Weir Premium plan
       (3) Rowan system
       (4) Barth variable sharing plan
       (5) Emerson efficiency bonus
       (6) Bedaux point premium system
       (7) Accelerating premium plan etc.
   (b) Group bonus :

4. Indirect Monetary Incentives.

The various schemes and premium bonus plans should combine time wages and piece rates. A brief explanations of them are given below :

1. **The Halsey Premium Plan :** This system is also known as Split Bonus Plan or Fifty-fifty Plan. The plan was introduced by *F.A. Halsey*, an American Engineer. In the plan, the task (standard) time, is decided on the basis of past experience, and scientific studies are set. Under this plan, a standard time is fixed for the performance of each job, and the worker is paid the agreed rate per hour for the time spent thereon plus a fixed percentage (may be 50%) of the time, he saved on the standard.

2. **The Halsey-Weir Scheme :** Here the worker gets a bonus of 30% of the time saved, against 50% in the Halsey Plan, Except for this point, Halsey Plan and Halsey Weir Scheme are similar.

3. **Rowan Scheme :** This scheme was introduced in the year 1901 by David Rowan of Glasggow. The guidelines of Halsey Plan have been followed. It is similar to that of

Halsey Plan except in regard to the determination of bonus calculation. Under this plan, the bonus is that proportion of the wages of the time taken which the time saved bears to the standard time allowed.

4. **Barth Scheme :** Under this plan, wages are not guaranteed. This system is suitable to beginners and learners. The earning is computed by multiplying the rate per hour by the geometric mean of standard hours and actual hours worked.

5. **Emerson Efficiency Bonus Plan :** Under this plan when the efficiency of the worker reaches 67% he gets bonus at the given rate. The rate of bonus increases gradually from 67% to 100% efficiency. Above 100% bonus will be at 20% of the basic rate plus 1% for each 1% increase in efficiency.

6. **Bedaux Premium Plan :** It is a combination of time and bonus scheme. Standard time for a job is determined by time study. Standard production per hour is determined and the unit of measurement is minute. An hour is taken as sixty minutes. Each minute of standard time or allowed time is called a point—Bedaux point. The number of points is being determined in respect of each job. If actual time is more than the standard time, the worker is paid on hourly basis. Excess production is counted in points, for which a bonus of 75% is allowed to the worker and remaining 25% goes to the employer. Thus hourly rate plus 75% of the points saved, multiplied by one-sixtieth of hourly rate is the earnings of a worker.

7. **Accelerating Premium Plan :** Under this premium plan, bonus increases at a faster and faster rate as output increases. The plan offers a higher incentive to the workers. The efficiency is determined on the basis of time saved or increased output. The plan is complex one.

The system of wage payment is of two types–time rate system and piece rate system. In the plan of incentive wage payment, both time and piece rate blended together. Under the time rate system, the worker is not benefitted for the time saved. Under piece rate system, the cost per unit falls, even though labour cost remains constant. This is due to savings in fixed overhead expenses, since the cost of overhead is distributed over all the units. The purpose of this scheme is to overcome the limitation of both the systems and combine the advantage of both the systems. In order to increase production through encouragement the benefits are shared by the employer and the employee. Before the introduction of incentive plan, the following factors may be taken into consideration:

1. It must be simple and understandable to workers.
2. It must be fair to both—employer and employee.
3. The standard should be fixed by time and motion study.
4. Standards once fixed may not be altered.
5. The cost of operating the scheme should be minimum.
6. The work must be repetitive by nature.
7. The workers should not raise objections.
8. The system must be permanent; once introduced should not be discontinued.
9. The system should also benefit the indirect workers.
10. It must reduce labour turnover.

A satisfied employee will give his best service and thus production will be increased, on the other hand, a dissatisfied employee will not give his service beneficially to the firm, thus production will be decreased. When the worker is dissatisfied because of insufficient incentives, he may go away whenever better opportunity arises elsewhere. When there is no chance of promotion, one may not take initiative to improve himself. But when there is a good system of promotion policies on the basis of better performance, naturally one will work hard to come up. Even today the problem of promotion of workers depends upon the will and pleasure of the management. If favouritism is shown in promotion, it will nurture jealousy, discontentment, etc. It is the duty of the personnel department to see that the right person is awarded suitably in order to cultivate goodwill among the workers.

When one does a job satisfactorily taking less time, he should be remunerated suitably in addition to the salary. Incentives are an encouragement for better work or greater effort in production. The extra payment of remuneration may be in the proportion of additional output or time saved.

Types of Incentives

Incentive may be financial or non-financial.

(a) **Financial Incentive :** Financial incentive is in terms of money and it provides higher emoluments for higher efforts or increased output. It includes money payments based on results in addition to wages and salaries. In this respect, piece rate system of wage payment provides greatest incentive to the workers as in this system remuneration is directly linked to their output. Similarly, there are many premium bonus systems, like Galsey premium system, Rowan premium bonus system etc. under which basic time wage is guaranteed and a bonus is paid, for achieving a saving in time, in proportion to the time saved.

(b) **Non-Financial Incentive :** Under this system, incentives are provided in the form of better facilities, instead of paying cash. The object is to attract the employees and such benefits may be in several ways:

1. Favourable working conditions
2. Free medical facilities to worker and his family
3. Rent free quarter
4. Free education to children
5. Welfare facilities
6. Subsidised canteen
7. Pension schemes
8. Protective clothing, liveries uniforms etc.
9. Opportunity for advancement
10. Subsidised transport facilities

Advantages of Non-Monetary Incentive Schemes :

(a) Reduce labour turnover
(b) Create a sense of loyalty and co-operation in them
(c) Enhance general goodwill of the company
(d) Reduce absenteeism
(e) The best labours are attracted.

Advantages to Workers

(*a*) **Increase in the wages of workers :** These systems increase the total wages of workers because workers get besides prescribed wages, the premium or bonus also. Different schemes have different premium amounts. An increase in total earnings improves their standard of living which eventually increases their efficiency.

(*b*) **Improvement in work capacity :** Every worker tries to work more and more and one who is unable to do his prescribed work, tries his best to reach the standard work level so that he may also get premium.

(*c*) **Improvement in standard of living :** This system increases the wages of the workers on one side while on the other hand, producer has to pay less for more work proportionately. This reduces the cost per unit. People get goods at cheap rates. Thus standard of living of workers, producers and buyers goes up.

Advantages to Producers

(*a*) **Minimum Supervision :** Workers work more themselves and do not waste time. Hence very less supervision is required.

(*b*) **Increase in Production :** When production increases, the cost of production decreases. Prices go down. Workers are happy. Buyers get goods at lower price. There will be more demand for goods. Sales are increased.

(*c*) **Good labour relations :** Workers and employers both have same interest. Both like saving in time and increase in output. Hence labour disputes come down automatically.

(*d*) **Improvement in organisation :** Wages according to work and extra motivation improve the climate of organisation. Misuse of time and such other bad practices are hardly visible.

(*e*) **Standardisation :** All premium schemes are based on standardisation. By time and motion studies, jobs are standardised and on this basis evaluation of work, labour is done. Further, standardisation improves the method of production.

QUESTIONS

1. What are the possible causes of "Labour Turnover"? How can the causes be ascertained? State the remedial action that can be taken.   (*ICWA Inter*)

2. "Pecuniary and non-pecuniary incentives are required to motivate the workers for harder work just as right and left foot both are essential for walking. Explain the statement.   (*ICWA Inter*)

3. What is meant by job grading ? State the usual procedure followed in job grading. Explain briefly the system of job grading.   (*ICWA Inter*)

4. What is Personnel Management ? Discuss its importance.   (*ICWA Inter MS, B. Com.*)

5. What is morale ? How is it related to productivity ?   (*CS, B. Com., Chennai*)

6. What is merit-rating ? What are the benefits of merit-rating plans ? How merit-rating differs from job evaluation?   (*ICWA*)

7. With what objectives job evaluation is carried out?   (*ICWA Inter*)

8. Explain briefly the factors influencing the morale of office staff. How is morale related to productivity ?   (B. Com., Delhi, Kerala)

9. What are the various methods of imparting personnel training ?   (MS, B. Com.)

10. What do you understand by 'Personnel Management' ? Discuss its importance in a modern office.   (B. Com., Madras)

11. Discuss the functions of the personnel department of a firm.   (B. Com., Madurai)

12. Differentiate between 'Financial' and Non-Financial incentives. Discuss their relative importance.

13. What is meant by employee welfare ? How would you plan employee welfare ?
                                                            (B. Com., Kerala, Delhi, Chennai)

13

CHAPTER

Office Services

INTRODUCTION

The purpose of office work is to render efficient' secretarial and clerical service' to functional departments–production, purchase, sales etc. In a large organisation, various functional departments may have sectional offices providing only the required clerical services to the corresponding departments. The services provided by each sectional office may be different. This necessitates complete decentralization of office work "However, this raises an important problem. That is, in-charges of functional departments, who are specialists in the field of their respective functions, cannot be expected to be specialist in the field of office management, say for example, correspondence, filing, data-processing etc. There are certain office services which are performed by all the offices which can be grouped together and centralised at one place known as 'central' or 'general' office. Such services, which can be centralised is as follows: (a few)

1. Typing and filing
2. Mailing
3. Computing
4. Control of forms
5. Correspondence
6. Collection of data
7. Maintenance and repairs

8. Duplicating services

9. Employment and training

10. Reception of visitors etc.

The above mentioned general services are required by all the functional departments directly or indirectly. If such general services are carried out efficiently, they can make a considerable contribution towards the efficiency of office management .But if such general services are ill-planned, the efficiency of other department will be adversely affected. It is important to note that all these services of different departments are inter-related and their efficiency is interdependent. If it is so, the management has to consider whether these services should be centralised or not–Centralisation and Decentralisation.

CENTRALISATION AND DECENTRALISATION

Centralisation

Centralisation in office can be defined as a process by which common office service or functions are centralised at one place–General Office. Again, office functions common to all sectional offices—typing, filing, duplicating etc, are physically concentrated in on department known as 'General Office'. For example, if the duplicating service is organised as a separate department no other department is authorised to purchase its own duplicating machine. Under centralisation, these common services are not arranged in the section offices. It is the duty of the general office to provide the common services to all departments as and when they are required by them. Centralisation of office services is desirable because it fixes responsibility on persons to do various jobs. It also avoids wastage and duplication of work and reduces cost of management.

Advantages of Centralisation

The centralised arrangement of office services has the following advantages:

1. Duplication of work is avoided. It results in lowering the investment and maintenance cost of office machine.

2. It is possible to bring specialisation in the centralised department. It becomes feasible to employ people with specialised knowledge. The efficiency and output go up and the cost of office management is reduced.

3. The total volume of work can be distributed evenly among the central staff. Equitable distribution of work load is possible. None will be over-worked nor will any-one sit idle.

4. The same type of machines and equipments can be used by all the employees and the supervision leads to standardisation of office procedures and methods.

5. It facilitates better and more scientific recruitment and training of employees.

6. It facilitates and ensures greater flexibility in the use of staff, machines and equipment.

7. Constant dealing with the same type of work makes 'The worker specialized and thus increases his efficiency and output and reduce cost of management.

Disadvantages of Centralisation

The disadvantages of the centralisation of office services are:

1. The personnel in the central office unit may lack personal interest in the work of other departments.

2. The work of a department may be of a confidential nature and there is no guarantee that its secrecy will be maintained.

3. Centralisation leads to frustration because of too rigid central control.

4. Work in the centralised office may be performed in that, order in which it is, received rather than in the order of its importance. This may result into less of business because of delay in the execution of orders.

5. Handling of mail, file, etc. is quicker in decentralised system than in a centralised system.

6. While writing correspondence or doing other work for the departments the central staff may have to frequently refer paper back to the operating departments for clarifications. Thus there may be greater delay in performance of work.

7. The technicalities of a particular department may not be properly understood by the general office, resulting in frequent references, which lead to delay in the execution of work.

Decentralisation

Decentralisation of office services refers to a situation in which each functional department has its own staff to perform activities like typing, filing, duplicating etc. with its own machines and equipment. Where an organisation has its plants and offices at different locations, centralisation of office services cannot be practised. In such cases, office activities have to be decentralised for their efficient performance. For example if the operations relating to handling of mail are performed by each department separately it will be said that mail handling is decentralised.

Advantages of Decentralisation

Centralisation is neither possible nor desirable for all type of activities. It can be better performed departmentally because of the following advantages :

1. Secrecy of departmental affairs is well maintained.

2. Delay in performing the operation is avoided because it is performed at the department where it is needed.

3. Staff attached to the department develops a sense of loyalty to it, and also develops personal interest in the work.

4. Since a worker is working, in a functional department, work can be performed promptly.

5. Departmental employees are conversant with the problems of the department and have knowledge of technicalities of the department. Therefore staff can perform the work more quickly and in a better way.

Disadvantage of Decentralisation

Disadvantages of decentralized arrangement are as follows:

1. The total workload of the office cannot be distributed among the personnel of different departments.

2. The quality of work may be poor because of lack of specialisation and specialised machines.

3. There will be duplication of efforts, equipments and machines etc., this leads to uneconomical operations.

4. There may not be uniformity of office procedure followed in different department.

5. Standardisation of the office procedure and equipment is not possible. The work may be done in different departments in different way and with different equipments.

6. Decentralisation creates problems of co-ordination of work among the different departments.

Complete physical centralisation or decentralisation is neither feasible nor desirable in a modern office of a large scale business. Theoretically, centralising the office work is desirable because it fixes responsibility under a capable executive, avoids duplication and permits better supervision with a more even distribution of the individual work load. In practice, the centralisation is not practicable in pureform. Office work is made up of a series of different activities such as filing, mailing, accounting etc. Again, some firms may have plant at one place, the others may have through out the country. In some concerns there is greater volume of work as compared to others. With all those variations the question of centralisation or decentralisation tends to became an individual problem for each firm. Therefore, common and routine office services - filing, duplicating typing etc. are centralised in the General Office, while separate staff is provided for individual departments for the performance of those activities which cannot be centralised. A co-ordination of the activities of the functional department is also affected by the General Office.

DEPARTMENTS OF A MODERN OFFICE

Functional departments require some clerical service which may be provided by creating a sectional office for each of these functional departments. The objective of the office is to provide clerical service to the operating or functional department. Some office work is invariably performed in the departments themself. However, for reasons of economy and efficiency, some office activities which are common to all the functional departments are centralised in the general office, under the supervision of an office manager, who is naturally a specialist. Office services common to all sectional offices – duplicating, typing filing, mailing etc., are centralised in the general office. The purpose of dividing the office on the basis of functions into sectional or departmental offices is to secure maximum efficiency in work at minimum cost. Each departmental office performs a specific function and the staff become specialised in that particular function. The important departments o sections of a modern office and their functions are as follows :

1. General Office

The general office deals with these office activities which are common to all the operating departments, *viz*, typing, correspondence filing, mailing etc. Generally, the general office of a large organisation is divided into the following sections:

(a) Typing pool

Typing pool consists of typists responsible for typing correspondence, preparing statements and doing such other works, relating to typing. When the volume of typing i large, a separate section is set up for looking after the work. This section deals with all typing work of all the departments including the general office.

Copying and Duplicating Section : It is a well-known fact that as an office expands there is greater need for copies of documents, bulletins, etc. Copying and duplicating service become an important activity of an office. Sometimes copying and duplicating may be created at a separate section. However, in a small office this section may be combined with the typing section or pool.

(b) Correspondence Section

A separate correspondence section may have to be organised in a large organisation. The main function of the correspondence section is to look into different letters, enquiries, memoranda etc. and prepare suitable replies. The work of preparing correspondence is performed by this section for the office as well as for other functional departments. The correspondence may be internal or inter departmental, where it concerns with the people within the organisation. The correspondence is external where it concerns outside people, outside organisations and the Government departments.

(c) Mailing Section

As the name implies, mail department handles incoming and outgoing mails relating to the entire enterprise. All the incoming and outgoing letters, parcels etc. are routed through this department. Chief functions are: (i) To keep record of all incoming and outgoing letters, (ii) To sort out incoming mail and send it to the concerned officials, (iii) Keep accounts of postal stamps, and (iv) To deal with post office.

(d) Filing Section

This department deals with the systematic preservation of all files and records of the business which concern all the departments. The activities include; Receiving papers and documents for filing; their classification indexing and cross referencing; filing the papers; issuing the files to departments; follow-up of the files issue to other departments etc.

(e) Secretarial Section/Department

This department is the secretary's own department. The main functions of this department are to deal with general administration and co-ordination of the activities of the other departments. It also deals with the issue, forfeiture, transfer etc. of shares, documents and papers relating to capital, finance and control of business, filing returns with the Registrar of companies, preparation of reports, budgets etc.

2. Purchase Department

Purchasing is an important function of modern office. This department is responsible for different kinds of purchases–assets (machines, plants etc.), consumable items (stationary etc) and raw materials for production etc. The other functions are: receiving purchase requisition, inviting tenders, placing orders, receiving ordered items, recording purchase details, issues, maintaining ledger and stock positions etc. it also advices the management on different matters concerning purchases and market conditions

3. Sales Department

This department performs a number of functions

  (i)   Advertising and publishing the firm's products;

 (ii)   Obtains and trains sales force;

(iii)   Keeping the selling expenses at minimum;

(iv)   Activities relating to exhibition, trade fairs etc., at the appropriate time; and place;

 (v)   Receiving, recording, replies to customers enquiries, complaints etc.;

(vi)   Conduct market research, survey etc.

(vii)   Collection of outstanding bills;

(viii)   Preparation of sales statistics;

    (*ix*) Despatching and transporting goods to customers.

    (*x*) Advice the management about sales policy etc.

4. Accounts Department

This department is concerned with the maintenance of books of accounts and the preparation of financial statements. The main functions include the following:

    (*i*) To keep records of all financial transactions;

    (*ii*) To deal with banks;

    (*iii*) To prepare profit and loss account, balance sheet and other financial statements

    (*iv*) To deal with wages, salaries, budgets etc.

    (*v*) To manage cash

        In very big concerns, there may be a separate Cash Department which deals with cash receipts and cash payments, but in small organisations, cash section is a part of the accounts section,

    (*vi*) To maintain cash vouchers;

    (*vii*) To maintain cash books, petty cash book etc.

5. Personnel Department

It is an important department of an organisation performing a number of functions- recruitment, training, placement and development of staff. They lay down procedures for transfers and promotions of staff. They maintain and keep the records of employees. In short, the chief functions of this department are:

    (*i*) To select people for employment;

    (*ii*) To provide training to staff;

    (*iii*) To administer wage and salary policies;

    (*iv*) To keep personal records of staff;

    (*v*) To help the management in the matters of promotion, transfer etc,

    (*vi*) To provide welfare facilities;

    (*vii*) To deal with labour problems and trade disputes;

    (*viii*) To prepare retirement and pension schemes etc.

6. Production Department

The production department deals with work concerning various activities of the production of finished products - Production control, quality control, material handling, control of stocks etc. It also prepares materials scheduled, maintain stock records, job cards, cost accounting records, wage and salary bills etc. It also provide relevant data for production planning and budgeting.

7. Export Department

A large organisation exporting goods on a large scale may have a separate export department to look after the exports of the organisations. Its function includes obtaining export orders, keeping liaison with importers, preparing export invoices, arranging insurance and shipment of goods, etc. **Public Relation Department :** The success of a business depends to a great extent on its ability to maintain good relations with the outsiders such as customers, suppliers, press, government departments,, general public etc.

QUESTIONS

1. List the office services suitable for decentralisation.   (B. Com., M.S.)
2. What are various departments of an office.   (B. Com., Madurai)
3. What are merits of decentralisation of office services?   (B. Com., Madurai)
4. What is meant by 'Centralisation of office services ? What are its advantages and disadvantages?   (B. Com., Kerala, Madurai)
5. Discuss the functions of a modern office. Also describe the relationship of office with purchase and personnel departments.   (B. Com., Delhi)
6. What do you meant by 'office service' ? Whether these services should be centralised or decentralised.   (B. Com., Delhi)

CHAPTER

Office Supervision

INTRODUCTION

Top management sets the objectives, middle management tries to achieve them and supervisory management actively helps the middle management in achieving the objectives set by top management. Supervisory management is represented by supervisors and departmental chiefs. The supervisors not only get things done but they get the things done willingly and harmoniously through employees. Supervision can be defined as the process in which an individual directs and control the work of others.

According to *Neuner* and *Keeling* "Supervision includes the planning of work. Supervision also involves securing actual performance that approximates, as closely as possible, desired performance. Planning includes setting up the best methods to produce an acceptable quality of office work in a standard quantity so that production may be measured in terms of these criteria. Maintaining such standards with due considerations of the human relationships existing in office work and supervision, should make it possible to reduce the cost of production."

Planning, organising and staffing can be considered preparatory managerial functions; the purpose of controlling is to find out whether or not the objectives are being achieved. The connecting and actuating link between these functions is managerial function of supervision which means the issuance of directives and the guidance and over-seeing of the subordinates. Thus supervision, in the context of office management, relates to provision of leadership, direction, guidance and motivation of office workers to better performance of office operations according to the plan and objectives.

Supervision in the office is the task of the supervisor. Little field and Peterson describe "a supervisor as a person who carries out lower level responsibilities for, higher level management and has a direct control over personnels." *Terry* describes a supervisory as a "Management member working at an organisational level where personal over-sight of tasks assigned to small groups is assumed in order to assure satisfactory performance."

CHARACTERISTICS OF SUPERVISION

The following are the characteristics of supervision:

1. The task of supervision is not concerned with materials and equipments but is primarily concerned with human relations that is, to get the work done through the efforts of other people.
2. Supervision is front-line management. It is that part of management function which is concerned with leading, directing, guiding and motivating of the office workers who are engaged in actual office operations.
3. Supervision is a delegated function. The authority enjoyed by supervisory management to exercise supervision over their subordinates, that is, workers engaged in operation, is delegated by higher levels of management. Conversely, supervisory management remains responsible or accountable to the next higher level of management.
4. The autocratic methods of getting the work done cannot succeed in the modern democratic environment. Effective supervision requires that supervisory management should be able to exercise dynamic leadership which alone will ensure effective co-ordination and co-operation among the workers and motivate them towards better performance of work.
5. The position of supervisory management is mid-way between higher level management and the workers. A supervisor is a representative of both man and management. Effective supervision depends a great deal on the supervisor's ability to interpret clearly and tactfully the view-points of management to the men and of men to the management.

OFFICE SUPERVISION

A supervisor is regarded as the key-man in management as he occupies a strategic position of strength in the organisation. He is the only member capable of linking management to operative personnel. The office supervisor, by whatever name he is called, occupies a very delicate and important position in the organisation structure of the office. He is the key figure in managerial actuating. Almost every plan and policy must pass through him for implementation. It is he who is responsible for the correct interpretation of plans and policies to his subordinates. For them, he is their guiding spirit. It is he who introduces team spirit among the subordinates. *Terry* summarises his position in these words "An organisation unit is what it is largely because of the supervisors influence." As a matter of fact, most of the problems are reduced to simple tasks when the supervisor is competent and gets full, co-operation from his subordinates. A supervisor is an individual who is at the critical, focal point where work is to be got done. He is the one who 'supervises' performance of tasks assigned to a group of workers and is 'responsible' for their performance. It is he who accounts for the performance of his subordinates to the management.

The place of supervisor in the organisation and the nature and scope of his responsibilities, primarily, depend upon the nature and size of the activities of an enterprise. In large sized offices there may be several levels of supervisory authority, *viz*, the first line supervisors, who are incharge of the office workers engaged in actual operations; second line supervisors, who deal with first line supervisors and as such act as connecting link between them and the higher management; in some concerns there may be third line supervisors also called top level supervisors, who deal with and co-ordinate and supervise the activities of the second line supervisors, "the pyramid of supervision is formed in this way."

Generally, a supervisor is a person who is primarily incharge of a group of workers in an organisation. He is responsible for the accomplishment of work and for the efficient performance of equipment and workers under his charge. He is the real executor of the plans., policies and programmes of the organisation. He is delegated authority by the departmental manager for getting the work done from the workers. He gives orders and instructions to the workers and is responsible to the departmental manager for their performance.

Effective Supervision

Following are the elements that should be considered for achieving effective supervision :

1. *Impartiality and fairness* in enforcing discipline and in dealing with employees are essential for securing the loyalty and confidence of the employees. All workers must be treated similarly.

2. The supervisor should *issue clear, simple and complete instructions* so that the employees are at ease to perform their work efficiently and speedily.

3. A supervisor must have the *knowledge of machines, equipments, tools, processes and materials* that are under his control.

4. He should *guard against waste of materials and time.*

5. He should be familiar with the *organisational rules and regulations and policies* which are applicable to his concern. He should also possess the knowledge of various labour laws that affect his section.

6. *Satisfactory work outputs* are the chief responsibility of the supervisor and therefore, he should stress upon the need for every employee to perform his best.

7. A supervisor should be a leader in the true sense of the term. As a leader, he will be able to *guide the subordinates* and promote harmonious relationship among them.

8. Employees should not be kept in the dark regarding *objectives, plans and policies* framed by higher management. If they are kept informed, this will enhance their sense of participation and loyalty and will improve employee morale.

9. A good supervisor should be able to *communicate clearly* with the subordinates and issue them *orders and instructions* in such a way that the subordinates feel like following them. He requires communication skill.

10. Performance of work efficiently, timely and according to standard, depends on the co-operation and *team-spirit among* the employees. Employees should be encouraged to get the best results.

11. The supervisor should see that the quality and output of work are strictly according to plan and standards set. He is the person *responsible to higher management* for achievement of work target. This is the *real test of his effectiveness.*

12. Every member of the work group is given the *right to make suggestions and discuss work methods.* This is will give them a sense of participation and improve their morale.

13. A supervisor must show his concern for the *welfare of the subordinates.* He should treat them as human beings if he wants to achieve good group relations. He should adopt a co-operative attitude with his subordinates.

14. Subordinates should be praised and given credit for good work. This will improve their morale and encourage them to keep up the good work.

15. The supervisor should be ready to take decisions on his own, in his sphere, as much as possible. Only *serious matters should be referred to higher management.* He will responsible for the work done in his department.

QUALITIES OF A SUPERVISOR

The role played by a supervisor in office management is that of a manager of people. That is, he is a manager of man-power, a specialist in human relations. A supervisor has to perform various functions. His responsibilities are mani-fold. He is responsible for getting work done by others and in order to do that he must be capable of motivating and leading his subordinates to give their best efforts. He is the key-man in the organisation. His performance directly affects the success of an enterprise. Thus, the person occupying the position of a supervisor must possess certain qualities, important of which are as follows :

1. **Knowledge of Responsibilities :** A supervisor should have sound knowledge of his organisation. It includes understanding the rules, regulations, plans, procedures and policies of the organisation, the extent of the authority and responsibility of the supervisor and the matters on which he can take final decisions. He should have complete information about his subordinates, that is he must know about their strong and weak points, their likings and disliking and their capacity to perform the job. He must acquaint himself with the basic information about the motives of organisation management.

2. **Technical Knowledge :** Firstly, a supervisor must know his job well. He should have technical knowledge relates to the knowledge of materials, equipments, systems, procedures and the manner in which results are used. A supervisor's job is not to do the work himself but to get it done by others. But he must have adequate experience and working knowledge of the job he is to supervise. He must be capable of demonstrating the best method of performing the work. He should be competent in his job having adequate professional knowledge, in addition to experience.

3. **Ability to Instruct :** A supervisor must be able to direct and guide the workers. He should have adequate knowledge and skill in teaching so that well-trained work force is available in the organisation. He must pass on the knowledge to others and develop them. The subordinates are more satisfied, more industrious and take greater interest in their work if they are clearly informed about the work to be done and the methods they would use.

4. **Administrative Ability :** He must be an efficient administrator. He must be recognised and accepted by his subordinates as a leader and not as a boss. Getting along with subordinates smoothly is very vital to the supervisor, without losing the dignity of his position. To be a successful supervisor he must be quick at making decisions.

5. **Ability to Communicate :** He has to work as a link between the management and the workers. He is a front line manager. "A good supervisor is a good communicator and a bad supervisor is a bad communicator." Instructions must be simple and clear. Clarity of instructions means that they are communicated in the way in which the management desires and the group understand them properly." In the words of Niles, "Good communications are essential to co-ordination. They are necessary upward, downward and sideways, through all the levels of authority and advise for the transmission, interpretation and adoption of policies, for the sharing of knowledge and information, and for the more subtle needs of good morale and mutual understanding.

6. A successful supervisor must also possess the following personal characteristics for improving human relations in his department :
   1. He should control his temper.
   2. He must have patience.
   3. He must be a leader rather than a driver.
   4. He should be straightforward, honest and loyal to subordinates.
   5. He must be interested in welfare of subordinates.
   6. He must give due weight to the opinions and suggestions of his subordinates before making final decisions.
   7. He must be able and competent to take quick decisions.
   8. He should be able to guide his subordinates towards organisational goal.
   9. He must be able to develop a team spirit in his workers.
   10. He must give clear and definite instruction to workers.
   11. He must give credit for the work done.
   12. He should not show favouritism and be fair in dealing with his subordinates.
   13. He should have a good sense of humour.
   14. He should not ask questions about private life of his workers.
   15. He must have courage to admit his errors, if any, of decisions.
   16. He should be able to judge his subordinates with regard to their capabilities, strong and weak points, likings and disliking and their efficiency.
   17. He must act as a friend, philosopher and guide to his workers.
   18. He, as a supervisor, has to listen to the complaints and grievances of workers. He should carefully enquire into a cause of grievances and those which are genuine should be handled and removed quickly.
   19. He should be able to avoid disputes between management and workers.
   20. He has to set an example to his group members by his own competence and willingness to learn.

FUNCTIONS OF A SUPERVISOR

As a part of management, a supervisor is responsible for discharging the managerial functions of planning, organising, directing and control. The main functions of a supervisor can be summed up as below:

1. Selection of Personnel

In large offices, there is a specialised personnel department for the selection of personnel. But the supervisor plays an important role in selection of personnel and help the personnel department in performance of their functions of manpower planning, recruitment, selection, training etc. He recommends transfer, promotions etc. of the staff, working under him. He should exercise great care in selecting right type of personnel. The supervisor not only get things done but they get the things done willingly and harmoniously through employees.

2. Organising the Office

The supervisor assigns the work among the various subordinates according to their skill, efficiency etc. while organising the work, the supervisor must see the arrangements of materials, tools, equipment etc. to ensure uninterrupted production. That is, the layout is such so as to ensure a smooth and straight-line flow of work, best utilisation of men, materials and machines and elimination of all wastages of time and effort.

3. Allocation of Work

The supervisor has to assign the tasks to his group members, set performance goals for them in clear terms and make them accountable for the results. He is required to guide and instruct workers in performance of their task towards the achievement of desired goals. He has to look ahead, anticipate problems, recognise contraints within and outside his work unit and plan in realistic but effective manner.

4. Motivating Workers

Motivating a worker is to create a need and a desire on the part of a worker to better his present performances. Motivation is an important factor which encourages persons to give their best performance and help in reaching interprise goals. A supervisor has to build confidence and zeal among workers so as to get the best out of them. A supervisor promotes morale when he helps the workers to satisfy their desires, interests and feeling. Morale contributes to a satisfied work group with greater, achievement in terms of goal attainment of the firm. He should also ensure that machines tools and equipment used by the workers are kept in good working condition. For this, he should provide for periodical check ups, repairs etc. of all equipments. Ensuring proper safety of his workers is also a very important function of a supervisor as lack of safety may cause damage to business property loss of trained personnel and payment of heavy compensations.

5. Office Procedures

The supervisor will have to devise procedures and routines to be followed by his subordinates for the best performance of the work. Improvement of the existing methods of working or introduction of new techniques is also an important function of supervisor. The supervisor holds the key to human relations not only at operative level but also at the organisation level as a whole. The success of an enterprise depends upon effective supervision. The best effort of the top management may fail to bring the desired results if the supervisor is not effective.

6. Training of Personnel

Training is an organised process for increasing the knowledge and skill of workers for doing a particular job. It is a learning process involving the acquisition of skills and attitudes and improve the current performance. A person never stops learning. As such, training is a continuous process. The supervisor should arrange for the training of staff not only at the time of their induction, but also when they are on the job. Training improves productivity, job satisfaction, and morale of employees. It helps in reducing accidents, costs, wastage etc. and facilitates growth and expansion.

7. Enforcing Discipline

The supervisor should take discipline as a means to assist, guide and train his workers to be devoted workers. Discipline is preventive. The rules, policies etc. of the firm towards workers should be such which are not resisted by workers. The supervisor should review the rules, policies etc. from time to time.

8. Effective Communication

An effective communication is the life blood of an organisation and its main purpose is to effect change and to influence action. Communication is our greatest source of power and the most significant characteristic of mankind. Without communication, we would not have formed community, bring up your children, work together in organised way and pass down ideas, innovations and inventions from generation to generation. A supervisor holds an intermediate position between management and the staff. It is his duty to communicate the decisions of management to the subordinate staff. It is also his duty to communicate the views of the staff to management. Therefore, it is more important for him to have an effective communication system.

9. Control Function

Another important function of the supervisor is to move the group towards performance of the assigned tasks and fulfillment of the set goals. This is basically a control function to ensure that what is planned is achieved at the level of the work unit.

10. Reporting to Management

It is the main function of supervisor to keep the management informed about the progress of work and staff as well as problems facing the section under his control. He must maintain and provide systematic reports to the management relating to performance of staff, attendance, machines and problems if any. This is essential for the management to take suitable decisions and to plan for the future. There may be complaints, grievances or problems of the staff. If so, the supervisor should bring such things to the notice of management so as to get them settled.

Responsibilities of the Supervisor

The work of the office supervisor differs from organisation to organisation, depending on the size of the office and the nature of its activities. In small offices, the office manager does the work of a supervisor. He himself is the first line supervisor. But in large size of offices, clerical works becomes so complex and volumious, requires the services of full time specialist supervisor. The supervisor has to protect and promote the interests of both, the management as well as the workers. He plays an important role in an organisation. The various responsibilities of a supervisor are stated below :

(A) Responsibilities towards his work group:

1. To train subordinate to assume greater responsibility.
2. To assist every employee to know what to do ?, how to do ?, and check the result too;

3. To assist new workers to get start quickly;

4. To act as a friend, philosopher and guide of the workers;

5. To delegate responsibility;

6. To build employee morale;

7. To handle grievances, complaints, problems, suggestions etc. of the workers and help them in performing their work;

8. To represent their problem before the management;

9. To create mutual trust and confidence;

10. To inform the workers about ideas, thoughts, plans etc. of the management;

11. To evaluate members and recommend promotions, transfer, dismissals etc.

12. To develop harmony and team work in his group;

13. To develop punctuality and maintain discipline;

14. To encourage and give credit for the work well done;

15. To take decisions without partiality.

(B) Responsibility towards management :

1. To know the plans and desires of the management;

2. To feed genuine information;

3. To convey workers needs to management and vice versa;

4. To ensure maximum utilisation of resources;

5. To implement plans of the management and achieve the desired result;

6. To inform the progress of performance of his work;

7. To maintain contacts at executive level.

(C) Responsibilities towards supervisors of equal rank

1. To work as a team with others

2. To accept responsibility for work in his section;

3. To work in co-operation and co-ordinating;

4. To provide information as and when required;

5. To understand the problems of colleagues.

(D) Responsibilities towards his own work

1. To ensure maximum utilisation of resources;

2. To enforce regulations and rules with justice;

3. To improve personality traits—punctuality, self-control, leadership, courtesy etc.

4. To assume active participation;

5. To attempt to reduce costs;

6. To plan his work properly;

7. To assign duties among staff according to their ability, interest etc.

8. To implement policies of the management.

9. To keep himself acquainted with the latest developments;

10. To develop maximum co-operation in his section,

(E) Responsibilities towards office work
1. To distribute the work fairly among his subordinates;
2. To plan the systems and routines for jobs to be done;
3. To set standards in order to maintain quality and quantity of work to be done;
4. To co-ordinate the work of different units;
5. To use new methods and machines to reduce costs;
6. To ensure the work done correctly and well in time;
7. To forecast difficulties and peak-loads of work.

TRAINING OF SUPERVISORS

Every organisation needs and services of trained persons for performing the activities in a systematic way. Training is an organised procedure for increasing the knowledge and skill of people for a specific purpose. The trainees acquire new skill, technical knowledge, problem-solving ability etc. while education improves the knowledge and understanding of employees in a general way, training aims at increasing the aptitudes, skills and abilities of the workers to perform specific job. Every concern has to arrange some kind of training for preparing workers for jobs and also keeping them acquainted with the latest technological advancements.

A supervisor is one who supervise the work of others. He is in the middle management cadre. He is the key figure on whose efficiency depends the efficiency of the office. A person, however capable and competent, cannot do his best at a job unless he is systematically trained in the correct methods of work. Training is necessary for the following reasons:

1. Training improves the performance.
2. A trained supervisor derives happiness and job satisfaction.
3. The degree of supervision required for a trained employee will be less.
4. A proper use of materials and machines in a systematic way causing less wastages.
5. A trained worker can be more adaptable to change them than an untrained one.
6. Training helps in reducing labour turnover and absenteeism.
7. Training helps in development of employees.
8. Training makes the personnel more skilled and accurate in performance.
9. It builds up confidence in the organisation, develops loyalty and improves team work.
10. Training facilitates to improve quantity and quality of output.

QUESTIONS

1. What is supervision ? What are the factors governing effective supervision ?
                                                                                (B. Com., Madurai)

2. Discuss the nature and objects of supervisory management in the office.
                                                                                (B. Com., M.S)

3. What qualifications should an office supervisor possess ?   *(B. Com., Kerala)*
4. Explain briefly the nature of duties of the office supervisor.   *(B. Com., Madurai)*
5. What are the responsibilities of an office supervisor.

6. "The main function of the office supervisor is to get things done by motivating the office workers." Explain in detail.   (B. Com., Madurai)

7. "The role played by the supervisor in office management is that of a manager of people." Explain the statement.   (B. Com., Kerala)

8. Discuss the position of a supervisor in a modern organisation. Is he a part of management ?   (B. Com., Punjab)

9. What are the qualities of a good supervisor ? What functions does he perform ?
                                                                            (B. Com., Madurai)

10. "Supervisor is the man in the middle." Discuss this statement by bringing out clearly the numerous functions that the office supervisor performs.
                                                                            (B. Com., Kerala)

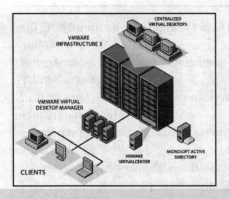

Collection of Data

INTRODUCTION

Collection of data and information are the most important tasks of a modern office, because all business operations depend on information. Data collection is a process of collection of numerical facts. Whether it is the Government or a business firm, statistical data form the basis of its functioning. The regular flow of information based on facts helps business executives in planning and co-ordinating activities and provide a sound basis of policy making and decisions. One of the major functions of the office manager is to supply of all kinds of information to the executives through reports and statements.

The bigger the concern, the greater is the need for statistics. In good old days, business was confined to limited units, when production was in handicraft stage. But today business people have to face cut-throat competition and similar problems. These problems will be solved through statistical analysis. To know if the losses were due to under or overstocking, untimely purchases, inexact estimates, uneconomic prices etc., a businessman analyses the problems with the help of statistics. Statistics to a great extent helps business to make maximum profits. A trader estimates the demand of his products. He decides the quality and quantity of goods to be produced. All the activities of the business are concentrated and helped by statistics. If the estimates of demand are correct, the businessman, makes good profits; if underestimated, he loses the chances of making profits; if overestimated, he finds it difficult to push the products; but simply blocks the finance in stocks. *Boddington* observes, "The successful businessman is the one, whose estimate most closely approaches the accuracy." Therefore, by looking to the statistics of past years, he predicts a good estimate for the future.

The office manager or secretary must collect facts and figures before preparing the report. The statistical data are needed in the office for preparing various types of reports and surveys. The reports cannot be prepared unless proper and adequate numerical data are available. Various types of data are needed for use by the office and the other departments of the business. Such reports cannot be drafted without the use of data.

Whenever management is in need of certain data, it will direct the office manager to submit to the management in the form of a report. Before preparing a report, the office manager is concerned with the collection of necessary data or factual information. Before the collection of data begins, the following steps or preliminaries need careful analysis :

1. **Object of Report :** If the purpose is not defined properly, then it is possible that irrelevant facts may be collected, leading to mere waste of time, energy and resources. Therefore, we have to pre-determine the purpose for which the facts are to be collected. The purpose of the report is to be well determined and states clearly, so that we can easily avoid errors and difficulties in the process of data collection. Pre-determined object of a report helps the office manager and enables him to decide as to what facts are to be collected and what facts are not to be collected.

2. **Statistical Units :** Unit of measurement applied to the data in any particular problem is called the statistical unit. Some of the illustrations of statistical units are kilogram, metre, hour, week, year, number of customers, geographical area etc. However, the problem of choosing the unit is not so simple as it appears to be. Before the collection of data the units may be clearly defined so that confusions can be avoided. The mistake in the selection of unit is more harmful than the mistakes in the collection of data. To find a solution for any problem, it is not enough that the data are collected accurately, but the units of measurements should also be appropriate.

3. **Sources of Data :** There are two sources of information—primary and secondary. Primary data mean the data collected for the first time, whereas secondary data mean the data that have already been collected and used by some agency. For instance, the statistics collected by the Government of India relating to the population, are primary data for the Government of India, as it has been collected for the first time. If the analysed data are used by a research worker to study a particular problem, then the data become secondary data to the research worker.

4. **Degree of Accuracy :** The standard of accuracy is to be maintained, in the enquiry to be planned beforehand. Perfect accuracy in enquiry is not possible; e.g. prices to be quoted to the nearest rupee. Perfect accuracy may not be possible, because the instrument of measurement may be imperfect or estimations may be resorted to. Because of many reasons, absolute accuracy is neither practicable nor even desirable. Accuracy desired depends upon the scope of enquiry. When we measure, say, wheat, a difference of a few grams is negligible; but when we measure, say, gold a difference of 1/5th or 1/10th gram goes to make a lot of difference.

5. **Method of Data Collection :** There are two methods for collecting data—Census Method and Sample Method. A census method is one in which all the items constituting the

population are studied and conclusions are drawn therefrom. Thus, if we want to find out the average height of all the sixty students of a class in a census method, we will measure the actual heights of all the 60 students and the aggregate will be divided by 60 which will give us the average height. On the other hand, in a sample method, only some selected representative units are studied and on the basis of this representative sample, conclusions are drawn for the whole population. The choice between the sample method and census method is to be made depending upon the object and scope of the enquiry, resources, time etc.

SOURCES OF DATA

Statistical data may be classified as primary and secondary. Primary data are those which are collected for the first time and they are original in character. If an individual or an office collects the data to study a particular problem, the data are raw materials of the enquiry.

Secondary data are those which already collected by someone for some purpose and are available for the present study. For instance, the data collected during census operations are primary data to the department of census and the same data, if used by a research worker for some study, are secondary data.

For the collection of primary data, the investigator may choose any one of the following methods:

1. Direct Personal Observation
2. Indirect Oral Interview
3. Information through agencies
4. Mailed Questionnaires
5. Schedules sent through enumerator.

1. **Direct Personal Observation :** Under this method, the data are collected by the investigator personally. The investigator must be a keen observer, tactful and courteous in behaviour. The enquiry is intensive, rather than extensive. There is face to face communication between the investigator and the respondents. The investigator asks questions and gathers required data. The interviewer can ask questions according to the reaction of respondents. This method is adopted in the following cases :

1. Where greater accuracy is needed.
2. Where the field of enquiry is not large.
3. Where confidential data are to be collected.
4. Where the field is a complex one.
5. Where intensive study is needed.
6. Where sufficient time is available.

Merits of Direct Personal Observation

1. Original (first hand information) data are collected.
2. True and reliable data can be had.
3. Response will be more encouraging, because of personal approach.
4. A high degree of accuracy can be aimed.
5. The investigator can extract correct information.

6. Misinterpretations, if any, on the part of the informant can be avoided.

7. Uniformity and homogeneity can be maintained.

Demerits of Direct Personal Observation

1. It is unsuitable where the area is large.

2. It is expensive and time-consuming.

3. The changes of bias are more.

4. An untrained investigator will not bring good result.

5. One has to collect information according to the convenience of the informant.

2. **Indirect Oral Interview :** When the informant is reluctant to supply information, the method of indirect oral investigation can be followed. Under this method the investigator approaches the witnesses or third parties, who are in touch with the informant. The enumerator interviews the people, who are directly or indirectly connected with the problem under study. For instance, we are asked to collect information relating to the gambling or drinking habits of people. In such cases, the informant will be reluctant to supply information relating to their own socially evil habits. On such occasions, we may approach the dealers of liquor shops, friends, neighbours, etc., to get the needed information. Generally this method is employed by different enquiry committees and commissions. The police department generally adopts this method to get clues of thefts, riots, murders, etc. The police interrogate third parties who possess knowledge about the happenings under study.

Suitability

This system is more suitable, where the area to be studied is large. It is used when direct information cannot be obtained. The system is generally adopted by governments.

Merits of Indirect Oral Interview

1. It is simple and convenient.

2. It saves time, money and labour.

3. It can be used in the investigation of a large area.

4. The information is unbiased.

5. Adequate information can be had.

6. As the information is collected from different parties, a true account can be expected and all aspects of the problem can be ascertained.

Demerits of Indirect Oral Interview

1. Absence of direct contact is there; the information cannot be relied.

2. Interview with an improper man will spoil the results.

3. In order to get the real position, a sufficient number of persons are to be interviewed.

4. The careless attitude of the informant will affect the degree of accuracy.

5. Witnesses may colour the information according to their interests.

3. **Information through Agencies :** Under this method, local agents or correspondents will be appointed. They collect the information and transmit it to the office or person. They do this according to their own ways and tastes. This system is adopted by newspapers, periodicals, agencies, etc., when information is needed in different fields, for example, riots, strikes, accidents, share markets, sports, politics, etc. The informants are generally called correspondents.

Suitability

This method is generally adopted in those cases where the information is to be obtained at regular intervals from a wide area.

Merits of Information Through Agencies

1. Extensive information can be had.
2. It is the most cheap and economical method.
3. Speedy information is possible.
4. It is useful where information is needed regularly.

Demerits of Information Through Agencies

1. The information may be biased.
2. Degree of accuracy cannot be maintained.
3. Uniformity cannot be maintained.
4. Data may be original.

4. **Mailed questionnaire:** In this method, a questionnaire consisting of a list of questions pertaining to the enquiry is prepared. There are blank spaces for answers. This questionnaire is sent to the respondents, who are expected to write the answers in the blank spaces. A covering letter is also sent along with the questionnaire, requesting the respondents to extend their full co-operation by giving the correct replies and returning the questionnaire duly filled in time. To get quick and better response, the return postage expense is borne by the investigator, by sending a self-addressed and stamped envelope. This method is adopted by research workers, private individuals, non-official agencies and State and Central Governments.

Suitability

This method is appropriate in cases where informants are spread over a wide area. This method should be preferred in such enquiries where there could be a legal compulsion to supply the information so that the risk of non-response is eliminated.

To make this method effective, the following suggestions are made :

1. The questionnaire should be so framed that it should not become undue burden on the respondents.
2. Self-addressed and stamped cover should be enclosed.

Merits of Mailed Questionnaires

1. Of all the methods, the mailed questionnaire method is the most economical.
2. It can be widely used, when the area of investigation is large.
3. It saves money, labour and time.
4. Error in the investigation is very small, because information is obtained directly from the respondents.

Demerits of Mailed Questionnaires

1. In this method, there is no personal contact between the investigator and the respondent. Therefore we cannot be sure about the accuracy and reliability of the data.
2. This method is suitable only for literate people. In many countries, there are illiterate people who cannot understand and reply the questionnaire.

3. There is long delay in receiving questionnaires duly filled in.

4. People may not give the correct answer and thus one is led to false conclusion.

5. The questionnaire is inelastic. Asking supplementary question is not possible.

6. Sometimes the informants may not be willing to give written answers, apart from causing delay.

5. **Schedules sent through enumerators.** It is the most widely used method of collection of primary data. A number of enumerators are selected and trained. They are provided with standardised questionnaires. Specific training and instructions are given to them for filling up schedules. Each enumerator will be in charge of a certain area. The investigator goes to the informants along with the questionnaire and gets replies to the questions in the schedule and records their answers. He explains clearly the object and the purpose of the enquiry. The difference between the former and this method is that in the former method, the questionnaire is sent to the informants, whereas in this method the investigator carries the schedule to the informant. This method is used by public organisations and research institutions.

Suitability

This method is quite popularly used in practice. The main reason for this is a very high rate of response because of personal contact of the enumerators.

Merits of Schedules sent through enumerator

1. This method is very useful in extensive enquiries.

2. It yields reliable and accurate results, because the enumerators are educated and trained.

3. The scope of the enquiry can also be greatly enlarged.

4. Even if the respondents are illiterate, this technique can be widely used.

5. As the enumerators personally obtain the information, there is less chance of non-response.

Demerits of Schedules sent through enumerator

1. This is a very costly method, as the enumerators are trained and paid for.

2. This method is time-consuming, because the enumerators go personally to obtain the information.

3. Personal bias of the enumerators may lead to false conclusion.

4. The quality of the collected data depends upon the personal qualities of the enumerator.

5. It is not suited to all persons due to its costliness.

SECONDARY DATA

Secondary data are those data which have been already collected and analysed by some earlier agency for its own use; and later the same data are used by a different agency. According to W.A. *Neiswanger*, "A primary source is a publication in which the data are published by some authority which gathered and analysed them. A secondary source is a publication, reporting the data which have been gathered by other authorities and for which others are responsible."

Sources of Secondary Data

The various sources of secondary data can be divided into two broad categories:

1. Published sources
2. Unpublished sources

1. **Published sources.** Various governmental, international and local agencies publish statistical data, and chief among them are:

   (a) **International Publications.** International agencies and international bodies publish regular and occasional reports on economic and statistical matters. They are the IMF, the IBRD, the ICAFE, and UNO, etc.

   (b) **Official Publications of Central and State Governments.** Departments of the Union and State Governments regularly publish reports on a number of subjects. They gather additional information. Some of the important publications are : the Reserve Bank of India Bulletin, Census of India, Statistical Abstracts of States, Agricultural Statistics of India, Indian Trade Journal, etc.

   (c) **Semi-official publications.** Semi-Government institutions, like Municipal Corporation, District Board, Panchayat, etc., publish reports.

   (d) **Publications of Research Institutions.** Indian Statistical Institution (ISI), Indian Council of Agricultural Research (ICAR) Indian Agricultural Statistics Research Institute (IASRI), etc., publish the findings of their research programmes.

   (e) **Publications of Commercial and Financial Institutions.**

   (f) **Reports of various Committees and Commissions appointed by the Government.** For example, Wanchoo Commission Report on Taxation, Pay Commission Reports, Land Reforms Committee Reports, etc., are sources of secondary data.

   (g) **Journals and Newspapers.** Current and important materials on statistics and socio-economic problems can be obtained from journals and newspapers like, Economic Times, Commerce, Capital, Indian Finance, Monthly Statistics of Trade, etc.

2. **Unpublished sources.** There are various sources of unpublished data. They are the records maintained by various government and private offices,, the researches carried out by individual research scholars in the universities or research institutes.-

Precautions in the use of Secondary Data

We must take extra care when using secondary data. According to *Simon Kuznets*, "The degree of reliability of secondary source is to be assessed from the source, the compiler and his capacity to produce correct statistics and the users also, for the most part, tend to accept a series, particularly one issued by a government agency at its face value without enquiring its reliability." *Prof. Bowley* points out that "Secondary data should not be accepted at their face value." Therefore before using the secondary data, the investigators should consider the following factors:.

   (a) **The suitability of data.** First, the investigator must satisfy himself that the data available are suitable for the purpose of enquiry. It can be judged by the nature and scope of the present enquiry with the original enquiry. For example, if the object of the present enquiry is to study the trend in retail prices, and if the data provide only wholesale prices, such data are unsuitable.

   (b) **Adequacy of data.** If the data are suitable for the purpose of investigation, then we must consider whether the data are useful or adequate for the present, analysis. It can be studied by the geographical area covered by the original enquiry. We must consider the time for which the data are available. In the above example, if our object is to study the retail price trend of India, and if the available data cover only the retail price trend in the State of Tamil Nadu, then it would not serve the purpose.

(c) **Reliability of data.** The reliability of data can be tested by finding out the agency that collected such data. If the agency has used proper methods in collecting data, statistics may be relied upon.

Without knowing the meaning and limitations, we cannot accept the secondary data. According to *Prof. Bowley*, "It is never safe to take published statistics at their face value without knowing their meaning and limitations, and it is always necessary to criticise arguments that can be based on them."

EDITING OF DATA

Editing of data is an important task which aims at detecting possible errors and irregularities. Once data have been collected, it is necessary that they should be edited. Editing is the first step in examining the collected data. Its purpose is to get rid of errors end irregularities. Editing of all kinds of data is important and more particularly that of the secondary data which have been collected second-hand in brief, editing is necessary to ensure that (1) the information gathered is complete. (2) it is reliable (3) the data is suitable and adequate for the purpose of investigation.

QUESTIONS

1. What do you understand by the term 'data collection'? State the factors that must be considered at the time of data collection.   (*B. Com., Punjab, Madurai*)

2. Write a note on Principle methods of data collection.   (*B. Com., Madurai, Chennai*)

3. What are the various methods used in collecting primary data? Examine the relative merits and demerits of each method.   (*B. Com., Delhi*)

4. Define 'secondary data'. State their chief sources and point out the dangers involved in their use and what precautions are necessary before using them.
     (*B. Com., Delhi, Kerala*)

5. Which method of collecting primary data would you suggest as the best and why?
     (*B. Com., Delhi, Madurai*)

6. What do you understand by editing of data? Explain the main point that you would keep in view while editing primary data.   (*B. Com., Chennai*)

CHAPTER 16

Presentation of Data

INTRODUCTION

The collected data in any statistical investigation are known as raw data. They are huge and confusing. As such they cannot be easily understood by persons, and are not fit for further analysis and interpretation. Thus, when the data have been collected for the office report, it becomes essential to present the data in a suitable form in order to facilitate interpretation. After the collection of data, classification is done to present the information in a precise and easily understandable form. Then data may be shown in tabular form or given diagrammatic presentation.

CLASSIFICATION OF DATA

Classification of data can be defined as the process of arranging facts on the basis of their common characteristics. It is necessary to classify the data on some suitable basis before it can be given a suitable presentation. The process of grouping a large number of individual facts or observations on the basis of similarity among the items, is called classification.

OBJECT OF CLASSIFICATION

The chief objectives of classification are:

1. To condense the mass of data;
2. To present the facts in a simple form;
3. To bring out clearly the points of similarity and dissimilarity;

4. To facilitate comparison;

5. To bring out the relationship;

6. To prepare data for tabulation;

7. To facilitate the statistical treatment of the data;

8. To facilitate easy interpretation;

9. To eliminate unnecessary details.

Classification serves a very useful purpose in the analysis of data. As such classification has its own importance. Masses of data without classification is not easily understood. Classification separates the essential data from the collected data. It gives them a definite shape for understanding and for making comparisons.

TYPES OF CLASSIFICATION

Classification of data primarily depends on the purpose and objectives of the enquiry. There are four important types of classification. (1) **Geographical Classification** is done on the basis of a geographical location of the items under study, for example, Districts, states, talukas, regions etc. (2) **Chronological Classification** is based on time, for example, years, months, weeks, days etc. (3) **Qualitative Classification** is made on the basis of attributes or qualities of the items, for example, sex, honesty, blindness, colour etc. (4) **Quantitative Classification** is based on quantitative characteristics of the data, for example, income, height, weight, price, production etc.

TABULATION OF DATA

After the data have been collected and classified, they have to be presented in a tabular form. In the broadest sense, "tabulation is defined as an orderly arrangement of data in columns and rows." It is the final stage in the collection and compilation of data, and is a sort of stopping stone to the analysis and interpretation of figures. Tabulation helps in understanding complex numerical data and makes them in a simple and clear way that their similar and dissimilar facts are separated, "The purpose of a table is to summarise a mass of numerical information and to present it in the simplest possible form, consistent with the purpose for which it is to be used,"

OBJECTIVES OF TABULATION

The main objectives of tabulation are:

1. To clarify the object of investigation;

2. To simplify complex data;

3. To clarify the characteristics of data;

4. To present facts in the minimum of space;

5. To facilitate comparison;

6. To detect errors and omission in the data; ,

7. To depict trend and tendencies of the problem under study; ,

8. To facilitate statistical processing;

9. To help reference.

PARTS OF A TABLE

A good statistical table is an art. The following parts must be present in all tables:

1. Table number
2. Title
3. Head Note
4. Caption
5. Stubs
6. Body of the table
7. Foot-note
8. Source-note

DIAGRAMS

One of the main functions of statistics is to simplify complex data. The classification and tabulation, discussed above, are devices of presenting the data in a neat, concise, systematic, intelligible and understandable manner. A large amount of information extending over a large number of columns often does not interest the public; and it is difficult for one to understand the significance of the data at a glance. Of-course, percentages, ratios, averages etc. reduce the complexity into a simple and single figure. Yet, the figures may not be interesting but confusing to many people. These have necessitated the statisticians to introduce methods of diagrams and graphs. Complicated data through a diagram or graph can easily be understood; at the same time appealing and convincing to the eye and mind. They are nothing but points, bars, squares, circles, pictures, maps, charts etc.

Classification refers to grouping of data into homogeneous class and categories. Tabulation is the process of presenting the classified data in tables. Classification and tabulation are applied in order to make the collected data understandable. Yet to many these figures may be uninteresting and even confusing, A better way of representing the data is by diagrams and graphs.

A diagram is a visual form for presentation of statistical data. Diagram refers to the various types of devices such as bars, circles, maps, pictorials, cartograms etc. These devices can take many attractive forms. Strictly speaking, these are not graphic devices. Diagrams do not add any new meaning to the statistical facts, but they exhibit the results more clearly. An ordinary man can understand pictures and diagrams more easily than the figures. The use of diagrams is becoming more and more popular in the present time.

IMPORTANCE OF DIAGRAM

Diagrams occupy an important place, because :

1. They are attractive and impressive.
2. They save time and labour.
3. They have universal applicability.
4. They make data simple.
5. They make comparison easy.
6. They provide more information.

LIMITATION OF A DIAGRAM

The following are the deficiencies or restricted uses:

1. Diagrams cannot be analysed further.
2. They show only approximate value.
3. The uses of certain diagrams are limited to the experts, for instance, multi-dimensional ones.
4. It exposes only limited facts.
5. To draw a table is easy but construction of a diagram is not so easy.
6. It is a supplement to the tabular presentation but not an alternative to it.
7. Minute readings cannot be made.
8. Diagrams drawn on false base are illusory.

TYPES OF DIAGRAM

There are various diagrammatic devices by which statistical data can be presented. We shall discuss a few of them, which are mostly used.

1. **One-Dimensional Diagram :** In one-dimensional diagram, the length of the lines or bars is considered and the width of the bars is not taken into account. The term 'bar' means a thick wide lines.
2. **Two-Dimensional Diagram :** In two-dimensional diagram, the area of the diagram represents the data, *i.e.* the length and breadth are considered.
3. **Three-Dimensional Diagram :** They are called so because length, height and width or depth are considered and these comprise of cubes, spheres, prisms, cylinders etc. Of all these cubes are the easiest to draw as the side of the cube can easily be found out by taking the cube-root of the data.
4. **Pictogram :** Pictogram is a device of representing statistical data in pictures. These are very useful in attracting the attention. They are easily understood. For the purpose of propaganda, the pictorial presentations of facts are quite popular and find place in exhibitions.
5. **Cartogram :** In cartograms, statistical facts are presented through maps accompanied by various types of diagrammatic representations. It presents the numerical facts in a pictorial form in a geographical or spatial distribution. Cartograms are simple and are easy to understand. They are generally used when the regional or geographic comparisons are to be made.

GRAPHIC PRESENTATION

Graphic presentation of statistical data gives a pictorial effect. It is a tool through which relationships between different factors or variables are presented, for example, revenue and profits, wages and productivity etc. Graphic presentation of numerical data is becoming popular because of various merits. A graph is a visual form of presentation. Graphs are drawn on a special type of paper known as graph paper. Each graph paper has thick horizontal and vertical lines of each division of a centimetre and thin lines for smaller parts of the same. A graph is divided into four quadrants but normally the first quadrant is used.

Advantages

When a graph is properly constructed, it readily shows information that might otherwise be lost amid the details of numerical tabulations. It also shows the tendency. In brief, the advantages are :

1. It provides an attractive and impressive view.
2. It simplifies complexity of data.
3. It provides easy comparison of two or more phenomena.
4. It needs no special knowledge of mathematics to understand a graph.
5. It saves the time and energy of the statistician as well as the observer.
6. It is probably the simplest method of presenting data.

QUESTIONS

1. What do you understand by classification and tabulation ? Discuss their importance.   (B. Com., Delhi)
2. "Diagrams help us to visualise the whole meaning of a numerical data at a single glance." Discuss.   (B. Com., Madurai)
3. What are the purpose for classifying the recorded observations ? What points will you take into consideration while tabulating classified observations ?
                                                                      (B. Com., B.A., Madurai)
4. State briefly the purposes served by the diagrammatic representation of data.
                                                                      (B. Com., Chennai)
5. What is meant by a Statistical Table ? Point out the objects of tabulation.
                                                                      (B. Com., Mumbai)

CHAPTER

Work Measurement and Standards

INTRODUCTION

Work measurement is *the application of techniques designed to establish the time for a qualified worker to carry out a specified job at a defined level of performance*. Work measurement involves determination of time required to do a job and it is also known as 'time study'. Here, time does not necessarily connote speed. Work measurement simply determines a rate of performance acceptable for the majority of workers. It may be used to determine desirable performance rates in particular areas and environment. It can also be used to establish an optimum work load for each worker.

In order to 'control' effectively, the office manager must know how the work should be done, what is currently being done, whether the work is being done according to plan. That is, he must ascertain the quantity and quality of the work performed, and the time spent on doing it. Attainment of the planned objective will be possible only if the work performed is of the right quantity and quality, and the work is performed within the required time so that the cost of performing it is kept within limits of economy. Thus 'work measurement' is an important tool in the hands of management for exercising effective control over office costs. That is, work measurement

233

is a programme of measuring the volume of work completed and the amount of time spent to complete it. This means assessment of work done by clerks and to know what is reasonable output expected of them.

Difficulties in Work Measurement

There is a resistance among office managers to the introduction of work measurement programmes. It is because of the widely held belief that office work is difficult of measurement, it is difficult to measure office work because:

1. **Difficulty in measurement :** Office work is not repetitive, it is so varied and complex that it does not lend itself to measurement, for example, clerks have to do different kinds of jobs at different time, sometimes they may be preparing an invoice, another time collecting data or at another time drafting a reply to a letter.

2. **Office employees' resistance :** White collar workers do not like to be bracketed with blue collar workers, whose work is measured on daily or weeskly basis.

3. **Office work can't quantitatively measured :** It is felt that clerical workers are closely related to management and they should be exempt from formal programme of measurement. They perform certain functions like planning, co-ordination or other work requiring prolonged mental effort. Thus such works cannot be quantitatively measured.

4. **Costly to measure :** Work measurement, even if practical in some cases, is a costly process. Managers feel that so long as the office work is going along well enough, there is no need of wasting money by attempting to measure it.

5. **Uneven flow of work :** It is possible that the flow of work may be uneven. It may be that a typist receives 40 letters for typing on one day and just 10 on the next day. Some persons are appointed to do a specific work, irrespective of quantity, for example, a receptionist will have to sit in the reception room, we cannot ask him "Why you have received 10 guests today when you received 20 yesterday ?"

MEASURABLE OFFICE WORK

Many management consultants feels that many of the reasons offered for the failure to establish a work measurement programme in office are more imaginary than real. Most of the office work is of repetitive nature and can be quantitatively and qualitatively measured. It is estimated that approximately 70% of all work done in offices is measurable. Following type of office activities are capable of measurement:

(a) The work of repetitive nature is capable of measurement. Much of the work done in offices is a uniform nature–work of typing, sealing envelopes, card punching etc. Such work can be measured.

(b) The work which is countable, that is, which can be measured in precise quantitative terms–like typing so many pages a day or entering so many cheques in the ledger etc.

(c) If the content of the work is consistently of same type over a long period of time, such work can be measured.

(d) If the volume of work is quite big, it is worthy of being counted and recorded.

IMPORTANCE OF WORK MEASUREMENTS

Work measurement is indispensable in carrying out the control function. It is an important management tool to control the size of workforce and improve the efficiency of workers and thereby control the labour cost. Work measurement can be used as a basis of incentive scheme in order to motivate the workers for better performance. Work measurement provides the relevant data for efficient work planning and control. Without work measurement, the manager cannot control the performance of workers. It is also not possible to lay down sound plans if there is no scheme for work measurement.

Work measurement can be used for effective allocation of work to workers and for preparing work schedules. Work measurement can be used in sending quotations as it makes it possible to know the time and cost involved in the proposed piece of work. In order to apply a proper incentive policy, the office manager must be able to judge the performance of each worker, to distinguish between a good worker and a poor worker so that the better worker receives due recognition and reward.

PURPOSE OF WORK MEASUREMENT

Work measurement establishes time standards for doing various jobs. The time standards so set help in planning and controlling. The basic objective of work measurement is to facilitate planning and controlling of office operations. In addition, work measurement can be used for the following purposes :

(a) To determine standard work load for each worker.

(b) To determine manpower needs or the number of persons required.

(c) To measure efficiency of employees, a department or the organisation as a whole.

(d) To serve as a basis for incentive wages.

(e) To help in simplifying office systems and routines.

STANDARDS OF PERFORMANCE

There is generally enormous waste in human efforts because many employees either do unnecessary work or do necessary work inefficiently. We shall analyse the first aspect under 0 and M and now concentrate on measures to be taken to remove inefficiency of office employees. For bringing efficiency in office employees, it is necessary to set up standards of performance and then to compare the actual performance with these standards.

The word 'standard' means a basis or criterion of measurement of performance of the employees. Different standards of performance are set up for various activities. A standard is a goal or objective of performance set up for men, materials and equipment. Setting of standards in terms of quantity, quality and time is necessary for effective control because it is essential to determine how the performance of work is to be measured before the actual process of control is to be put into effect. But work measurement has no sense unless it can be compared with some predetermined standards to know whether the work has been performed in the best possible manner or not.

Standards are constituents of a large programme of scientific analysis. They are necessary for management control. "The standards should be accurate, precise, acceptable and workable and to certain extent they should be flexible. To make the standards more effective, production standard should be developed for each activity. This should not be borrowed from past work. A standard is bound to fail if it is based on records of past performance that are poor.

UNIT OF MEASUREMENT

There must be different unit for measuring different kinds of work. For example, there must be one unit for measuring drafting work, another for measuring typing work and yet another for measuring ledger posting etc. While selecting the unit of measurement for a particular type of office work, it should be seen that the unit selected fulfils the following points :

(a) The unit selected must be standard. It must not be changed from time to time.

(b) One unit of a particular class must be comparable with another unit of the same class.

(c) The unit selected must be suitable for measuring the work with a reasonable degree of accuracy.

(d) The unit selected must be easy to understand and use.

METHODS OF WORK MEASUREMENT AND SETTING STANDARD

Several methods or techniques are used for measuring work and setting standards. A brief description of methods of measuring efficiency and setting standards on office are given below :

1. Past performance method. Under this method, past record about the performance of the workers on the job is methodically kept. It is found out how much time does a normal worker takes to complete a particular volume of work. For example, the output of typist may be measured, over a period of time, on the basis of pages he typed in one day. If the quantity of work is to be measured more accurately, the typed work can be measured on the basis of lines or words or square inches of matter typed in one day.

In past performance method, performance of the best worker is used as standard but, it may prove too harsh for average workers. The answer to his problem is that the average work of the best and of the poorest may be used as standard. The main advantage of this method is that it can be easily installed, at a very low cost and there is no need for highly qualified and trained personnel to administer it.

2. Time analysis method or time log method. Under this method a record of actual time spent and the unit of work done, over a period of time by various employees is kept. On the basis of this a time analysis list for the entire department is prepared.

The next step is to find out how many units of work, do the workers complete in one hour. This is done by dividing the total quantity of work completed by total hours spent. From these figures, it is possible to establish standard time for each item of work being done.

The main advantage of time analysis method is that its installation does not involve much additional cost. By maintaining continuous record of work of employees, a permanent control over their activities can be maintained.

3. Work sampling method. In work sampling method of measuring work, a trained analyst first "breaks down" the various jobs which are to be studied. The next step is to prepare a report about each individual employee to determine how he spends his time. The analyst also records the number of items produced during a specified time. The point to note here is that the analyst not only studies the number of items produced but also sees how an employee spends his time. It may be that an efficient worker produces 10 units in 8 hours but of these 8 hours he spends two hours on gossiping. As the name, work sampling method suggests, the analyst does not study each and every job, he selects a few samples and bases his conclusion on those samples.

The data obtained under work sampling method are more reliable than those secured under time analysis method. The main disadvantage of this method is that it proves quite costly, specially, if the number of samples to be studied is large. Moreover, the work of analysis has to be done by a trained analyst.

4. Motion study and time study. Under this system an attempt is made to find the minimum time required to do a work through a study of the motions of the worker and time taken by him.

Through motion study. "The one best way to do the work is found out by avoiding unnecessary movements. In motion study analysis a job or an office procedure is divided into small operations and each operation is studied visually by means of stop watch. For example, it was noticed that if sponge; for moistening gummed flaps of envelopes was out of normal reach of the hand, it involved waste of activity and caused fatigue.

To get more accurate results it is better to study movements by motion picture camera, this method is known as Micromotion Study. Micromotion techniques are used to study office work of repetitive and costly nature.

Following either a motion study or a micromotion study, a standard time for doing a job can be determined. This standard time does include proper rest pauses and delays due to machine difficulties.

Time study is the means of measuring job performance in terms of time. Its object is to establish the time required for performing each operation at an average speed. The purpose of time study is to find out the output of a worker of average skill, under normal conditions. Since the worker cannot produce steadily and uninterruptedly throughout the day, additions to normal working time must be made for delays, fatigue and personal needs such as going to take water, washing face and hands or taking a cup of tea etc.

For measuring time, use of stop watch is generally made. When making observations for time study, stop watch is started at the beginning of each operation and is kept running during the entire work cycle till the last element is completed. All these readings are recorded in the data sheet. Similar records are maintained for all subsequent work cycles and by summing them up we get standard time for doing a job. Time study by stop watch is based on scientific approach and can give reliable results.

Time studies can bring good results only if office personnel have confidence in the fairness of these studies. The time analyst must be capable of dealing with people honestly and sympathetically. He must earn a reputation for making fair and accurate studies.

5. Predetermined Elemental Time Data. To standardise time studies in relation to different kinds of jobs performed under same conditions, *"Predetermined Elemental Time Data"* has been developed on the assumption; that if the same motions are used for performing various jobs under the same conditions the standard time for these motions would be the same. There are a large number of basic motions which are common to many operations. If a job consists of a series of such basic motions, it will be more appropriate to add up the time taken in doing these motions and find out the total standard time required to perform the full job (of course special motions required for doing that job will be studied separately).

Various methods available for finding predetermined elemental time data. Among them "Methods Time Measurement" (MTM) is the most commonly used method. Under this method the motions required to complete a given activity are analysed and by applying standard time values for each motion a theoretical standard is derived for each element of operation. It is possible to maintain uniform standard because there are no chances of analyst's personal judgement entering into the study.

BENEFITS OF WORK STANDARDS

Setting up of standards is a basic prerequisite of management control. Work measurement is an effective tool of management control. The work standards help the management in planning and control in the following ways:

1. Determination of Personnel Requirement

Standards help in determining the number of employees required to perform various office activities. By measuring the work and setting standards, the office manager can know the volume of work that has been done and that ought to have been done. On the basis of this, he can know the number of staff required in the office.

2. Measurement of Effectiveness of Departments

Work measurement and standards serve as a basis of measuring effectiveness of all the departments in the office. The efficiency of office employees can be assessed by measuring their work and comparing it with standards. Corrective action to rectify the causes of inefficiency in any department can be taken on the basis of work measurement and its comparison with the standards.

3. Determination of Office Cost

Standards help in determining the cost of the office work. By measuring the quantity of work performed it is possible to determine the cost of the work. The management can prepare budgets regarding office costs. By knowing the difference between standard cost and actual cost of performing office work, it is possible to ascertain the reasons for the differences and take corrective action. Standards can thus, help in reducing office costs.

4. Help in Planning

Standards help in planning, scheduling and routine work in the office. The office manager can know when the required work is likely to be completed and how much time it is going to take. The employees can also know by what time their individual work should be completed.

5. Installation of Incentive Schemes

Standards are helpful in installing incentive wage systems. On the basis of time standards laid down, incentive wage plans for rewarding increased production or performance beyond standard, by means of piece rate or wage bonuses can be introduced.

6. Improvement in Morale

Standards and work measurement help in improving morale of office workers. The employees know, what is expected of them, both in terms of volume and quality. They know what is the fair amount of work and if they done it, they will be termed as good workers and this gives them self-confidence. Under this system, recognition does not depend on the whims of supervisor, the superior worker automatically receives recognition for a job well done, and the inefficient worker is rated accordingly.

7. Development of Systems and Procedures

Standards can help in the development of newer or more efficient office systems and procedures. Through the analysis of cost and time involved in performing office work, office manager try to find better systems and procedures which reduce cost of performing office work.

QUESTIONS

1. What are the techniques of work measurement of office work ? Discuss them in brief.
   (B. Com., Delhi)
2. Enumerate the purposes for which work measurement programmes are set up.
   (B. Com., Chennai)
3. What are the different ways in which office work may be measured ? *(AIMA)*
4. What is a 'Work Standard' ? State the importance of standards in measurement of office work. *(B. Com., M.S)*
5. Briefly explain the techniques used for work measurement. *(CS)*
6. What is the Time Log or Time Analysis method of setting standard ? What steps are necessary for setting standard under this method. *(B. Com., Delhi)*
7. What is understood by time and motion study ? *(B. Com., M.S)*
8. What are the benefits derived by management from work standards ? *(CS)*
9. What are the main purposes of measurement in office management.
10. Why is a unit of measurement needed ?

Office Report and Precis Writing

INTRODUCTION

Every management needs accurate and up-to-date information, on the basis of it, formulates policies for future business. Formulation of policies may not be practicable in the absence of information. For the growing needs of the organisation, increase in the professions, widening activities of the business, etc. it has become essential to look for the information. Executive or the management will look into the information, and on the basis of that, policies are drawn. The office superintendent or the manager has to present the up-to-date information in the form of report, to the management who do the needful at their end. A report is a presentation of facts, which have been drawn from investigation, inspection, experience, research, survey, interviews, etc. A report must be based on actual facts, but not on mere opinion.

With the increase in the size of modern business organisation and their activities, there has been a growing need for communication within a group. Decentralisation compels delegation of authority. Therefore, each executive, supervisor or foreman is a manager—a manager who is accountable for results in his own sphere of operations. Each manager should report on those operations of the firm for which he has accepted the responsibility and the authority. A regular flow of such information and communication—report or statistical data—to different executives is essential for a sound basis for policy decision, planning and the successful attainment of business objectives.

MEANING OF REPORT

What is a report ? A report is a summary of information. "A report can be described as a statement prepared to present facts relating to planning, co-ordinating, performance and general state of business in an organisation. It is thus a summary of managerial performance." According to *Littlefield*, "Organisational distance, specialisation, and limitations of human comprehension force management to reply heavily upon reports in communicating information both downward and upward. Reports are basically summaries of information. A system of reporting is vital to any management information system but especially to a responsible, decentralised management. It logically follows then that each manager not only should, but must report on those operations for the firm for which he has accepted the responsibility and authority."

According to *George R Terry*, "A written statement based on a collection of facts, events and opinions and usually express a summarised and interpretative value of this information. It may deal with past accomplishments, present conditions, or probable future developments." According to *Johnson*, "A good business report is a communication that contains factual information organised and presented in clear, correct and coherent language." A report is an organised statement of facts relating to a particular subject, prepared by an individual or a constituted body after an independent investigation and presented to the interested persons with or without recommendations.

FUNCTIONS OF REPORT

Reports have the following functions :
1. Reports are prepared to help the process of planning in an organisation.
2 . It serves as a means of communicating information to those who need and use it. It provides the required information to creditors, investors, share-holders and the general public.
3. It aims at measuring executive performance and how such a performance may be improved.
4. The act of co-ordinating is best performed with the help of reports.
5. It presents factual information to management in order to exercise control.
6. A system in which regular reports are sent can check unsatisfactory trends in performance and corrective steps can be taken.

TYPES OF REPORTS

Reports are usually of two types: (*a*) Routine or Ordinary Report and (*b*) Special Report.

a) Routine Reports :

Routine reports are generally prepared by the clerks of the concern and submitted to the officer concerned. Many such reports may be daily, weekly, monthly, quarterly, etc., dealing with specified topics — sales, production, cost of manufacturing, etc. Such reports generally do not contain comments, suggestions or recommendations etc., and may be generally in figures. This report is meant to inform the management position of the business.

"A report is submitted by a lower authority to a higher authority."

(b) Special Reports :

The name suggests that such reports are drafted for special purpose and not as a regular or routine nature. When a circumstance arises and some decisions have to be taken, usually special reports are prepared. For this purpose, a particular person or a committee is appointed to look after the job of preparing report. Such occasions may be the opening of new branches, changing the production line, shifting of business, etc. A person or a committee after its appointment, makes the enquiry and finally has to submit the report to the appointing authority or to the authorised person.

It usually contains the opinion or recommendation of the reporter on a certain matter of special, *i.e.* non-routine nature for example, market research report, product development report etc.

A report may also be : (*a*) Formal or (*b*) Informal.

(*a*) **Formal Report** is prepared in the prescribed or recognised form and is presented according to the established procedure. Such report is presented to the reader in a rather formal format.

(*b*) **Informal Report,** on the other hand, does not follow any prescribed form or procedure. It may involve verbal reporting in person or over the telephone or may take the form of a letter.

SOURCES OF DATA : The reporter must find the sources from where he can collect information and interpret it. The following are the sources of information.

1. Primary Data

Primary data are those which are to be collected for the first time and they are original in character. Therefore, this type of data can also be known as original data or first-hand information. Primary data can be collected by following methods.

(*a*) Direct personal observation

(*b*) Indirect personal interviews

(*c*) Local reports

(*d*) Questionnaires

(a) Direct Personal Observation

The investigator has to meet the informants personally and collect the data. When the enquiry is intensive, the result will be more accurate. If the field of enquiry is big, this type of enquiry is not possible as it takes much time to complete the reports.

(b) Indirect Personal Interview

When the first method of collection is not possible because of the vast enquiry, an indirect personal investigation is carried out. In this method, information is collected from the informant about the matter of enquiry. The correctness of the enquiry will depend upon the interviewing person. If the informant knows the information needed—not prejudiced in his mind and is ready to give correct information—one can have reliable and correct information. This type of enquiry is expensive, because many enumerators have to be appointed under the investigator. If the enumerators are biased, the collected data may be misleading.

(c) Local Reports

Local correspondents or agents collect the data and report them to the investigator. This is a cheap method. Correspondents may be biased in collecting the information. The are directly or indirectly not interested in the enquiry, as such furnished data may not be correct. This method is suitable where approximate data or figures are required.

(d) Questionnaires

This type of enquiry is popular. Questionnaires are sent either by post or by enumerator to the persons who are in possession of information. This method can cover a larger area. If the questionnaire is sent by post, the informants are requested to fill in the forms and return them to the investigator. If the informants are illiterate, this type is not practicable. There will also be delay in getting the information. Sometimes incomplete questionnaire may be returned. If the questionnaire is sent through the enumerator, the informant will be helped by him in filling the required information. This method is definitely better. The questionnaire may be printed or cyclostyled and should have enough space to write the answers for the questions. The enumerators must be courteous in approaching the informant and should not be biased or prejudiced. The reliability of data is based upon the training, qualification and competence of the enumerators. If the questionnaire is sent by post, the response will be very poor.

DRAFTING A QUESTIONNAIRE

The selection and framing the questions are important. The questionnaire may be in print or cyclostyled. The correctness and accuracy of the information collected depend upon the questions themselves. The drafting of the questions may be made after choosing all the questions. The following few hints may be of assistance in drawing proper questionnaire:

1. The question may be understandable even to a layman.
2. The question must be selected so as to give answers in a few words, e.g., "Yes" or "No" or in Figures.
3. They should not hurt the pride of the informant.
4. The purpose of the survey may be informed to the informant.
5. If any clarification is needed, it must be given under footnote.
6. Questions must be in logical order.
7. The informant must feel easy to fill the forms.
8. Each question must contain a different idea. Many questions should not be mingled in one question.
9. As far as possible, avoid questions which require much time in filling in the answers.
10. The informant must be informed that the information will be kept confidential.

1. Secondary Data

Secondary data are those which are already collected by someone and are available in finished form. The method simplifies and makes easy the job of the investigator. It is less expensive. The following are a few examples of secondary data :

1. Official publications of Central and State Governments.
2. Reports of committees.
3. Commercial and economic journals like "Commerce", "Capital", etc.
4. Report of Bankers, Reserve Bank and other institutions.
5. Publications brought out by research institutions, universities, etc.

Secondary data may also be available in an unpublished form. It is always better to make use of primary data instead of secondary data. Secondary data should not be used blindly. A careful enquiry may be made as to the purpose and limitation of secondary data.

GUIDING PRINCIPLES FOR A GOOD REPORT

All the essential data must be included in the report so as to give effectiveness and completeness to the report. The report may be in the form of a letter or in any other form. Whatever it may be, report must contain some conclusions or recommendations from the facts investigated. The following **general rules** may be noted while drafting a report.

1. A report should be addressed to a particular person or group of readers. Example, to the General Manager or the Board of Directors.
2. It must have a short title.
3. The reference to which the report is drawn, must be quoted.
4. Following the title, a report should have a table of contents, consisting of headings and sub-headings describing various topics along with the page number so that readers can know the pattern of the report and reference to various topics.
5. It must contain introductory paragraphs, a brief description about the matters dealt with problems solved, etc.
6. The language of the report should be simple and unambiguous.
7. The rules of punctuation should be strictly followed so as to avoid confusion of change of meaning, when it is read.
8. The report must be readable and understandable, especially for whom it is meant.
9. If the report is lengthy, each paragraph should be numbered.
10. The report should deal with the matter as concisely as possible.
11. The facts drawn in the report should be reliable, complete and true.
12. Technical terms must be avoided in a report. Clarity is essential. Presentation of the report must be in a systematical order.
13. The completed report must be signed by the person responsible alongwith date.
14. The recommendations or suggestions must be based on the factual data, of course, supported by reasons with investigated result.
15. The recommendations and suggestions may be within quotation marks or in capitals, so as to draw the attention of the readers.

PRESENTATION OF REPORTS

The main purpose of a report is to help the recipient to know the facts relating to the subject under consideration. He draws his own conclusion from the report and takes suitable action. A report which does not stimulate thought and lead eventually to action may be of passing interest to the reader; it serves no useful purpose. It does not justify the cost incurred on its preparation. Therefore, a good report should contain all the relevant facts, it should marshal the facts in logical order, discuss them in simple language and arrive at some conclusion.

FORM OF REPORT

The form of the report will vary according to its purpose. However, a formal report generally contains the following:

1. **Introduction :** It contains the purpose and name of the report and the terms of reference.

2. **Heading :** The report should give a main heading and sub-headings which should indicate, as concisely as possible, its contents.

3. **Address :** The report should be addressed to some definite reader or readers—the Board of Directors, Managing Director etc.

4. **Table of Contents :** In case of a lengthy report, the topics or chapters alongwith their page numbers should be given.

5. **Body of the Report :** It should state the terms of reference which the reporter was given and define the problem to be solved and all other relevant facts.

6. **Findings :** This part of the report contains the findings of the reporter. Findings should be based on the facts and the data collected by him.

7. **Conclusion :** This section contains the conclusions and suggestions of the reporter.

8. **Summary :** In case of a long report, a brief summary of the report should be given.

9. **Appendices :** This may consist of statistical tables, graphs, list of witnesses etc.

10. **Signature and Date :** The report should be signed by the person responsible for it and dated.

Specimen :
Report on the location of a new branch
Nikhil Kumar   Chennai-600 001
                                                                          10th Jan.

The Director,
Ramlal Publications,
New Delhi-110 040

Sub : Opening of a branch in Chennai

Sir,

In accordance with the resolution dated 20th December, I take pleasure in submitting a report upon the suitability and desirability of opening a branch office in Chennai for our publications.

Existing Position :

From Chennai alone, our firm has been getting an annual business amounting to Rs. 2 crores.

Figures for the last five years show a tendency of increase of our sale and printing publications.

I have received repeated requests from customers of this area and surrounding areas to open a branch office in Chennai so that parties can deal directly.

Work Done :

I have the complete data on the subject from our office. The data were useful to me. 1 visited several schools, colleges, local book-sellers and markets. I had the clear suggestions from many in favour of opening a branch office in the Chennai city. The people wish to see the books directly and buy them on the spot, without wasting time in unnecessary correspondence.

Facts Finding :

A building near the Railway Station is lying vacant and the rent will be Rs. 5,000 per month. I have contacted the owner of the building, who is ready to spare it on a rent basis for a period of 5 years. One gentleman, a retired manager of M/s. Jyoti Press Ltd., is willing to act as a manager of our branch in Chennai. His salary can be fixed at Rs10,000 plus 2% commission on sales.

Conclusion :

Our initial expenditure will be Rs. one lakh, provided machineries and furnitures are to be transferred from Head Office. Moreover, I am sure, the sales of our publications will increase, if such a branch is opened in Chennai.

If my opinion is acceptable, a branch may be opened before March.

Yours sincerely,

Model : Investigation regarding decline in sales.

Gram : Chopra

CHOPRA & SONS ENTERPRISES

(Washing-soap Manufacturers)

No. Sales 71-72/47

Cantonment,
Bazar Street
Kolkata-1.
10th Oct. 2009

Shri R.C. Jain
Sales Representative,
29, West Street,
Agra-282008
Dear Sir,

We have been watching your reports of monthly sales sent by the Regional Manager. From the statements, it is understood that the sale of the washing-soap has been decreasing steadily for the last three months. If the decrease in sales goes on at this rate, we will have to face much difficulty to get a smooth running of the establishment.

We, therefore, entrust you to find out the cause of the decrease in sales and send your report to us with suitable suggestions and recommendations in order to arrest the present undesired trend.

Thanking you.

Yours faithfully,
for Chopra & Sons Enterprises

....

(Sales Manager)

Model : Reply to the sales manager

CHOPRA & SONS ENTERPRISES

(Dealers in Washing-soap)

H.O. Cantonment,   29, West Street,
Kolkata-1.   Agra.
                                                                    20th Oct., 2009.

Dear Sir,

    Ref : Decline in the sales of washing-soap. Detailed report with suggestions

In accordance with your letter No. Sales 71-72-47 dated on 10th Oct., I have undertaken a careful study of the general trend of our business. I contacted the local dealers and collected the shortcomings in respect of our own products. The following are the results of my investigation :

1. There is a general depression in the trade. It has affected our business as well as others.

2. There is a flow of substitute products in the market. Owing to this, a high competition is being experienced at present.

3. Our advertisement policy is ineffective. Other firms are coming forward with new advertisements to attract the customers.

4. Our products are at a disadvantage, because of the outmoded designs and packing. But other firms are adopting the best designs with attractive packings.

Under these circumstances I suggest the following remedies, which I hope, if put into practice, would give higher sales and will enable us to compete with similar products :

1. In order to overcome the present position, the prices may be reduced temporarily. A free gift of a soap box may be given to those, who buy at least six numbers of soaps. This may be continued until the sales boost up.

2. A more scientific way of advertisement should be adopted. The superiority and the usefulness of our products be brought in the minds of the public, through regular advertisement. Of course, there is a considerable expenditure, but this will, I am sure fetch a good sale.

3. In local exhibitions, our stalls may be opened to promote the sales.

4. The present design and shape of soap may be changed to a better design, with an attractive packing.

5. Frequent changes in the design and shape will also create a good impression in the minds of the people.

I am sure, if these are put into effect, we can easily arrest the undesired situation, we are facing now. Thus, we shall create a favourable position in order to have the best sales in future.

Yours faithfully,
for Chopra & Sons Enterprises
R.C Jain
Sales Representative

Model : Report on the need for computerisation

ALLIED SALES COMPANY LTD
(H.O. Mumbai)

P.B. No.240,
Nagercoil.
629 001.
6th June, 2009.

The Managing Director,
Mumbai.
Sir,

Sub : Urgent need for computerising the Accounts Department.

As you are well aware that our branch has achieved tremendous growth during the last two years. The sales volume, number of customers, turnover, the staff of this branch etc., have doubled. The auditors report clearly shows this. The Accounts Department is over-loaded with more and more responsibilities. The present staff position is quite unsatisfactory. The Accounts Department finds it difficult to keep up-to-date records of purchases, sales, salary bills, remittances of amount, receipt of cash etc. Apart from Head Office, we have three branches including this one. The other two branches were computerised last year. It is a fact that this branch is doing more business than the other two. Although the Head Office has appointed additional hands in the Accounts Department, the staff are unable to cope with the increasing work-load. The staff in the department continue to work till late hours, yet fail to keep up the work up-to-date.

The only way to overcome this situation is to computerise the Accounts Department. When it is done, it will lead to a reduction of staff strength and at the same time we can keep up the records of every transaction at our finger tips with the help of computers. In the long run it will be economical, apart from modernisation.

The proposal may please be given top-priority.

Thank you.

Yours truly,

Model : Opening of branch

Brooke Bond Layout,
Coimbatore-641009
3rd March, 2009.

The Director,
Gandia Press Ltd.
Madurai 625002
Sir,

Ref : Opening of a branch in coimbatore

In accordance with the resolution dated 18th December, 2008, take pleasure in submitting a report upon the suitability and desirability of opening a branch office in Coimbatore for publications.

Existing position :

From Coimbatore alone, our firm has been getting an annual business amounting to Rs. 35 Lakhs.

Figures for the last five years show a tendency of increase of our sale and printing Publications.

We have received repeated requests from customers of this area and surrounding areas to open branch office at Coimbatore, so that parties can deal directly.

Work done :

I have the complete data on the subject from our office. The data were useful to me. By staying in Coimbatore I visited several school, institutions, local booksellers and markets. I had the clear suggestions from many, and am in favour of opening a branch office in the city. The people wish to see the books directly and buy them on the spot, without wasting time in unnecessary correspondence.

Fact finding :

A building near the Railway station is lying vacant and the rent will be Rs. 800 per month. I have contacted the owner of the building, who is ready to spare it on a rent basis for a period of 5 years. Mr. M.S. Nadar, a retired superintendent of M/s. Jyoti Press is willing to act as the manager for our firm. His salary can be fixed at Rs. 5,000/- plus 2% commission on sales.

Conclusion :

I find that the condition is very nice to open a branch. Mr. M.S. Nadar is an able hand to deal our business. Our initial expenditure will be less than Rs. 25,000 provided machines are transferred from the head office. Moreover, I am sure, the sales of our publications will increase, if such a branch is opened.

If my opinion is acceptable, a branch may be opened before June, 2009.

Yours faithfully,

Sangaralingam.

Report on the declining sales

Udith Kumar

Bangalore-560009

10th February.

The Sales Manager

Black-bird Company,

Mumbai-400001.

Ref. : Causes of declining sales and suggestions for improvement.

Sir,

In accordance with your letter of 25th Jan., I have undertaken a careful study of the general trend of our business. I contacted the local dealers and collected the short-comings in respect of our products. The following are the results of my investigation:

Findings :

1. There is a general depression in the trade. It has affected our business as well as others.

2. There is a flow of substitute products in the markets. Owing to this, a high competition is being experienced at present. The increased competition from new multi-national companies, in recent years, is one of the prime causes for decline in sales.

3. Our advertisement policy is ineffective. Other firms are coming forward with new advertisements to attract the customers.

4. Our products are at a disadvantage, because of the outmoded designs and packing. But other firms are adopting the best designs with attractive packings.

Suggestions :

Under these circumstances I suggest the following remedies, which I hope, if put into practice, would give higher sales and will enable us to compete with similar products:

1. Sales efforts should be intensified with greater emphasis on services to customers.

2. In order to overcome the present position, the prices may be reduced temporarily, by 10% or a free gift of a soap box may be given to those, who buy at least six numbers of our product. This may be continued until the sales boost up.

3. A more scientific way of advertisement should be adopted. The superiority and the usefulness of our products be brought in the minds of the public, through regular advertisements. Of course, there is a considerable expenditure, but this will, I am sure to fetch a good sale.

4. In local exhibitions, our stalls may be opened to promote the sales.

5. The present design and shape of our product may be changed to a better design with an attractive packing.

6. Frequent changes in the design and shape will also create a good impression in the minds of the people.

7. Feed-back of information on the results of the .above steps should be carefully examined and corrective measures adopted as and when necessary.

I shall be glad to give you any other information or clarification needed, on hearing from you.

Thank you.

Yours sincerely,

PRECIS WRITING

A precis means a summary or an abstract. The word summary is an exact synonym for precis, a French word. *Collins* says that precis is the extract of the given passages. In actual sense, a precis is just a straightforward statement of the mere facts without adding any unnecessary explanations. The length of passage can be reduced to one-fifth or to one-third of the original passage.

Precis is a condensed piece of composition, giving a precise or exact idea of the original passage. It should be brief to the point, including everything important and excluding everything unimportant. The importance of precis applies to us in our everyday life. Everyone reads the newspapers. We find in it the summarised accounts of the events of the world. Precis-writing goes on endlessly in press offices daily and efficiently.

Essentials of a Good Precis Writer

1. In the first, the writer must possess the power of thorough understanding and judgement, and also the correct and quick grasping power of facts in full. He should know what is important and what is unimportant.

2. He must have good vocabulary which he can use correctly. Mere stock of words is not enough, he must be sure about their meanings and use.

3. He must possess the ability to compress the passages in a few words. When one word can be sufficient, never use two words. Padding, flourishes of style, uses of metaphorical language should be strictly avoided.

4. He should remember that brevity is the main theme of his work. But telegraphic language will be vagueness.

Essentials of Precis Writing

1. The precis must be a true summary of the given passages. No hard and fast rule can be laid for the summary to be written.

2. If no word limit for precis is asked in the passage, precis must be one-third of the original passage. In order to count the number of words of given passage, we need not spend our time to count exactly. For this, we can count the words in an average line and multiply by the number of lines. This will give more or less correct number. But as far as the precis is concerned, count exactly the number of words in a precis.

3. Whatever the matter may be, the summary must be in indirect form and in past tense.

4. As far as possible, the original words of the passages should be avoided. Sometimes certain words cannot be changed; in such cases, they can be used.

5. Order of the ideas in a precis can generally be that of the original. But for effectiveness, the ideas can be written in any order. Sometimes, the writer uses his own skill to arrange or rearrange the idea in the precis.

6. The precis must be continuously written and create a good impression of patch work. The reader of the precis must easily understand it without trouble.

METHOD OF APPROACH

1. Read the passage carefully in order to grasp the central and the general meaning.

2. Read the same again and try to pick up essential ideas, and underline most important points.

3. Sum up the points in short.

4. Make a rough draft. Make sure that there is no repetition of ideas.

5. Keep the original passage aside, then look at the draft whether it is clear, logical, and carries good summary. Modify it, by adding or deducting.

6. Make sure that no important ideas are left out. If it is alright in all respects, then write the precis in good and legible handwriting.

7. Do not forget to suggest a suitable title for the precis. It should be written as a heading and then write your precis.

Illustration

Make out a precis of the following with suitable title

One spring morning–I am not sure, but I think it must have been in April, because it was one of those days when rain and sunshine follow each other at frequent intervals–my brother and I, after much discussion as to how we should spend the day, thought we would go for a walk as far as the nearest town, which was situated about three miles away. We were staying at a large and somewhat dilapidated farm house, which had been in the possession of the same family for several generations but which, like its present owners, had gone down in the world. The house was situated at a distance of a mile or so from the main road, with which it was connected by a narrow, muddy lane, thickly overshadowed by trees. Along this lane accordingly we trudged, clad in thick shoes and mackintoshes, being resolved that we would take no chances with the weather.   (156 words)

Answer :

A JOURNEY IN A SHOWERY MORNING

Precis

One showery morning my brother and I decided to walk to the neighbouring town. Wearing thick shoes and mackintoshes, we left the old farm house where we were staying and proceeded along a dark and muddy lane leading to the main road.   (41 words)

Illustration

Make out a precis of the following :

I feel that India can play a big part and may be, an effective part, in helping to avoid war. Therefore, it becomes all the more necessary that India should not be lined up with any group of powers which for various reasons are full of war, preparing war. This is the main approach of our foreign policy and I am glad to say that I believe that it is more and more appreciated.   (75 words)

Answer :

INDIA'S FOREIGN POLICY

Precis

India can play an important role in avoiding the war. She should avoid alignment with war-mongering powers. And this policy is gaining much appreciation.   (25 words)

Illustration

Make out a precis of the following :

All of us are engaged in an unconscious endeavour to distract attention from the respect in which we are inferior to others and to emphasis the respect in which we believe ourselves to be superior. Each of us must feel superior in some respect; and we try, perhaps unconsciously, to convince the world that this is really the one thing that matters. If we are physically superior, then we believe–and try to make others believe–that physical fitness and strength are, after all, the real test of a man. If, on the other hand, we are physically inferior but intellectually superior, then we tend to disparage physical prowess and emphasis the importance of mental ability. If we are bad workmen or bad farmers, then we may try to shine as parlour politicians. If we are uneducated but (self-made), wealthy, well, what is the use of education, anyhow ? There's far too much education — and it only spoils a man. If, on the contrary, we are educated, but unsuccessful in the business of life, then we never lose an opportunity of belittling business success. Generally, if we are successful at anything, we believe that success is won by industry, ability and character, while if we have been unsuccessful, we believe that success is a matter of luck! Isn't that so ?

Answer :

PRECIS

It is a fact of human psychology to give more importance to one's plus points while denying it to those that are minus. It is never a matter of principle or logic. Instinct leads us to rate ourselves higher because of those qualities which we have and to run down others for the ones they have but which we lack. There are plenty of examples to prove the truth of this unconscious aspect of our mind.

Illustration

Make out a precis of the following :

I have often heard people say how disappointed they will be if they never see a certain place which they have for years dreamed of visiting. I sometimes wonder whether, if we got all we dreamed of, we might not be even more disappointed than if we failed to get it. I, for example, longed for years to go to Rome; yet, when at last I arrived at the Eternal City and drove through its streets, I wondered whether it was worthwhile going so far to see a city which appeared to me to be so unworthy of its history. This disappointment, I may say, did not last; but famous cities, famous objects, famous views do not always kindle at first sight the emotions we expect them to kindle. People used to think that a famous author was being funny when he said that he was disappointed with the Atlantic Ocean. To me this seems to be a straightforward confession of a disappointment that must have been experienced by thousands of people. The Atlantic Ocean, to my mind, looks its best from the shore; but even when it is seen from the shore for the first time by someone who has lived till manhood in an inland district, it does not always come up to expectations. Its very bigness is against it. It is easier to see at first sight the charm of a little lake, nestling among the mountains, than to drink in the vast beauty of the Atlantic. In the same way, I have never been disappointed in a hill; I have often been disappointed in a mountain. Although mountains are undoubtedly impressive, they have a kind of dreadful monotony that makes people like myself feel hostile to their beauty. While I like reading about mountains, nevertheless, outside books, I prefer the pleasures of the plain.

Answer :

PRECIS

It should cause no disappointment if a dreamt of place is never visited. On the contrary visiting it may prove disappointing as was the case with the author initially when he visited Rome. Another case in point is the Atlantic turning out to be very unlike what one imagined it to be. It is its size that is against it. Even as a hill is more satisfying than a mountain, a lake is more pleasing than a vast ocean. The author in fact prefers plains in actual life even though he enjoys reading about the mountains.

QUESTIONS

1. Define an office report ? What purposes can it serve ?   (B.Com. Delhi)
2. From which sources and by what methods can an office manager collect various types of information and data to meet business requirements ? Discuss in brief.
                                                                            (B.Com. Kerala)
3. Distinguish between routine and special report. Set out the stages in which you would proceed for drafting a report.   (B.Com. Punjab)
4. What are the important principles which should be borne in mind while drafting business reports ?   (B.Com. Madurai)
5. What are the functions of a report ? State what principles would guide you while drafting a report.   (ICWA Inter)
6. Draft a report as secretary of your company for submission to the Board on the recent trend of sales of your company, suggesting steps for improvements. (B. Com. Mumbai)

7. What forms a good report ? What are its different types ? Describe briefly special reports. *(ICWA Inter)*

8. You are asked by the Director of your company on desirability of acquiring new premises for the office. Draft a suitable report in this regard. *(B. Com. Delhi)*

9. **Make a precis of the following passage to one-third of its length and give a suitable title to it**

The industrial system, besides providing conditions of work, should also guarantee labour the higher satisfaction that, by doing their work well, they are rendering service to the community not as slaves of the system but as freemen. In order to give them greater satisfaction and to remove their fear of the future, workers should be given a voice in the shaping of the industrial system.

It is admitted on all hands that maintenance of satisfactory industrial relations between employers, and workers forms an important principle in the labour policy of every civilized nation. Success of an industrial development generally depends upon the harmonious relations and co-operation between employers and the human element of the industry. Such industrial relations in their turn depend upon many factors. In the first place there should exist properly developed organisations or workers appreciating the value of rule of law. Secondly, the employers and their organisations should recognize and appreciate the value of the human element and they must realize their responsibilities to their workers. Thirdly, there must be adequate machinery for the settlement of threatened or existing trade dispute.

Employers in India are fairly organised on national and industrial lines. Many employers in the past have failed to recognize the human element in the industry and their responsibility to provide proper working conditions and welfare of their workers both inside and outside the factory. The establishment of the Tripartite Labour Conference has, however, brought about a change in the employers' attitude towards their workers and their organisations. They are becoming more and more responsive. It will thus be seen that the first two essentials for the maintenance of good industrial relations are not altogether absent in India, although they have not yet fully and adequately developed.

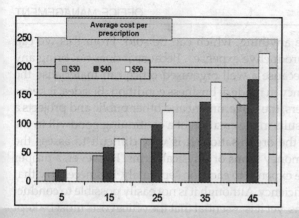

Office Cost Reduction and Cost Saving

INTRODUCTION

Office work is generally branded as unproductive activity of the organisation though it provides valuable services to different functional departments. This is because of the fact that there is no 'cost consciousness' in most of the offices and there are always inexcusable waste in the offices like installing machines which are not needed, buying services which do not contribute to the effective operation of the business and placing on the pay roll employees who are not needed. Moreover, office employees misuse their time and the stationery and other items which are at their disposal. Many a time, this happens because of lack of proper supervision in the office, lack of training to employees and existence of defective systems and routines in the office. As a consequence, the office costs increase miserably and they reduce the overall gains of the organisation. Therefore, it is one of the important tasks of the office manager to keep the costs of running the office under control.

Cost reduction and efficiency are closely interlinked. Cost reduction means, can be defined, "planned and positive approach to the improvement of efficiency." To spend something to increase the sales is obvious. To spend something to increase the production is also obvious. However, the office does not sell any thing and it does not make anything, which can be sold. From this we can understand that the cost of office is "unproductive expense". Because it does not bring any income directly. "This view is wrong. Because a well organised office can materialise the policies and plans to achieve more efficiency in modern business condition. Besides, it keeps the organisation in touch with its customers, the Government and other public and projects a good image of the organisation which results in the creation of a continuing goodwill in the minds of all the people who deal with the organisation. It is very difficult to assess the contribution of office to each activity in money terms or physical terms. However, a proper costing system may help to allocate office expense to each job separately. It is necessary that the office costs must be correlated with efficiency. Although it is not easily possible to conduct a cost-benefit analysis in quantitative terms, yet it is essential that the office costs must be kept at a reasonable minimum level without, of course, sacrificing the efficiency.

COST REDUCTION

Cost reduction is an extention of cost control. It aims at effecting economies in costs or alternatively at cost savings. It is an attempt to bring costs down, generally and permanently. The steps for the purpose are the elimination of waste and inefficiency and effecting major changes in product content and operating methods. For this purpose, a good number of devices could be employed such as search for cheaper materials, improved methods of production and inspection, and improved standard of quality and timing. The emphasis all along is on permanent savings, and thus increasing profit margin. Hence, cost reduction is a much wider concept than cost control, Cost control is essentially a short term programme in as much as it relates costs to objects and standards. But cost reduction could have both short-term and long-term dimensions.

Importance of Cost Reduction

Savings is a good habit. "A rupee saved is a rupee earned." It does not mean parsimoney, which spends little or nothing. Cost reduction or cost savings cannot be equated with miserliness. The office manager should scientifically assess the possible benefits of an expenditure and incur it without reservation once he feels that it is necessary. Where he feels that an expenditure is unnecessary and is not needed, he must not incur it even if it is an insignificant amount. The cost reduction or cost saving is important because:

1. Wasteful expenditure is eliminated.
2. Economical use of resources take place.
3. Productivity increases.
4. Management gets regular information on cost analysis.
5. A good cost reduction or cost saving develops cost, consciousness among employees.

TYPES OF WASTEFUL EXPENDITURE

The office manager should properly understand the problem of wasteful expenditure before he takes up the question of cost saving. All wastes in an office may be divided into three classes :

1. Waste of Money
2. Waste of Time
3. Waste of Effort.

Since time is money, the single waste is of money in various forms. Waste of materials is a waste of money (paid for materials). Waste of efforts due to faulty office procedure is a waste of time, which ultimately leads to waste of money.

PROGRAMME OF COST REDUCTION AND COST SAVING

There must be a definite programme of cost saving and cost reduction. The programme must have the following features :

1. **Employee's Participation :** Every employee of the organisation should be encouraged to give suggestions for cost reduction and cost saving. Suggestions should be welcome and can be implemented if they are suitable. Co-operation at every level is essential for the effective implementation of the programme.

2. **Cost Consciousness :** A habit of cost consciousness should be developed among the managerial and other personnel in order to make the programme successful.

3. **Responsibility :** It is essential to identify the key persons who will be responsible for cost saving. The supervisor who actually oversees the office work is the right person who can be assigned the responsibility of cost reduction.

4. **Continuous Programme :** The programme should be continuous in nature so as to create cost consciousness among the office staff. *Leffingwell and Robinson* observed, "An economy wave soon passes, as all waves must and the organisation resumes its old wasteful habits until the next economy wave comes along".

TECHNIQUES OF COST REDUCTION

It is very difficult to achieve 100% utilisation of men and machines in the office. Following are the means which can be used to achieve the object of cost reduction :

1. Organisation and Methods (O & M)
2. Work Simplification
3. Budgetary Control
4. Supervisory Control
5. Cost Control

ORGANISATION AND METHODS (O & M)

Organisation and methods refers to the systematic attempt on the part of an enterprise to improve organisation, to improve methods and to maintain administration at great level of efficiency. O & M covers everything that contributes to efficiency, however, it mainly deals with office organisation, office systems and routines, Methods of operation, uses of mechanical devices etc. The main objectives of O & M are elimination of unnecessary operations, simplification of procedures and ensuring proper flow of work. Every organisation while working involves certain systems, once efficient become inefficient, outmoded or uneconomic and sometimes, a source of trouble. The main reasons for this is as follows:

1. Changing Circumstances

The circumstances are always changing. To day, the change seems to be faster than in the past. The change is faster with the higher levels of education, faster transportation, faster communication, greater human aspirations about what we should have as an expected part of our life and with increased emphasis on human rights. New products come up. It increases the work of the office. There arise potential change in the office work.

2. New Development

To day we live in a world of rapid technical advance in every field including office. What was the most modern method ten years back, is almost certain to be outmoded now. Due to continuing change and speed of change, a continuous reeducation and retraining have become essential.

3. New Demands

Change is quite complex and a difficult problem. The changes in the industrial sector include the creation of new products, obsolescence of others changes in the techniques of production, changes in marketing and distribution technique changes in organisational structure etc. The application of scientific management principles has led to entirely new kind of clerical system. There is more paper work and more clerical operations. The office procedures and methods keep on changing.

The O and M refers to the systematised attempt on the part of an enterprise to improve and maintain office administration at a high level of efficiency. The term O and M can be described as "the activities of groups, of people in Government or other public bodies or in private firms, who are asked to advise administrators or managers on questions of organisation and methods so as to increase the efficiency of the work for which the manager is responsible, either by providing a better service or a cheaper one, or both."

Objectives of O & M

The aims or objectives of O & M are as follows :

1. Elimination of waste, in all activities, is the primary objective of O & M.
2. Improvement of existing output—improvement in work efficiency.
3. It is concerned with efficiency of services as well as efficiency in the manner of providing it.
4. To make the staff efficiency conscious and to improve their work efficiency.
5. To simplify the procedures and to ensure proper flow of work.
6. All operations should be made as simple as possible.
7. It checks wasteful expenditure to the minimum or to zero.

Principles of O & M

The following are the guiding principles of O & M.

1. Employees must be properly prepared to co-operate in the task of O & M.
2. All work should be studied and combination of work must be done.
3. Work must flow to an employee in a regular manner.
4. Unnecessary activities must be eliminated.
5. People and papers in the office must follow the shortest routes.

Steps in O & M Work

A separate department may be set up by large concerns to carry out the O & M work. However, O & M work can also be performed by supervisors in small organisations. It would be better if a separate department is created so that the department can devote full time and energy for O & M work. O & M is mainly concerned with planning a new system and procedures and routines. The O & M officer and the team adopt the following procedures :

1. Object of Assignment

The area to be selected for assignment is one which is bound to prove most fruitful. The purpose must be written down clearly. It is necessary to define the purpose at survey, scope, period within which it is to be completed, probable cost and the authority to whom the recommendations should be submitted.

2. Planning the Assignment

Drawing up a plan of work, indicating the general and specific purposes of the task involved, the nature of information to be obtained and the sources of information to be tapped. A preliminary enquiries to be made to get better understanding of the problems involved and the way to conduct the work.

3. Studying the Existing Procedure

It is necessary to prepare correct specifications of duties and responsibilities of staff. The procedures and actions must be studied from the point of view of the staff and the customers. An effort should be made to find out simpler ways of doing the work. A careful study of every operation is needed. The study may be with reference to the followings :

(a) Object of each operation,

(b) Persons engaged in the operations,

(c) The place of doing the work,

(d) The amount of skill required,

(e) Nature and frequency of the occurrence of the operation,

(f) Forms used in relation to the operation,

(g) Degree of supervision needed,

(h) Cost of operation,

(i) Degree of mechanisation etc

4. Collecting the Facts

The O & M officer should collect the facts regarding : (a) the nature of work, (b) the amount of work, (c) the purpose of work, (d) the people who do it, (e) the place of doing it, (f) the time of doing it and (g) the methods used for work. The methods of getting facts involve: (a) direct observation of work, (b) interview and discussion, (c) study of records, (d) Sampling techniques, (e) checklists and (f) written questionnaires.

5. Analysing the Facts

Study of the data is a basic O & M work. It is only through this process that generalisation can be made and conclusion can be drawn. The data can be studied with the help of statistical tools, for examples, averages, correlation, skewness, dispersion etc. The process of framing ideas is a difficult one. The O & M officer should not lose sight of objectives. He should set out the purpose of the work in a few words.

6. Submitting the Proposal

Sound ideas are converted into specific proposals. The O & M officer should weigh all the pros and cons of each proposal or suggestion. The proposal must be well tested. It must be practicable. The proposal or suggestion must be sound and capable of being implemented smoothly. It must fulfil the objectives of O & M exercise. The final decision is shown to the manager of the department and then it is submitted to the management.

7. Implementation

The task of the O & M officer does not end with the report. If the proposal is accepted by the management, the O & M officer may have to be associated with the implementation. Once the new system or procedure is approved, it must be given trial for some time. After the trial period, if it is found satisfactory the O & M officer will propose for incorporation in the office manual.

8. Review

O & M officer must inspect the working of the new procedure when it is fully operative and review the procedures periodically and modify them if necessary.

Advantages of O & M

O & M has the following advantages:

1. It eliminates wastes and results in saving of office costs.
2. It not only eliminates wastes but also introduce improved procedures and systems.
3. It aims at improving the services rendered by office staff.
4. It facilitates higher output with greater accuracy.
5. It helps the management to evaluate the performance of the staff.
6. It projects a scientific approach to the problems of the office as well as the whole organisation.
7. It keeps the staff alert regarding efficiency.
8. It reduces wasteful expenditure by suggesting ways of using office resources efficiently.

Disadvantages of O & M

O & M has the following limitations :

1. In many cases, it may not be possible to measure the work.
2. The procedure suggested may not be easily practicable.
3. Clerical staff feels insecure and usually do not co-operate with the O & M Staff.
4. O & M costs may be very heavy and not suitable to small offices.
5. The office staff feels that it is subjected to "snooping raids" by the management, and this lowers morale of the staff.

PAPER-WORK SIMPLIFICATION

Motion and time studies help us to find easier, simpler and safer ways of doing work. Methods improvement is non-stop and not one shot approach. Work simplification or work improvement is an important aspect of scientific office management. Work simplification may be defined as the organised application of common sense to find a better and easier way to do a job. The main aim of work simplification is to improve the effectiveness of office work at reduced cost. The object of paper work simplification involves two factors: (i) Elimination useless and outmoded procedure of paper work and (ii) minimising delays. The following are some measures, if adopted, can effect considerable savings in costs. (There may be many more such possibilities).

1. Wherever possible envelopes can be eliminated for letters, more particularly within the organisation. If the letter is confidential, it can be stapled.
2. Covering letter for outgoing statements can be eliminated. This is because the statements are self-explanatory.

3. When goods received from supplier, goods received contained the list of each item serially. This can be eliminated and replaced by a simple report stating only "Goods received as per Bill No...Dated...."

4. When goods taken out, an additional copy of cash memo can be used as gate pass, instead of issuing a separate gate pass.

5. Delivery challan can be eliminated. The order from the seller with an endorsement of the supplier regarding delivery can serve as a delivery challan.

6. Irregular circular letters do not catch any attention of busy dealers. Personal letter can be written, monthly or quarterly.

7. Minor typing errors in letters can be corrected with ink instead of re-typing, etc. etc.

BUDGETARY CONTROL

Modern business world is full of competition, uncertainty and exposed to different types of risks. This complexity of managerial problems has led to the development of various managerial tools, techniques and procedures useful for the management in managing the business successfully. Budgeting is the most common, useful and widely used standard device of planning and control. The budgetary control has now become an essential tool of the management for controlling costs and maximising profit. Costs can be reduced,: wastage can be prevented and proper relationship between costs and income can be established only when the various factors of production are combined in profitable way. The resources of a business can be effectively utilised by efficient conduct of its operations. This requires careful working out of proper plans in advance, co-ordination and control of activities on the part of management.

A proper planning and control are essential for an efficient management. A good number of tools and devices are available. Of all these, the most important device used is budget. Cost accounting aims not only at cost ascertainment, but also greatly at cost control and cost reduction. Thus the management aims at the proper and maximum utilisation of resources available. It is possible when there is a pre-planning. Modern management aims that all types of operations should be pre-determined in advance, so that the cost can be controlled at every step. The more important point is that the actual programme is compared with the pre-planned programme and the variances are analysed and investigated. All are familiar with the idea of budget at every walk of life—state, firm, business etc.

Definition

A budget is a detailed plan of operations of some specific, future period. Many of us are familiar with the term "Budget". For instance, if we want to have a holiday trip to Kashmir, we are to estimate the cost of travelling, boarding, lodging etc. so as to have sufficient amount for the trip. On return from the trip, we may like to compare the actual amount spent with the estimated or budgeted figures. Similarly we can know the importance of budgets even from the household management.

The word 'budget' is derived from a French term "Bougette" which denotes a leather pouch in which funds are appropriated for meeting anticipated expenses. The same meaning applies to the business management. A budget is a numerical statement expressing the plans, policies and goals of the enterprise for a definite period in the future. It is a plan laying down the targets to be achieved within a specified period. It is a final and approved share of a forecast. When forecasts are approved by the management as a tentative plan for the future they become budget. The following are some of the important definitions :

1. "budget is an estimate of future needs arranged according to an orderly basis, covering some or all of the activities of an enterprise for definite period of time".

—George R. Terry.

2. "A budget is a comprehensive and co-ordinated plan, expressed in financial terms, for the operations and resources of an enterprise for some specific period in the future."

—James

3. "A budget is a pre-determined statement of management policy during a given period which provides a standard for comparison with the results actually achieved."

—Brown and Howard

4. "A financial and/or quantitative statement, prepared prior to a defined period of time, of the policy to be pursued during that period for the purpose of a given objective."

—ICMA, England

A study of the above definitions reveals the following basic elements of a budget:

1. Budget is a comprehensive plan of what the enterprise endeavours to achieve.
2. It is a statement in terms of money or quantity or both.
3. It is prepared for a definite future period.
4. It is prepared prior to the defined period.
5. It provides yardsticks and measures for the purpose of comparison.
6. It is prepared in advance and refers to the future course of action.
7. It indicates the business policy which has to be followed so as to achieve a given objective.

Forecast and Budget

Forecast is mainly concerned with probable events; but budget is concerned with planned events. Forecast may be done for longer time; but budget is prepared for shorter periods.

Forecast is only a tentative estimate and can be revised; but budget remains unchanged for the budget period.

Forecast results in planning and the planning results in budgeting. Forecast is a prediction or an estimate of changes, if any, in characteristics, economic phenomena which may affect one's business plans. It is a study into the future, when the forecasts are given a shape and approved by the management as a commitment, they become budgets. For example, sales forecast is an estimate for future sales, while a sales budget is a commitment with an objective to reach certain sales figures.

Forecast is the base while a budget is the structure built on the base.

Forecast is not used for evaluating the efficiency of performance while a budget is always used for this purpose.

Forecast refers to the events over which there is no control, (for example, forecast of restricted import) while a budget .is an endeavour to control the events.

Objectives of a Budget

1. It directs the attention of all concerned to the attainment of a common goal.
2. It leads to the disclosure of organisational weakness. The budgets are compared with actual performance; and variances, if any, are investigated. This step helps in taking corrective and remedial measures.

3. It aims at careful control over the performance and cost of every function.

4. It contributes to co-ordinated efforts of all departments in order to achieve an integrated goal. Budgets grow from bottom and are controlled from top level.

Budgeting

A budget is essentially a statement of the intention of management. Budgeting refers to the management action of formulating budgets. Preparation of budgets involves study of business situations and understanding of management objectives as also the capacity of the enterprise. It includes the entire processing of making the budget plans. Preparation of budgets or budgeting is a planning function, and their application or implementation is a control function. When plans are embodied in a budget and the same is used 'as the basis for regulating operations, we have budgetary control. Budgetary control starts with budgeting and ends with control. Budgeting is defined as:

1. "The entire process of preparing the budgets is known as budgeting".   —Batty

2. "Budgeting may be said to be the act of building budgets".   —Rowland and Harr

Objectives of Budgeting

The main objectives of budgeting are :

1. To obtain more economical use of capital.

2. To prevent waste and reduce expenses.

3. To facilitate various departments to operate efficiently and economically.

4. To plan and control the income and expenditure of the firm.

5. To create a good business practice by planning for future.

6. To fix responsibilities on different departments or heads.

7. To co-ordinate the activities of various departments.

8. To ensure the availability of working capital.

9. To smooth out seasonal variations, by developing new products.

10. To ensure the matching of sales with productions.

Types of Budgets

Budgets are classified according to their nature and purpose. Some of their types are given below:

1. Materials Budget

The materials budget is concerned with determining the quantity of raw materials required for production. The programme for purchasing raw materials is adjusted according to the production department. The materials are purchased as per the requirements of production department. The requirements of materials are determined product wise and the rate of consumption.

2. Production Budget

The production budget is prepared in relation to the sales budget. Whatever is to be sold should be produced in time so that it is sold to the customers. It is forecast of the production department.

3. Sales Budget

A sales budget is an estimate of expected sales during the budget period. A sales budget is known as a nerve centre of the enterprise. A sales budget is the starting point on which other budgets are based.

4. Selling and Distribution Cost Budget

Selling and distribution cost budget forecasts the costs of selling and distributing the products. This budget depends upon the sales budget. These expenses will vary with the expected sales figures during the period.

5. Cost of Production Budget

The production budget determines the number of units to be produced. When these units converted into monetary terms, it becomes a cost of production budget. The cost of production budget is the total amount to be spent on producing the units stipulated in the production budget.

6. Cash Budget

A cash budget is an estimate of cash receipts and payments during a future period of time. The functional budgets may be adjusted according to the cash budget. The available funds should be fruitfully used and the concern should not suffer for want of funds.

There are many other types of budgets.

What is a Budget ?
1. Budgets are blueprint of the desired plan of action.
2. They are means of communications.
3. They indicate the business policies.
4. They serve as declaration of policies..
5. They provide a means of co-ordination of the business as a whole.
6. They are instruments of managerial control.
7. They are controlling tools.
8. They provide yardsticks for comparison.
9. They set definite goals.
10. They fix responsibilities and direct to profitable direction.

BUDGETARY CONTROL

"Budgetary control means the establishment of budgets relating to the responsibilities of executives to the requirement of a policy, and continuous comparison of actuals with budgeted results either to secure by individual action the objective of that policy or to provide basis for its revision."

Budget, budgeting and budgetary control, according to *Rowland and William* H. Harr is that,

"Budgets are the individual objectives of a department etc., whereas budgeting may be said to the act of building budgets. Budgetary control embraces all this and in addition includes the science of planning the budgets themselves and the utilisation of such budgets to effect an overall management for the business planning and control."

A budget is a numerical statement expressing the plans, policies and goals for a definite future period. Budgeting means the process of preparing budgets. Budgetary control is a system of controlling costs which includes the preparation of budgets, co-ordinating the departments and establishing responsibilities, comparing actual performance with the budgeted; and acting upon results to achieve maximum profitability.

Characteristics

1. *Establishment.* Budgets are prepared for each department and then the plans and objectives are presented before the management.

2. *Co-ordination.* The budgetary control co-ordinates the plans of various departments and the master budget is prepared.

3. *Continuous comparison.* The essential feature of budgetary control is to conduct continuous comparison of actual performance with budgeted figures, revealing the variations.

4. *Revision.* Budgets are revised, if necessary, according to changed conditions.

Advantages

The advantages and benefits of budgetary control are summarised below :

1. Budgets fix the goals and targets, without which operation lacks direction.

2. Reduction in cost and elimination of inefficiency is achieved automatically.

3. The budget facilitates to maintain ordered effort and brings about efficiency in results.

4. An effective system of budgetary control results in co-ordinated effort of all persons involved.

5. Budgetary control enables the management to decentralise responsibility without losing control of the business since it pin-points inefficiency.

6. The budgetary control and standard costing go hand in hand and the combination of the two gives the most effective results. It promotes mutual co-operation and team spirits among the persons involved.

7. Budgetary control ensures that the capital employed at a particular level is kept at a minimum level.

8. It facilitates an intelligent and planned forecast for future.

9. It is a good guide to the management for making future plans. It is on the basis of budgetary control, realistic budgets can be drawn.

10. It aims at maximisation of profit through cost control and proper utilisation of resources.

11. It brings to light the inefficiencies and weaknesses on comparing actual performance with budget. Thus management can take remedial measures.

12. It is a guide to the management in the field of research and development in future.

13. It evaluates the performance.

14. Since budget provides advance information, financial crises can be avoided

15. It acts as a safety signal for the management. It prevents wastages of all types.

Essentials of a Successful Budgetary Control

A budget is both a plan as well as a control tool. A business budget is a plan covering all phases of operations for a definite period in future. It is a formal expression of policies, plans, objectives and goals laid down in advance by the top management for the concern as a whole and for every sub-division thereof. For an effective system of budgetary control, certain pre-requisites must be present. These essentials are :

1. The budgetary control system should have full support of top management.
2. There should be well-planned organisational set-up, with responsibility and authority clearly demarcated.
3. The accounting system should provide accurate and timely information.
4. Variations should be reported promptly and clearly to the appropriate levels of management.
5. Budgets have no meaning unless they lead to control action as a consequence of feedback provided.
6. Staff should be strongly and properly motivated towards the system.
7. The budget should lay down the targets which are realistic and attainable.
8. It is most desirable that there is full and meaningful participation of all concerned.
9. Budgets should actually aim as a co-ordinating device rather than control device.
10. The budgets should be flexible enough to permit the adjustments in the light of changed operational circumstances.

Limitations of Budgetary Control

Budgetary control is a sound technique of control. But it is not a perfect tool. Despite the appreciation, it has its own limitations which are as follows,:

1. Budgets deal with future. Forecasting is necessary for budgeting. Forecasts and estimates are rarely cent per cent accurate. The success largely depends upon the degree of accuracy of the estimates.
2. Budgeting is time consuming process. During the preparation period, the business conditions may change and estimates may go wrong by that time.
3. The successful operation and execution of budgets depends upon the efficiency of the executive personnel.
4. Budgetary control is essentially a tool of decision-making and it helps the management in taking sound decisions. But it cannot replace the management.
5. Budgeting necessitates the employment of specialised staff and this involves expenditure which small concerns may not afford.
6. A budget programme should be dynamic, capable of being adapted to changing conditions. But when budgets are prepared with pre-determined targets, there is a feeling that the budgeted figures are final. Thus budgetary programme is bound to become rigid.
7. The success of the budgetary control largely depends upon willing co-operation or team work of all concerned. If there is no co-operation, the whole system collapses.

Organisation

The following are the essentials for a sound system of budgetary control:

1. Chart. There must be an organisational chart to show the authority and responsibility of each executive of the firm. This will enable him to know his relationship with other executives. The budget director derives power from the chief executive, helps in co-ordination and drawing up of all budgets and suggests changes, if necessary. The sales manager, production manager, purchasing manager, personnel manager and accountant will prepare their budgets.

2. Budget Centre. For the purpose of effective budgetary control, budget centres are defined. A budget centre may be a department or a section of the undertaking. Separate budgets are prepared for each department and the departmental head is responsible for carrying out budgets. Departmental heads should have effective control over the execution of the budget, to prevent unfavourable variation.

3. Budget. In small firms, the chief accountant prepares the budgets and co-ordinates various activities. In big concerns, a committee is appointed for this task. The committee consists of various section heads, the chief executive and the budget controller. The budgets are prepared by section heads and submitted to the committee for approval, changes are made, if necessary, and approved.

4. Budget Manual. It is a document which sets out the responsibilities of persons engaged in the routine work. Budget manual lays down the objectives of the organisation, responsibilities of all executives and the procedure to be followed for budgetary control. Duties, authorities, powers of each official of the different departments are clearly defined, so as to avoid conflicts among the personnel. It also specifies different forms and records to be used for the purpose of budgetary control.

5. Budget Period. This is the period or time for which the budget is prepared and remains in operation. The length of period depends on the nature of business, the production period, the control aspect etc. There is no definite rule as regards the duration of a budget period. Generally, the budget is prepared for a year, which is preferred by most concerns. For example manufacturers of consumer goods may prepare budgets for a year, whereas in industries like ship-building the period of the budget may be 5 to 10 years.

6. Key-Factor. Key-factor is also known as 'limiting factor' or 'governing factor' which means this is the factor, the extent of whose influence must first be assessed, in order to ensure that the functional budgets are reasonably capable of fulfillment. The key factor may be, shortage of raw materials, non-availability of labour, limited sales, government restrictions etc. The key factor is a limitation on production or sales. First locate the key factor, before preparing the budget, as if influences all other budgets for example, shortage of power supply leads to under utilisation of plant capacity. Therefore, the concern will have to first prepare a budget for plant utilisation and later the other budgets say sales will be prepared.

Master Budget. A master budget is the summary budget for the entire enterprise and embodies the summarised figures for various activities. This is also known as summary budget or finalised profit plan. This budget includes the budgeted position of the profit and loss as well as balance sheet. Master budget is prepared by the committee and becomes a target for the company.

Preparation of Office Budget. Proper care should be taken to prepare the office budget. To achieve the objectives of the budgets, the following steps may be followed :

1. Classification of Office Expenses

Where office expenses are an important part of the organisation, it would be proper to define them. There are three types of office expenses : Fixed, Variable and Semi-variable. Classification of expenses are needed for better control.

2. Allocation of Office Expenses

The budget must allocate the expenses to various sections carefully. There are two types of office expenses: (*i*) Direct expenses can be charged directly to the operating section and (*ii*) Indirect expenses cannot be charged directly and are allocated to sections on suitable basis.

3. Consultation

The supervisors are consulted about the various aspects of the budgets. The office manager is responsible to prepare a sound budget. On the basis of past performance of each section, target for the future is laid down.

4. Final Budget

The office manager takes every care while preparing the budget. After the preparation of the final budget, it is incorporated into the master budget. Office budget is a financial statement.

It is an important device exercising control over expenditure. It provides a standard by which actual operations can be measured and variations checked. An office budget should not be considered as a rigid plan. The budget must be flexible to accommodate adjustments. The person preparing the budget should ensure that only those items are included in the budget which are really required by the office otherwise the purpose of the office budget will be lost.

SUPERVISORY CONTROL

An office supervisor is an executive who gets work done through the operative employees in the office and has direct control and authority over them. It is the office supervisor who decides work schedules, assigns work to different employees and oversees the performance of the employees. He gives guidance to the employees and takes corrective steps, when the quantity and quality of office operations are not upto the mark. Thus, an office supervisor plays an important role in getting work done from the employees. If he is efficient, the employees will do their duties by following right methods and procedures and they will not indulge in wasteful operations. Effective supervision can keep down costs of office operations by making best possible use of office stationery and machines and other equipments.

Items offering Cost Reduction

Certain items such as those of a repetitive and cumulative nature usually offer the best opportunities for lowering costs. Major expenses are the amount spent on staff as salaries and wages: it may about 75% of the office costs. The salary and wages are increasing tremendously due to many reasons. However, efforts should be made to keep the number to the minimum possible. The following items offer cost reduction opportunities *i.e.* to keep down the office expenses and to increase office efficiency. A few examples:

In the field of personnel

1. Time and motion study helps to eliminate unnecessary motions of staff.
2. Setting standards and close supervision to achieve standards.
3. To provide good working condition so as to increase efficiency in performance.
4. Providing moving group to meet peak load works.
5. Proper planning of daily work.

In the field of stationery :

1. Use both sides of paper for correspondences extending beyond one page.
2. Eliminate extra file copies of correspondence.
3. Type answer on original letter received and return where no file copy of reply is needed.
4. Substitute postal cards for letters.
5. Eliminate the use of envelopes for internal mail.

6. For internal correspondence, make endorsement on the original letter rather than writing a separate reply.

7. Eliminate return envelopes from advertising mailings.

In the field of forms

1. Revise existing forms only when essential.
2. Carry out a form reduction and elimination programme.
3. Establish centralised control at all printed forms.
4. Reduce the quantity and increase frequency of ordering forms to minimise deterioration in store and obsolescence.
5. Use both sides of the forms.

In the Field of Machine and Furniture

1. Centralise operations involving machines to permit greater utilisation of them.
2. Provide for multiple shifts as a means of utilising machines
3. Standardise and simplify varieties at office machines, furniture and equipment to provide greater flexibility and facilitate maintenance.
4. Substitute wooden equipment for metal.
5. Substitute chairs with writing arms for salesmen's desk.

In the field of general

1. Hold employees responsible for turning off lights when leaving decks or room.
2. Take daily record of meter reading for comparison.
3. Shut off motors on office machines when not operating.
4. Disconnect water coolers at night.
5. Use re-inked ribbons.
6. Issue new items on the return of stubs.
7. Arrange annual servicing of machines by recognised agencies.
8. Instruct staff to use more day light, keeping lights off.
9. Use window envelopes so as to reduce clerical work.
10. Consider fewer private offices.

COST CONTROL

While cost accounting is concerned with cost finding for a product or process, cost control attempts at reducing cost by informing as to what should be the cost of products or services under improved conditions. Thus the aim of the cost control is to reduce the cost of products or services and to guard against wastage and extravagance. Effective control over the actual cost of production is possible only by comparing the actual cost with the standard costs, which is arrived at after making a careful study and analysis of cost figures of the past years.

Cost control can be defined as the control of all items of expenditure by regular and frequent comparisons of actual expenditure with pre-determined standards or budgets, so that undesirable trends away from standards can be detected and corrected at an early stage. Thus, cost control involves the following steps:

1. Determination of cost standard for each item,
2. Finding out variation in costs from the standard, that is, comparing actual cost with standard cost.
3. Taking corrective steps to ensure that actual cost is the same as the standard cost in future.

Cost control is a control of all the costs of an enterprise in order to achieve cost effectiveness in business operations. Cost can be classified as : fixed cost, variable cost and semi-variable cost. The fixed costs are incurred over a period of time and are not directly related to production. The fixed cost remains the same even if there is an increase or decrease in production. Variable costs, on the other hand, change in the proportion of output. Semi-variable costs are fixed as well as variable in nature.

Problem of Office Cost

Office has a variety of activities and it is not easy to establish rigid classification and unit costs. Office activities are composed of many factors. Costing cannot be done on the basis of specifically identifiable units of operations. The cost analysis in the office is a big problem since office costs are often small items and detailed analysis often more expensive than the savings realised. Costs can obtained on all kinds of office operations but it is difficult to decide as to which operation should be costed.

Cost Control Programme

In establishing an effective Cost Control Programme the following three steps are necessary:

1. Determining cost wise what is being accomplished.
2. Evaluating it, and
3. Applying corrective action, if necessary.

Cost comparison is inherent in cost control, because it is only then that a basis for cost control is obtained. Past records furnish the data for cost comparison. All changes in cost should be investigated. A cost comparison chart can be devised to serve the purpose.

As far as possible office cost should be charged to the user department and they should not be considered as overhead. Many office costs are of variable nature and they can be easily allocated to the user departments.

QUESTIONS

1. What is the significance of office cost reduction and cost saving in a modern organisation?
   (B. Com., Madurai)
2. Outline the features of an adequate programme of cost saving and cost reduction. What are the areas of opportunity for office economies.
3. Why is there need for O & M? What qualities should be O & M officer possess in order to succeed in his task ?
   (B. Com., Madurai)
4. What is O & M ? What are its advantages ?
5. What are the different kinds of budgets ? Outline the principles of preparing a budget of administrative office expenses.
   (B. Com., M.S.)

6. Explain the significance of controlling office costs. Enumerate areas of cost control.
   (B. Com., Punjab)

7. What is cost control ? Explain the steps in cost control. *(B. Com., Mumbai)*

8. How can budgetary control help in controlling office costs ? Discuss the limitations of budget. *(B. Com., Punjab)*

9. Briefly explain the importance of office cost reduction and cost saving. What are the main methods of cost reduction and cost saving ? *(B. Com., Chennai)*

10. What do you understand by "work simplification"? What are the fundamental principles of work simplification ? Briefly outline the major benefits of the work simplification programme. *(B. Com., M.S.)*

11. "The office is really a money maker and a money saver." Explain. *(B. Com., Chennai)*

12. How the waste of money can be prevented in office work ? *(B. Com., Punjab)*

CHAPTER

Modern Technology

There have been dramatic changes in information technology over the past ten or fifteen years. Consumers and business people no longer need to be near a computer to send and receive information. All they need is a cellular phone. While they are on the move, they can be in touch with their field personnel no matter where they are. Advances in information technology are revolutionising the *modus operandi* of marketing and the business system. The business horizon is humming with buzzwords like internet, world wide web (www), cyberspace, information superhighways, etc., which are changing the way of contacting customers; order receiving and processing; and networking and intergrating business system. The revolutionary changes being ushered in by the internet are indeed exciting. The revolutionary changes in the information technology is sweeping across the global business. New information technology modes include electronic mail, corporate and public databases, application systems, fax, video and computer conferencing. These modes are considered to be some of the driving forces of internationalisation. These new information technology modes have a major impact on the co-ordination of head-quarter-subsidiary relations. In fact, most of the MNCs have developed these new modes of information technology. The internet is a world wide, self-governed network connecting thousands of smaller networks and millions of computers and people to mega sources of information. Quite simply, it is a technology no nation or enterprise can ignore. Technology experts are anticipating that the internet and the www would become the centre of commercial universe. Electronic markets will eliminate the need for the intermediaries and that direct contact between manufacturer and customer will bring down the cost of transaction and the cost of final product. The internet has the potential to evolve into an inter-connected electronic market place (cyberspace) bringing buyers and sellers together to faciliate commercial exchanges.

It is needless to say that the internet is a world-wide network of computer networks. Imagine a network of five computers in your office which are linked up together in a manner that you can exchange data, correspondence (mail) and even soft-ware, between these computers. Now imagine that you have a business associates or friends who also have several computers in their homes or offices organised pretty much like yours. Now imagine all these computers spread over different locations linked up in manner so that they (meaning you) can communicate between each other. This is what Internet is all about. Except as mentioned earlier, this is a global network linking millions of computers and people cutting across all barriers and boundaries of countries, race, class or sex. The networking of computers that allow the managers, employees, customers, vendors, dealers, bankers, suppliers to deal with each other even across the globe. The networking of ATMs allow the customer to deposit money in Mumbai, to withdraw money in Delhi, to deposit cheques for clearance in Kanpur and to get his statement of accounts in Chennai.

COMPUTER

We live in the computer age. Most of our day-to-day activities are being influenced by the use of computers. While in areas like science and technology improvements cannot be achieved without computers, it has become necessary for everyone to have a basic knowledge of computers.

In simple words, a computer is an electronic device which processes information based upon the instructions provided and generates the desired output. Like any other system, a computer system also requires an input which is processed to get the desired output. In the case of computers two kinds of inputs are required. One, the basic or raw data, and two, a set of instructions containing the methodology to process this data. This set of instructions is called a programme or software in computer speak. That is, it accepts, stores and processes the data (input) as per instructions (programme) and communicate the information (output) at very fast speed.

INTERNET

Internet is the network that connects other networks of computers around the globe into one seamless network. Like an electronic cloud, it enriches the earth. Many different networks operated by different organisations are connected together to form the internet.

The conventional and commonly used method of accessing the internet is dialing up via phone. The requirements for establishing this conventional dial up connection to the internet are, a telephone, a computer with a slot for internet modem or a serial port for external modem and an account with an internet access provider. A modem is device that translates between the digital format for data/information which is used by computers and the analog signal used over telephone lines. The modem regulates the speed of interaction over the phones.

Since the Internet consists of not one but multiple data system, which were developed independently, it allows users to access a variety of services. The most important ones are:

1. We can send E-mail across the world.
2. Internet can be easily used for publicity and advertisement.
3. Tele-conferencing is possible.
4. We can touch with people around the world.
5. We can provide technical support to the customers.
6. We can do electronic commerce on the Internet.

It is easy to find information on the Internet. A person who wants to buy any products– Car, scooter, TV, etc. does not have to visit the showroom or even scan the advertisements for information. The Internet has all the information needed.

Buying tickets for travel by air or train is a simple matter of going to the website and click the needed buttons. Besides, hotel booking, site-seeing tours, etc. can be done very easily. Job seekers can also use the information not only to seek jobs but also to decide which companies to work for ' and which not to work for. Bio-data posted on the Internet also make it easy for companies to find suitable candidates for recruitment

Internet is "the world wide collection of networks and gateways that use the TCP/IP suite of protocols to communicate with one other. At the heart of the Internet is a backbone of high-speed data communication lines between major modes or host computers, consisting of thousands of commercial, Government, educational and other computer systems, that route data and messages. One or more Internet nodes can go off line without endangering the Internet as a whole or causing communications on the Internet to stop.

TELEX

Telex services provide automatic communication through printed words from one place to another with the help of a teleprinter. Teleprinter consists of two parts: (*i*) a keyboard transmitter and (*ii*) a receiver. Under telex system, the sender presses a button, waits for the dial tone, dials the desired number and if the number is contacted, types the message. The message so typed is presented in a small strip of paper at the receiver's end. This is one of the quickest and most accurate method of transmitting written communication .

Advantages of Telex Service

Telex services provide the following advantages to its users :

1. The written message is transmitted quickly and accurately.
2. It is much quicker than a letter and cheaper than the Trunk Call Service.
3. In case the receiver is not available, the message can be left as neatly typed on the teleprinter.
4. The message can be transmitted or received at any time of day and night. Thus telex service is useful for large business houses, news agencies, stock exchange dealers etc.
5. Telex services provide direct automatic interconnection with the called party.

TELECONFERENCING

Telephone technology has so advanced that it is now possible to link one telephone number with several other numbers simultaneously, which means that people can hold a conference over the telephone without meeting each other in person. Video facilities also being available, people can not only confer with but even see each other on telephone screens. People can hear and see each other and share information with one another as if they were all placed together in one room. Teleconferencing can lead to substantial saving both in terms of money and time.

Advantages of Teleconferencing

1. It is almost like communicating face to face.
2. It makes discussion more meaningful.
3. It enriches communication in several ways.
4. The interaction allows people at distant locations to understand one another better.
5. It helps people feel connected and goes a long way in building relationships in a way that telephone and e-mail cannot do.

CELLULAR (MOBILE) PHONE

The cellular (mobile) phone is based on a combination of the old radio technology and emerging telecommunication technology. The person holding mobile phone can be contacted at any time and at any place. The possessor can talk and transact even during driving car or travelling in train.

Cellular phone instruments have facilities for storage of numbers, record of missed calls, for receiving text messages (SMS), and for receiving information given by the network about the weather, about conditions on the road and other vital news needed while travelling

Now, most of the business transactions and exchange of information take place on mobile phones because of individual's accessibility at any time and at any place. With the introduction of new technologies such as digital photography, electronic messaging, gaming support and internet access in consumers' bands, the mobile phones are outperforming PCs and Internets. They have become today's true personal digital device.

Marketing persons who visit customers can instantly get in touch with their home office to consult. Most importantly, travelling representatives have instant access to data and information from the home office as well as other information through the internet which can be accessed from the mobile phone.

ELECTRONIC MAIL (E-Mail)

It is the fastest growing value added communication service and an important element in office automation. Electronic mail or E-mail is a technique for distributing mail electronically. It can function solely between one computer terminal and another or between computers linked in a local area network (LAN). It can also be used to send messages world wide through the Internet system. The message is typed on a computer screen at one end, and is conveyed to the other end through electric impulses. The person operating the computer terminal at the receiving end is alerted by a signal that a message or mail meant for his is in the electronic mailbox. Or he can occasionally see his mailbox to check for any incoming mail. Then he can get flashed on to a screen immediately or keep it stored, and attend to it at leisure.

Advantages of E-mail

1. It is the quickest means of transmitting messages.
2. It is cheaper.
3. The messages can easily be stored for future reference.
4. E-mail messages are always clear and easy to read.
5. You can send an E-mail message whenever you like and the person at the other end can receive it the next morning when he comes to work.

VOICE MAIL

Voice mail is a communication service on a telephone line. The simple answering machine which can be attached to a telephone is a form of voice mail it allows a caller to leave a name or number and message if you do not answer the phone. The message can be retrieve and answered later, at a more convenient time. Like E-mail, it is very easy to use and is a convenient way of leaving short messages for someone who is not immediately available.

SHORT MESSAGE SERVICE (SMS)

The short message service (SMS) is the ability to send and receive text messages to and from mobile telephones. This text may be in the form of words or numbers or an alpha-numeric combination. Some of the benefits of SMS to the mobile owner or subscriber includes:

* Guaranteed message delivery;
* Reliable and cost effective communication device for concise information;
* Convenient to use;
* Delivery of message to multiple subscribers at a time;
* Ability to receive diverse information;
* Seamless integration with other data and Internet applications.

FACSIMILE (FAX)

Many organisations are now going in for facsimile (fax) transmission facilities. Fax machines are very useful for transmitting visual material such as diagrams, illustrations, photographs or copies of artwork visuals. All that we need for it is the fax machine with a connected telephone. As the document to be transmitted is fed through the machine, it is electronically scanned and signals are transmitted to the receiving end, where an identical copy of the document is reproduced on a blank sheet of paper by the receiving machine. The fax machine has made it possible to send copies of important documents including certificates, testimonials, agreements contracts etc. from one place to another at high speed.

WORLD WIDE WEB (WWW)

The internet system got a great boost with the development of World wide Web (WWW or W_3 or simply Web). The Web technology was developed by a Swiss scientist at the European Nuclear Research Laboratory in Geneva, as part of nuclear particle research.

Almost every business has a web site today. A web site is an excellent medium for reaching all segments of the company's public. A good web site can include all information and pictures of products, price-lists, catalogues, order forms, instructions on how to place orders, methods of payment and any other information that customers might need.

All public notices, press releases, bulletins and other company publications can be put on the web site. A web site may include organisational information about the company, with names of directors, location of branches and so on. Web sites are the best source of information about the company for job applicants preparing for interviews.

TELEMARKETING

Telemarketing, sometimes called telephone selling, refers to a sales person initiating contact with a shopper and closing a sale over the telephone. That is telemarketing involves the use of the telephone and call centres to attract prospects, sell to existing customers, and provide service by taking orders and answering questions. Many products that can be bought without being seen are sold over the telephone. Telemarketing helps companies increase revenue, reduce selling cost and improve customers' satisfaction.

Today some companies have a sales force that goes to the customers, but not in person. These sales representatives, "going to the customers" by means of telephone, computer, etc. Thus, outside selling is becoming electronic, and the term telemarketing describes such communication systems. Telemarketing has become a major marketing tool. Telemarketing is increasingly used in business as well as consumer marketing. Telemarketers should have pleasant voices and project enthusiasm. Effective telemarketing depends on choosing the right telemarketers, training them well and providing performance incentives. Telemarketing is growing because: (a) many buyers prefer it over personal sales calls, and (b) many markets find that it increases selling efficiency. Sellers face increasingly high costs keeping sales people on the road; selling by telemarketing reduces that expense. Also routine selling by telemarketing allows the field sales force to devote more time to creative selling, major account selling and other more profitable selling activities.

E-BUSINESS

As computers became common business tools in the late 1950s firms were able to collect, store and manipulate larger amounts of data to aid marketing decision makers. Out of this capability developed the marketing information system—an ongoing, organised procedure to generate, analyze, disseminate, store, and retrieve information for use in making marketing decisions. Information is recognised as an important resource. A wide variety of information needs of a business are organised into what is called "Management Information System" (MIS). A management information system consists of inter connected subsystems. They provide the information necessary to stay competitive. The computer is an electronic tool that is used to collect, organise, analyse, interpret and communicate vast amounts of information with great speed.

E-business describes the use of electronic means and platforms to conduct company's business. The advent of the Internet has greatly increased the ability of companies to conduct their business faster, more accurately, over a wider range of time and space, at reduced cost and with the ability to customize and personalize customer offerings. Many companies have set up Web site to inform and promote their products and services. IBM defines e-business as "A secure, flexible and integrated approach to deliver differentiated business value by combining the systems and processes that run core business operations with the simplicity and reach made possible by Internet technology."

E-business can be (a) Within the organisation, that is, Intranets facilitate employees communicating with one another and to facilitate downloading and uploading information to and from the company's computers, (b) Business to Business dealings, that is Extranet consists of two Intranets connected *via* the Internet, whereby two organisation are allowed to see confidential date of the other. (c) Business to customer transations, that is, selling the goods and services through Internet to the innumerable customers spread all over the world.

Electronic business is a super-set of business cases. E-commerce is one of the aspects of E-business. Some other important aspects of E-business, which are successfully carried through the Internet are e-auctioning, e-banking. e-mailing, e-learning, e-marketing. e-trading, etc.

AUTOMATIC VENDING

The sale of products through a machine with no personal contact between buyer and seller is called automatic vending. The appeal of automatic vending is convenient purchase. Products sold by automatic vending are usually well-known, presold brands with a high rate of turnover. Automatic vending is used for a variety of merchandise, including impulse goods like cigarettes, soft drinks, coffee, newspapers, magazines, etc. Vending machines can expand a firm's market by reaching customers where and when they cannot come to a store. Thus vending equipment is found almost everywhere, particularly in schools, factories, offices, large retail stores, gasoline stations, hotels, restaurants and many other places. They offer 24 hour selling, self-service and merchandise that is always fresh. Automatic vending has high operating costs because of the need to replenish inventories frequently. The machines also require maintenance and repairs.

E-COMMERCE

Prashant Jain defined Electronic Commerce (E-Commerce) as "The exchange of business information using electronic formats, including Electronic Mail, Electronic Bulletin Boards and Electronic Funds Transfer. E-Commerce technologies are designed to replace traditional paper-based work flow with faster, more efficient and reliable communications between computers." He further stated that "e-commerce" is the process of two or more parties making business transactions *via* computer and some type of network, *e.g.*, a direct connection or the Internet.

E-commerce (electronic commerce) is the buying and selling of goods and services *via* the communications capabilities of private and public computer networks including the Internet. Global business indeed is increasingly becoming e-business. This helps both the parties to efficiently co-ordinate their activities. Extranet also links dealers, retailers and distributors so that the company can have better controls on the delivery of finished goods. All consultants, ad agencies and market research agencies are linked with the company through the extranet making it possible for them to provide service of value to the company,

E-commerce is more specific than e-business; it means that in addition to providing information to visitors about the company, its history, policies, products and job opportunities, the company or site offers to transact or facilitate the selling of products and services online. E-marketing describes the company efforts to inform, communicate promote, and sell its products and services over the Internet. The 'e' term is also used in terms such as e-finance, e-learning and e-service. But as someone observed, the 'e' will eventually be dropped when most business practice is online.

ELECTRONIC DATA INTERCHANGE

The term electronic data interchange has many definitions. American National Standards Institute has defined it as: "Electronic Data Interchange (EDI) is the transmission, in a standard syntax, of unambiguous information of business or strategic significance between computers of independent organisations."

The principle of EDI is simple. It is a set of standards that define the way the paper forms should be rendered electronically. For example, EDI can be used to send an invoice or an order form from one company to another. The "sending computer" located at a customer's premises, used telecommunication technology to transfer order data instantly to the "receiving computer", located at the supplier's distribution centre. Software on each company's computer translates the item into standard codes, so it would not matter if one company calls a product a cog and the order calls the same thing a sprocket, EDI will make sure that the right part is ordered. After the order is received data are manipulated and formatted to match the order entry files, in the "order data base" of the supplier. The information is then transferred into the data base and appropriate error messages, and/or exception reports are generated. The "sending computer" stores the order and follows up on it. The "receiving computer" automatically transfers the data to the warehouse of the factory, the accounting and billing department and the shipping department. Electronic Data Interchange is the transfer of business documents, such as purchase orders and invoices, between computers as per a set of standards. EDI facilitates the transfer of business documents stored in structured format through mutually agreed messaging protocols - from one computer application to another.

E-AUCTIONING

Auctioning on the Internet has become popular nowadays. In traditional methods of auctioning all those who would like to participate in the auction either assemble at one place or bid over the phone. Some one who are busy may find it difficult to spare time to participate in the auction. But nowadays all those who have Internet connection can participate in the auction by sitting in the home itself. The Internet enables everyone, irrespective of the country to which he belongs and where he is located, can visit the auction web site with a click and participate in the auction. In e-auctioning the people who want to participate in the auction visit the web site with a click, go through the details of the goods offered on the concerned web pages and place the price or price they would like to offer on the web page.

E-MARKETING

In traditional marketing the marketing team could not get immediate results on the customer reaction. They conducted market, surveys processed the data and prepared the reports. On the basis of those reports the management took decisions, formulated the policies, prepared the plans and implemented them. For all these they took lot of time. The Internet allows companies to react to individual customer demands immediately without any loss of time. It does not matter where the customer is located. This is called e-marketing.

E-BANKING

Electronic banking is one of the most successful online businesses. E-banking allows customers to access their accounts and execute orders through a simple-to-use web site. Electronic banking saves individuals and companies' time and money. Online banking allows the customers to self-service themselves. Customers can get money from an Automated Teller Machine (ATM) instead of walking upto the cash counter in the bank, can view their accounts, transfer funds and can pay bills.

E-TRADING

E-trading where the basic requirements are a PC, a modem and the Internet connection, the investor can log on to an online trading portal, go through a comprehensive database of information, use the online analytical tools and pass on instructions to a friendly and reliable online broker. Online trading is the perfect combination of the medium of net catering to a real life concept. Online trading is the perfect solution to investor needs. It brings together under one site all the relevant factors to enable an informed investment, rather cheaply to the user.

Common Abbreviations

a/c	:	Account
A/C	:	Account Current
Advt.	:	Advertisement
Amt.	:	Amount
Apr.	:	April
A/S	:	Account Sales
Aug.	:	August
Approx.	:	Approximate
Admin.	:	Administration, Administrative
Agcy.	:	Agency
Art.	:	Article
Assn.	:	Association
a.m.	:	Ante Meridian (before noon)
Asst.	:	Assistant
Agt.	:	Agent
amp.	:	Ampere (Electrical unit)
Ans.	:	Answer
Abt.	:	About
Align	:	Alignment
Bal	:	Balance
b/d	:	Brought Down
B/D	:	Bank Draft
B/E	:	Bill of Exchange
Eq#	:	Equalise Spacing
"	:	Put inverted Comma
B/L	:	Bill of Lading
B/O	:	Brought Over

B/P	:	Bill Payable
B/R	:	Bill Receivable
B/S	:	Balance Sheet
Bros.	:	Brothers
B/F	:	Brought Forward
B.O.T.	:	Board of Trade
bdl.	:	Bundle
Bk.	:	Bank
B.O.	:	Branch Office
brl.	:	Barrel
C.A.	:	Chartered Accountant
Cap.	:	Capital
Capt.	:	Caption
C.B.	:	Cash Book
Cat.	:	Catalogue
c/d	:	Carried down
Cent.	:	Centigrade
cert	:	Certificate
c/f	:	Carried Forward
chq.	:	Cheque
C/N	:	Credit Note
Co.	:	Company
C/o.	:	Care of
C.O.D.	:	Cash on delivery
Cont.	:	Continued
Cr.	:	Creditor, Credit
Col.	:	Column
Comm.	:	Commission
C&F	:	Cost and Freight
C.I.F.	:	Cost, Insurance & Freight
Consgt.	:	Consignment
C.W.O.	:	Cash with Order
D/A	:	Document Against Acceptance
D/D	:	Demand Draft
deb.	:	Debenture
dely	:	Delivery
Dept.	:	Department
Dft.	:	Draft
Dis.	:	Discount
D/N	:	Debit Note
D/O	:	Delivery Order
do	:	Ditto

doz.	:	Dozen
Dr.	:	Debtor
Dec.	:	December
D.L.O.	:	Dead Letter Office
D/W	:	Dock Warrant
ed	:	Edition
e.g.	:	Exempligratia, Example
E. & O.E.	:	Errors and Omissions Excepted
Enc. & Encl	:	Enclosure
esp.	:	Especially
Esq	:	Esquire
etc.	:	Et Sequens (and so forth)
Excl	:	Exclusive or Excluding
F.O.R.	:	Free on Rail
F.O.B.	:	Free on Board
Feb.	:	February
Ft.	:	Foot
Fol.	:	Folio
Fig.	:	Figure
Fri.	:	Friday
Govt.	:	Government
G.P.O.	:	General Post Office
Gro.wt.	:	Gross Weight
Gal.	:	Gallon
Gm.	:	Gramme
Grs.	:	Gross, Grains
Gen.	:	General
Hr.	:	Hour
i.e.	:	Idest (that is)
I.O.U.	:	I owe you
in.	:	Inch
insce.	:	Insurance
Inc.	:	Including
Inv.	:	Invoice
I/C	:	Incharge
incorp.	:	Incorporated
inst.	:	Instant
In toto	:	In total
int.	:	Interest
Insert Space	:	Insert in sign & symbol
Jan	:	January
Jr.	:	Junior
Jun	:	Junction

Kilo	:	Kilogram
Kg.	:	Kilogram
kw	:	kilowatt (1000 watts)
km.	:	kilometre
Ib	:	Pound
L/C	:	Letter of Credit
L/A	:	Letter of Authority
Lcm	:	Least Common Multiple
Ltd.	:	Limited
LL.B.	:	Legum Baccalaureucs
M.	:	1,000
Mar.	:	March
Max.	:	Maximum
Min.	:	Minimum
mfg.	:	Manufacturing
Messers.	:	Messieurs (Fr.) (Gentlemen)
mm.	:	Millimetres
m .p.h.	:	Miles per hour
Mr.	:	Mister
Mrs.	:	Mistress
M/s.	:	Messers
Med.	:	Medium
No.	:	Number
N.B.	:	Note Bene
Net, Nett	:	Netio (lowest)
Nov.	:	November
nr.	:	Near
Nom.cap.	:	Nominal Capital
N.R.	:	No risk (insurance)
O/O	:	Order of
ord.	:	Ordinary
o/c.	:	Overcharge
O.K.	:	All Correct
Oct.	:	October
oz.	:	Ounce
p.,pp.	:	Page, Pages
p.a.	:	Per Annum, Yearly
P.A.Y.E.	:	Pay as you earn
p.c.	:	Per centum, Per cent
pd.	:	Paid
per	:	By
per pro	:	Per procuralionem, On behalf of

Pkg.	:	Package
P.M.	:	Post Meridian
P/N	:	Promissory Note
Pref.	:	Preference
Prof.	:	Professor
prox.	:	Proximo, Next month
P.T.O.	:	Please turn over
Qlty.	:	Quality
Qnty.	:	Quantity
Rs.	:	Rupees
Recd.	:	Received
R/R	:	Railway Receipt
R.S.V.P.	:	Reply if you please (Repondez, s' il vous plait)
R.P.M	:	Revolutions Per Minute
retd.	:	Retired
rept.	:	Receipt
Sch.	:	Schedule, School
Sec., Secy	:	Secretary
Sgd.	:	Signed
sq.	:	Square
St.	:	Street, Straite
stet	:	Let it stand
Sept.	:	September
Std.	:	Standard
Supdt.	:	Superintendent
T.T.	:	Telegraphic Transfer
T.M.O.	:	Telegraphic money order
U/w	:	Underwriter
ult., ultp.	:	Ultimo, Last month
Via.	:	By way of
V.I.P.	:	Very Important Person
viz.	:	Namely
vol.	:	Volume
v.	:	Versus, Against
wk.	:	Week
w.p.m.	:	Words Per Minute
wt.	:	Weight
w.e.f.	:	With effect from
x.c.	:	Ex (without) Coupon
x.d.	:	Ex (without) Dividend
x.i.	:	Ex (without) Interest
Xmas	:	Christmas

Yd.	:	Yard
yr.	:	Year
yrs.	:	Years

SIGN AND SYMBOLS

@	:	At the rate of
&	:	And
C	:	Copyright
£	:	Pound setting
£A	:	Pound Australian
$	:	Dollar
4to	:	Quarto
8to	:	Octavo
%	:	Percent
0/00	:	Per mile, per thousand
∴	:	Because
∵	:	Therefore
'	:	Feet
"	:	Inches
X	:	By
o	:	Degrees
" "	:	Put inverted comma